VOLUME 2

DAILY READINGS

from the Life of

CHRIST

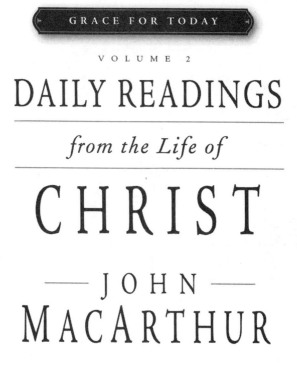

GRACE FOR TODAY

VOLUME 2

DAILY READINGS

from the Life of

CHRIST

— JOHN — MACARTHUR

MOODY PUBLISHERS
CHICAGO

All Scripture quotations, unless otherwise indicated, are taken from the *New American Standard Bible®*, Copyright © 1960, 1962, 1963, 1968, 1971, 1972, 1973, 1975, 1977, 1995 by The Lockman Foundation. Used by permission. (www.Lockman.org)
Scripture quotations marked KJV are taken from the King James Version.

Cover Design: Kirk DouPonce, DogEared Design, www.DogEaredDesign.com
Cover Image: iStockPhoto
Interior Design: Ragont Design
Editor: Garry Knussman

Published in association with the literary agency of Wolgemuth & Associates, Inc.

Library of Congress Cataloging-in-Publication Data

MacArthur, John, 1939-
    Daily readings from the life of Christ, vol. 2 / John MacArthur.
    p. cm.
    Includes bibliographical references.
    ISBN 978-0-8024-5601-4
    1. Jesus Christ—Biography—Meditations. 2. Devotional calendars. I. Title.
BT301.3.M33 2008
232.9'5—dc22

2008025053

This book is printed on acid free recycled paper containing 30% PCW (Post Consumer Waste) and manufactured in the United States of America by Lake Books.

We hope you enjoy this book from Moody Publishers. Our goal is to provide high-quality, thought-provoking books and products that connect truth to your real needs and challenges. For more information on other books and products written and produced from a biblical perspective, go to www.moodypublishers.com or write to:

Moody Publishers
820 N. LaSalle Boulevard
Chicago, IL 60610

1 3 5 7 9 10 8 6 4 2

Printed in the United States of America

*To Don Green, a friend, uniquely gifted
as a strong and wise scholar, teacher,
counselor, and leader.*

INTRODUCTION

The rapid pace of twenty-first-century living is not very conducive to setting aside time to slow down, read the Bible, and pray and mediated on God's Word. Yet such activity ought to be the daily priority of every Christian—it is the primary way God leads us in our sanctification. Just as physical nourishment is essential to physical life, so spiritual nourishment is essential to spiritual life—your growth in Christ depends on it.

The frustration comes for many Christians when they're unable to find the time to study God's Word as they would like. I certainly understand that frustration. While I think you should be striving to carve out as much time as possible to spend with the Lord, which you can do by letting go of less important priorities, I do realize that's not easy to do.

That's why I offer you this new book of daily readings from God's Word. Its goal is to help you develop a consistency in reading and mediating on the truths of the Bible—yet this does not mean a large time commitment on your part.

However, that doesn't mean this is like other devotional books that merely offer inspirational thoughts and meditations to help you feel good about your life. This book contains substantial, thought-provoking selections that come from my commentaries on the gospels, which are products of my lifetime of study in God's Word.

The focus of this volume as with the first one and a third to follow, is the life of our Lord and Savior, Jesus Christ. My greatest joy in the pulpit has been teaching from the gospels and seeing how our Lord lived and interacted with all sorts of people, from the disciples who truly loved Him, yet were weak in their faith, to the masses of people who were mesmerized by His miraculous acts, yet many of whom never believed in Him, and to the religious hypocrites who pretended to want to know Him, yet always wanted to kill Him. In short, by observing how Christ interacted with people you'll gain great insight into how you can live as He did.

In each of the selections that follow, you'll draw daily nourishment from a nugget of God's Word. In this volume I focus on the later Galilean, Judean, Perean activities of Jesus' life and ministry, along with some new entries on His incarnation (birth). Each entry will challenge you to meditate and act on significant truth. My desire for you as you conclude this second year of reading and meditating is a growing commitment to deeper, subsequent study, meditation, and prayer with our great heavenly father.

THE PREEXISTENT WORD, PART 1

In the beginning was the Word, and the Word was with God, and the Word was God. He was in the beginning with God. —JOHN 1:1–2

The concept of "the Word" (*logos* in the Greek) was meaningful to both Jewish and Greek readers of this gospel. Greek philosophers defined it as the abstract principle of order and reason in the universe. Even laymen understood the term as one of the universe's most important principles, the source of wisdom.

Thus to John's Greek audience, he presented Jesus as the embodiment of the *logos* concept, though not as an impersonal force or emanation. God, the true *logos*, became a man, Jesus Christ. This concept was something new to Greek thought.

To his Jewish readers, on the other hand, John presented Jesus as the incarnation of divine power and revelation, a continuation of the Old Testament "word of the Lord" concept (cf. Gen. 15:1; Ex. 24:3–4; 1 Sam. 3:21; Ps. 33:6; Jer. 1:2). Among other things, Jesus was the agent of creation (Col. 1:16), inspired the New Testament through the Holy Spirit whom He sent (John 14:26; 15:26), initiated the new covenant (Luke 22:20), and was the One who instructed believers (John 10:27). As God's incarnate Word, Jesus is His final word to humanity: "God, after He spoke long ago to the fathers in the prophets in many portions and in many ways, in these last days has spoken to us in His Son" (Heb. 1:1–2).

Although Jesus was intimately with the Father from eternity past, He willingly left that glorious privilege and "emptied Himself, taking the form of a bond-servant, and being made in the likeness of men. . . . He humbled Himself by becoming obedient to the point of death, even death on a cross" (Phil. 2:7–8).

ASK YOURSELF

Jesus is not all things to all people, yet He meets each of us at our individual points of need and our unique frames of reference. If you were to describe how Jesus proves His Word true in your own life, what ideas would come most quickly to mind?

THE PREEXISTENT WORD, PART 2

In the beginning was the Word, and the Word was with God, and the Word was God. He was in the beginning with God. —JOHN 1:1–2

John restates the profound truths of verse 1 in verse 2. He underscores again the eternity of the Word—Christ existed "in the beginning" when everything else was created. And as noted in verse 1, that existence was one of intimate fellowship with God the Father.

Jesus' deity and full equality with His Father is a truth of the Christian faith that can't be compromised. The apostle John later warned the readers of his second letter, "If anyone comes to you and does not bring this teaching [the biblical truth of Christ's deity; cf. vv. 7, 9], do not receive him into your house, and do not give him a greeting" (2 John 10). Such seemingly unloving actions are justified toward heretics who deny the Lord's deity and His gospel, because they are under God's curse:

> There are some who are disturbing you and want to distort the gospel of Christ. But even if we [Paul], or an angel from heaven, should preach to you a gospel contrary to what we have preached to you, he is to be accursed! As we have said before, so I say again now, if any man is preaching to you a gospel contrary to what you received, he is to be accursed! (Gal. 1:7–9)

We must not be confused about the deity of Christ, because the Bible teaches it clearly and unmistakably. Jesus is the eternally preexistent Word, who has always enjoyed full communion and divine life with the Father, and is Himself God.

ASK YOURSELF

Are you ever in danger of limiting the power, rule, sovereignty and, yes, even the goodness of God? Though your belief and profession may be biblically sound and solid, does your daily interaction with life's circumstances reveal a complete trust in God's preeminence?

THE WORD'S CREATIVE POWER

*All things came into being through Him, and apart from Him
nothing came into being that has come into being.* —JOHN 1:3

Here John declares the weighty truth that Jesus, the eternal Word, created everything that "came into being." This truth provides two more
proofs of His deity. First, if Christ is Creator of all things, He must be
uncreated, and only God is uncreated. This verse uses a different verb
from "to be" in verses 1 and 2, which denotes a state of being. Here the
verb ("came into being") describes the creation of the universe, thus emphasizing the divine creative act distinct from that state of being. The
verb also points to a second proof of deity—Jesus is Creator ("through
Him") and thus is God. Elsewhere in Scripture the Creator is likewise
portrayed as God (Gen. 1:1; Isa. 40:28; Rom. 1:25; Rev. 4:11).

With this clear verse, John strongly rejected the developing heresy
of Gnosticism, which claimed that matter was evil and spirit was good,
and therefore a good God could not have created the universe.

Today's world, however, is obviously radically different from the
Lord's original good creation (Gen. 1:31). The fall not only affected humanity adversely but the whole creation as well. Because of that, Christ
will eventually redeem not only believers but also the created world, as
Romans 8:19–21 teaches:

> For the anxious longing of the creation waits eagerly for the reveal-
> ing of the sons of God. For the creation was subjected to futility, not
> willingly, but because of Him who subjected it, in hope that the crea-
> tion itself also will be set free from its slavery to corruption into the
> freedom of the glory of the children of God.

ASK YOURSELF

The concept of God as Creator comes with many practical, daily
implications since we live inside His created order at all times. How does
the creation itself—even in its fallen state—continue to reflect the
grandeur and careful oversight of its and your Creator?

The Word's Self-existence, Part 1

In Him was life, and the life was the Light of men. The Light shines in the darkness, and the darkness did not comprehend it. —John 1:4–5

God's and Christ's having life in themselves—self-existence—is a foundational truth to our faith. We can describe everything created as "becoming," because nothing created is unchanging. But the divine, eternal, nonchanging being or life, such as the Father and the Son, is distinct from what is becoming—and is actually its source. It is what distinguishes creatures (us) from the Creator (God).

There was a point when the universe did not exist (Gen. 1:1), but never a point when God did not exist (cf. Ex. 3:14). Acts 17:28 says, "In Him we live and move and exist." We can do nothing apart from Him, but He has always lived and moved and been.

This verse is one of the purest descriptions of deity—and to say Jesus is "the life" is the purest statement about His deity and His role in creation. As Creator He is the source of everything and of everyone who has life. Furthermore, John's gospel often uses the form of the word "life" that denotes spiritual or eternal life (1:12; 3:15–16; 6:37, 39–40, 44, 47; 20:31). Christ came into the world to impart spiritual life to sinners who "were dead in [their] trespasses and sins" (Eph. 2:1; cf. John 6:33; 10:10).

ASK YOURSELF

Of all the things we forget to be grateful for and most often take for granted is the simple gift of life. May you stop at frequent moments of the day simply to give glory to God for the gift of breath, of sight, of hearing, of life itself . . . and the privilege of enjoying it with Him.

THE WORD'S SELF-EXISTENCE, PART 2

*In Him was life, and the life was the Light of men. The Light shines
in the darkness, and the darkness did not comprehend it.* —JOHN 1:4–5

John's statement "the life was the Light" says that life and light are essentially the same. It basically has the same construction as "the Word was God" (v. 1)—divine life and light share the same essential properties.

The divine life is true and holy. "Light" is that truth and holiness displayed against the darkness of lies and sin. In John 8:12 Jesus declares, "I am the Light of the world; he who follows Me will not walk in the darkness, but will have the Light of life" (cf. Ps. 36:9).

This Light is no less than the manifest life of God shining in His Son: "The light of the gospel of the glory of Christ, who is the image of God" (2 Cor. 4:4; cf. v. 6). "The Light" is simply the Father's divine light revealed in His Son, Jesus Christ.

Satan's kingdom is the "domain of darkness" (Col. 1:13), but Christ is the source of life (John 14:6) and the Light that "shines in the darkness" of a lost world (cf. 12:35–36). Despite the devil's intense assaults on the Light, "the darkness did not comprehend it." The word translated "comprehend" is better rendered "overcome." A very small candle can dispel darkness from a room; the Lord Jesus, the glorious Light of saving truth, will destroy the satanic realm of spiritual darkness. In fact, since Jesus' earthly ministry, "the darkness is passing away and the true Light is already shining" (1 John 2:8).

ASK YOURSELF

What effect does Jesus' being "the Light" have on your life? How does He brighten the path you walk? What does His light expose, both in the world and in yourself, refining your approach and strengthening your confidence as you journey through each day?

The Word's Self-existence, Part 3

In Him was life, and the life was the Light of men. The Light shines in the darkness, and the darkness did not comprehend it. —John 1:4–5

Because they understand so well the final judgment awaiting them, Satan and his forces have tried desperately throughout redemptive history to destroy the self-existent Word of life and light, the Lord Jesus. First they attempted to destroy the nation of Israel, from which Messiah would arise. They also targeted the royal line from which Christ would descend (2 Kings 11:1–2).

Shortly after Jesus' birth, Satan prompted Herod's vicious but futile attempt to murder Him (Matt. 2:16). Prior to the start of Jesus' ministry, the evil one tried in vain to turn Him aside from His mission (Matt. 4:1–11). Later he worked through Peter in an effort to accomplish the same objective (Matt. 16:21–23). Likewise, Satan's children, those who refuse to believe the truth, are eternally lost because they reject the Word of Light and life:

> For the wrath of God is revealed from heaven against all ungodliness and unrighteousness of men who suppress the truth in unrighteousness, because that which is known about God is evident within them; for God made it evident to them [through Jesus Christ]. For since the creation of the world His invisible attributes, His eternal power and divine nature, have been clearly seen, being understood through what has been made, so that they are without excuse. For even though they knew God, they did not honor Him as God or give thanks, but . . . their foolish heart was darkened. (Rom. 1:18–21)

Anyone who rejects the deity of the Logos, Jesus Christ, will be lost: "For unless you believe that I am He, you will die in your sins" (John 8:24).

ASK YOURSELF

In what ways do you continue to see the enemy at work, combating and contradicting Jesus, His gospel, and His people? We know he cannot ultimately succeed, but what can we do as Christ's followers to stand against the onslaught of Satan's attacks and accusations?

GOD'S GRACE ON MARY

Jacob was the father of Joseph the husband of Mary, by whom
Jesus was born, who is called the Messiah. —MATT. 1:16

When God chose Mary to be the mother of His Son, He showered much grace upon her. And although a descendant of King David's family, she was a humble, obscure young woman, just as much a sinner as all other human beings ever born. She was likely a superior person morally and spiritually than her contemporaries, but she was not sinless. Mary demonstrated her faithfulness and obedience to God by her humble and submissive response to the angel Gabriel's announcement (Luke 1:38).

Mary herself, in her song of praise called the Magnificat, acknowledged her need of a Savior: "My soul exalts the Lord, and my spirit has rejoiced in God my Savior. For He has had regard for the humble state of His bondslave" (Luke 1:46–48). These words refute any ideas of her being co-redemptrix and co-mediator with Jesus. Such beliefs are not scriptural and were never contained in early church doctrine. The Catholic Church embraced such false concepts several centuries later by accommodating pagan myths from the Babylonian mystery religions.

According to Scripture, Mary never did dispense grace but only received it from the Lord. "Favored one" (Luke 1:28) literally means "one endued with grace." Just as every other sinner, Mary needed God's grace and salvation. That's why she "rejoiced in God [her] Savior" (Luke 1:47). Mary realized what an unequaled privilege she enjoyed being a sinful woman chosen by the Lord to give birth to the Messiah, Jesus.

ASK YOURSELF

Are you encouraged by realizing that even the most revered figures in biblical history were just as much in need of God's grace and mercy as you are? Humility is the shared property of all who possess an appropriate view of themselves and of their incredible debt to God.

GOD'S GRACE ON TWO MEN

*The record of the genealogy of Jesus the Messiah,
the Son of David, the son of Abraham.* —MATT. 1:1

Although they were sinful men, David and Abraham, by God's grace, both were ancestors of Jesus Christ.

David sinned against Bathsheba and her husband, Uriah. He was also a poor father who failed to discipline his children. One of those (Absalom) even tried to wrest the throne from David by armed rebellion.

Abraham on two different occasions (Gen. 12:11–19; 20:1–18) told pagan kings that his wife Sarah was his sister. This brought shame on Sarah, himself, and God, the One he claimed to trust and serve. In spite of these sins, God made Abraham the father of Israel, the chosen people from whom Christ would arise. The Lord appointed David head of the kingly line from whom Messiah was promised.

Furthermore, God's grace extended to specific descendants of these two men. Abraham's son Isaac was the son of promise and a type of Christ, willingly offered up to God (Gen. 22:1–13). Isaac's son Jacob (later renamed Israel) and his sons were leaders of the people of Israel. God's grace was always with them, even when they needed discipline or rebuke.

David's son and royal successor, Solomon, was peaceful and wiser than most men but also foolish and sinful in many ways. His hundreds of wives, mostly pagan, turned his and the people's hearts away from the Lord (1 Kings 11:1–8). The kingdom of Israel soon became divided, but the royal line remained and God eventually fulfilled His promise to David, God's grace prevailing in the person of Messiah Jesus.

ASK YOURSELF

All the way back, we see humanity's inconsistency and God's faithfulness, intertwining into the merciful, purposeful outworking of His plan for the ages. Far from being an excuse to slack off, how does this realization infuse you with new zeal to trust, obey, and follow?

GOD'S GRACE IN THE HISTORY OF THREE ERAS

So all the generations from Abraham to David are fourteen generations; from David to the deportation to Babylon, fourteen generations; and from the deportation to Babylon to the Messiah, fourteen generations. —MATT. 1:17

Matthew's summary of Jesus' genealogy shows us God's grace working in three eras of Israel's history. First was the period of the patriarchs, Moses, Joshua, and the judges. During that time God's people found an identity, served as slaves, wandered after their deliverance, received divine law and covenant, and conquered the Promised Land.

The second era was one when Israel became a monarchy similar to her neighboring nations. But the Israelites soon discovered that sinful kings more often led them away from God instead of toward obedience and peace. There was much decline and apostasy, followed by defeat, exile, and the destruction of Jerusalem and the temple. Kings David, Jehoshaphat, Hezekiah, and Josiah were notable exceptions to the pattern of ungodliness.

The third period, concluding with the time of Christ, was one of captivity, frustration, and the marking of time. It was a period generally cloaked in spiritual and cultural darkness and marked by many inconsequential years. Most of the men of this period are unknown and unnamed apart from the genealogy. Essentially it was Israel's Dark Ages.

Christ's genealogy contains elements of pathos and glory, listing persons of disgrace and heroism, obscurity and renown. The Messiah's nation rose, fell, stagnated, and eventually rejected and crucified the One the Father sent to His people. In spite of it all, God's grace was at work during all three periods through His Son and the promise of His Son.

ASK YOURSELF

What spiritual markers and descriptions could be given to the age in which we currently live? Even in spite of our failings and the evidence of much falling away, what are some of the singular examples of faithfulness you see in the world at large, as well as close to home?

GOD'S GRACE SEEN IN
OUTCASTS TAMAR AND RAHAB

Judah was the father of Perez and Zerah by Tamar. . . .
Salmon was the father of Boaz by Rahab. —MATT. 1:3a, 5a

The first outcast through whom Christ would descend and in whom God manifested His grace was Judah's daughter-in-law Tamar. Because of their evilness, God had killed Tamar's husband, Er, and allowed his next oldest brother, Onan, to commit suicide. As a result, Judah promised her that his third son, Shelah, would become her husband when he came of age and would produce children for her in place of the deceased Er (Gen. 38:6–11). When Judah didn't keep that promise, Tamar posed as a prostitute, had intercourse with Judah, and bore twin sons, Perez and Zerah (vv. 13–30). Despite such sinful activities, God graciously allowed Judah, Tamar, and Perez to join the messianic line.

A second Gentile woman outcast in the genealogy is Rahab, the prostitute from Jericho. In order to save the lives of the two spies Joshua had sent to the city, Rahab lied to messengers of Jericho's king (Josh. 2:1–21). Because she feared God and was kind toward His people, He spared Rahab and her family when He destroyed Jericho (Josh. 6:22–25). Beyond that, divine grace brought Rahab into the messianic genealogy as wife of Salmon and mother of Boaz, David's great-grandfather. Thus it is documented that God used undeserving sinners in His plan to give all sinners His Son, the Savior.

ASK YOURSELF

Are there individuals in your family, workplace, or community whom you've basically given up on? Could it be that God still has plans to capture their hearts and use them for His glory? How might they see this kind of hope in your eyes as a result of your dealings with them?

GOD'S GRACE SEEN IN
OUTCASTS RUTH AND BATHSHEBA

*Boaz was the father of Obed by Ruth . . . David was the father of Solomon
by Bathsheba who had been the wife of Uriah.* —MATT. 1:5b, 6b

Like Tamar and Rahab, the third outcast, Ruth, was a Gentile (a
Moabite). After her husband (an Israelite named Mahlon) died, she went
to Israel with her mother-in-law, Naomi (Ruth 1:22). Ruth was a godly,
devoted woman who had accepted by faith the Lord as her own God (v.
16). Mahlon had married Ruth in violation of the Mosaic law (Deut. 7:3;
cf. Ezra 9:2; Neh. 13:23), and many believe his early death, and that of his
brother, were God's judgment on their disobedience. Though she was a
Gentile Moabite who had no right to marry an Israelite, God's grace
made Ruth one of His people and later, through Boaz, brought her into
the royal line as grandmother of King David.

The fourth outcast is Bathsheba, with whom David committed adultery (2 Sam. 11:2–5). He then sent her husband, Uriah, to the front lines
to be killed and took her to be his own wife. The son of the adultery died
in infancy, but the next son, Solomon, succeeded to David's throne and
continued the messianic line. God's grace was again abundant as
Bathsheba became an ancestor of Jesus Christ.

Jesus' genealogy is far more than merely a list of ancient names that
identifies His forbears. It is a wonderful testimony to the Father's grace
and the Son's ministry—the Son who is the friend of sinners, who "did
not come to call the righteous, but sinners" (Matt. 9:13).

ASK YOURSELF

Have you felt as though your sins of the past or your sinful struggles of
the present have shipwrecked your spiritual future? To remain in sin is to
give up on God (and yourself) too easily. To believe that you have no
choice is to fall for one of Satan's favorite deceptions.

CONFRONTING THE VIRGIN BIRTH

Joseph her husband, being a righteous man and not wanting to disgrace her, planned to send her away secretly. But when he had considered this, behold, an angel of the Lord appeared to him in a dream, saying, "Joseph, son of David, do not be afraid to take Mary as your wife; for the Child who has been conceived in her is of the Holy Spirit." —MATT. 1:19–20

Although they were only betrothed at this time, Mary and Joseph were considered husband and wife according to Jewish custom. Because he was a righteous man, Joseph felt he faced two difficult dilemmas in this situation. First, his high moral standards would not allow him to proceed with his marriage to Mary because of her pregnancy. Second, his strong love for Mary would not allow him to shame her publicly, much less to demand her death, as provided by the law (Deut. 22:23–24).

Joseph's concern was not for his own shame but for Mary's. Therefore, "not wanting to disgrace her" by public exposure to her alleged sin, he "planned to send her away secretly." The word translated "send away" was the common term for divorce—Joseph planned to divorce Mary secretly so that at least for a while she would be protected.

In the midst of these considerations, an angel from heaven instructed Joseph on what to do: "Joseph, son of David, do not be afraid to take Mary as your wife; for the Child who has been conceived in her is of the Holy Spirit." These words emphasize the supernatural character of events and give ultimate testimony to the truth of the virgin birth. Furthermore, to underscore the divine encouragement and verify Jesus' royal lineage, the angel called Joseph "son of David." The Lord's rightful place in the Davidic line came through Joseph, even though He was just Joseph's legal son and actually God's Son by the power of the Holy Spirit.

ASK YOURSELF

Integrity is usually one of several options available to you in tough, complex situations. If you find yourself rarely choosing the highest road in circumstances like these, to what would you attribute your reluctance—not knowing what to do, or just not wanting to do it?

The Virgin Birth Predicted

Now all this took place to fulfill what was spoken by the Lord through the prophet: "Behold, the virgin shall be with child and shall bear a Son, and they shall call His name Immanuel," which translated means, "God with us."
—MATT. 1:22–23

Here Matthew, under the Spirit's inspiration, clearly identifies the birth of Christ as a fulfillment of Old Testament prophecy. Thus the prophetic text of Isaiah (7:14) must be interpreted as predicting Jesus' virgin birth.

The prophet used the Hebrew word *alma* in Isaiah 7:14. The word can mean "virgin," which is how the Jewish translators of the Greek Old Testament rendered it in 7:14 (by the Greek *parthenos*)—several centuries prior to the birth of Christ. The "sign" Isaiah referred to was specifically for King Ahaz, who feared that Syria and Israel might destroy Judah's royal line. Isaiah assured Ahaz that God would protect that line and the future Messiah—through the birth of a son and the death of the kings. The future birth of a far greater Son, the virgin birth of God incarnate, would ensure the covenant with His people. Matthew did not simply give *alma* a Christian "twist." He used it with the same understanding that all his Jewish readers would have had for it.

But Matthew's teaching of the virgin birth of Jesus does not rest solely on the usage of *alma*. The case is made unquestionably clear by his previous statements that Jesus' conception was by and of "the Holy Spirit" (1:18, 20). And Matthew reinforced the case by reminding us that the Son would also be known as Immanuel ("God with us"), which was an honored and descriptive title more than a proper name. In His virgin birth and incarnation, the Lord Jesus was in the most literal sense "God with us."

ASK YOURSELF

We admittedly serve a God who is invisible to our human eyes. Thus, like Moses, we must live as though "seeing Him who is unseen" (Heb. 11:27). But in what ways does God reveal to you that He is "with us"? How does He help you counteract your doubts?

The Virgin Birth Consummated

And Joseph awoke from his sleep and did as the angel of the Lord
commanded him, and took Mary as his wife, but kept her a virgin until
*she gave birth to a Son; and he called His name Jesus. —*MATT. 1:24–25

That "Joseph awoke from his sleep" confirms that God had spoken to
him in a dream. Such extraordinary communication occurred on other
occasions (cf. Gen. 20:3; Job 33:14–16; 1 Kings 3:5).

We don't know much about Joseph's reaction to God's words except
that right away he obeyed. He must have had feelings of amazement, relief, and gratitude that he could marry Mary with honor. He undoubtedly
also would have been pleased that he could care for the Son of God while
He grew up. Joseph's obedience demonstrates his godliness and proves
the trustworthy, faithful kind of man he was and the reason God chose
him as earthly father for His Son.

Joseph took the baby Jesus to the temple for dedication (Luke 2:22–
33), to Egypt with His mother to flee Herod (Matt. 2:13–23), and to
Jerusalem when He was twelve (Luke 2:42–52). Beyond those events,
Scripture says virtually nothing about Joseph.

Joseph likely took Mary as his wife shortly after the angel's message to
him, and he was faithful to keep Mary a virgin "until she gave birth to [her]
Son." And, as a final obedience to the dream's instruction, Joseph called that
Son Jesus, which indicated He was to be the Savior of His people (v. 21).

An unbeliever reportedly asked a believer, "If I told you that child
over there had no human father, would you believe me?" The Christian
answered, "Yes, if he lived as Christ lived." One of the best proofs of our
Lord's supernatural birth and deity was His earthly life.

ASK YOURSELF

You probably haven't received a dream lately with specific instructions
from God on how to handle a certain situation. (You may wish you had!)
But how well are you following the instructions already given to you in
His Word? Are you in the habit of doing what He says?

MAGI FROM THE EAST

Now after Jesus was born in Bethlehem of Judea in the days of Herod
the king, magi from the east arrived in Jerusalem, saying, "Where is
He who has been born King of the Jews? For we saw His star in the
east and have come to worship Him." —MATT. 2:1–2

This is one of the most myth-shrouded yet well-known accounts in all
of Scripture. The only sure facts we know about these magi, or wise
men, are the ones in Matthew 2:1–12. We don't even know their number,
names, mode of transportation, or specific country from which they trav-
eled. Most would have assumed they came "from the east" since people
knew the magi constituted the priestly-political class of the Parthians,
who lived east of Palestine.

The Bible also does not tell us how God revealed to the magi about
Messiah, only that He gave them the sign of "His star in the east." As
with the identity of the men, little is known about the star's nature. Some
claim it was Jupiter, the largest of the planets. Others say it was the con-
junction of Jupiter and Saturn. But since the Bible simply mentions the
star, we can't be dogmatic about its characteristics—it might have been
the same divine glory that shone around the shepherds when the angels
announced Jesus' birth (Luke 2:9).

Because they had to ask about where Jesus was born, it's clear the
magi did not actually *follow* the star. Only after they heard of the prophesied birthplace of Christ (2:5–6) did the star reappear and guide them to
the precise place where Jesus was.

That the magi came to worship Christ shows they were genuine seekers after God. With limited spiritual light, they recognized God's light
when it shone on them and they found Him in the person of His Son.

ASK YOURSELF

You may not think of yourself as a very wise person, but the Bible
teaches us that "the fear of the Lord is the beginning of wisdom" (Prov.
9:10). If that's where it starts, what could you do with that piece of
information to make some wise choices and decisions today?

THE MAGI'S ADORATION, PART 1

After hearing [Herod] the king, they went their way; and the star, which they had seen in the east, went on before them until it came and stood over the place where the Child was. When they saw the star, they rejoiced exceedingly with great joy. After coming into the house they saw the Child with Mary His mother; and they fell to the ground and worshiped Him. —MATT. 2:9–11a

The unique star's reappearance to the magi gave them unprecedented joy and enthusiasm. Matthew is almost at a loss for words, saying that "they rejoiced exceedingly with great joy." Such superlatives indicate the magi's extremely strong interest and exhilaration in this event. And such reactions were justified, because God somehow used the special star to lead them directly to Jesus and His family.

Joseph had apparently taken his family from the stable to a house, where they lived until the Lord instructed them on their next move. It was at this house that the pilgrims finally found the object of their search—"the Child with Mary His mother." By God's grace they were allowed to see His promised Son in person. They experienced firsthand Charles Wesley's great lyrics, "Veiled in flesh the Godhead see; hail the incarnate deity."

Matthew carefully points out that the magi "fell to the ground and worshiped Him"—only Jesus and not His mother or father. They were more discerning than Cornelius, who wanted to worship Peter (Acts 10:25), or the Lystrans, who attempted to worship Paul and Barnabas (14:11–13). They likely were respectful of Mary and Joseph, but they reserved their true adoration for the Christ Child, because as God, only He was worthy of worship.

ASK YOURSELF

When was the last time you "rejoiced exceedingly with great joy" or "fell to the ground and worshiped Him"? What keeps you from sensing this kind of awe on a regular basis? And what could help to keep you in a state of mind and spirit that is routinely amazed at who Jesus is?

The Magi's Adoration, Part 2

Then, opening their treasures, they presented to Him
gifts of gold, frankincense, and myrrh. —MATT. 2:11b

Proper divine worship is always, and must be, the only basis for proper giving, proper learning, and proper service. The magi's giving was not so much an extension of their worship as an element of it, given as an expression of their adoring and grateful hearts. Any giving, even though generous, that is done apart from a worshipful relationship to God is empty giving.

Throughout history people have considered gold the most valuable of metals, the universal symbol of value and wealth. The Israelites used it extensively in the construction of the temple (1 Kings 6–7, 9; 2 Chron. 2–4). And here we see Matthew implicitly presenting Jesus as not only King of the Jews but as King of kings and appropriately receiving a royal gift of gold.

Frankincense was a fragrant and expensive incense used only on very special occasions. The Jews used it for tabernacle and temple grain offerings (Lev. 2:2, 15–16), in certain royal processions (Song of Sol. 3:6–7), and sometimes at weddings. The church father Origen believed frankincense was the incense of deity, which suggests just how important and special people viewed it.

Myrrh was a slightly less expensive perfume than frankincense but still highly prized. According to many commentators, myrrh was the gift for mortals and emphasizes here Jesus' humanity. As a mixture with other spices, it was later used in the burial preparation of Jesus' body (John 19:39).

Thus these three items were the magi's gifts to Christ: gold for royalty, frankincense for deity, and myrrh for humanity.

ASK YOURSELF

Rather than looking at our regular disciplines of prayer, worship, and Bible study—or even our acts of service and obedience—as duties and obligations, how might our attitudes change if we saw those as gifts to God? What gifts could you give to Him today, tomorrow?

Out of Egypt—Fulfilling a Type

*Now when they had gone, behold, an angel of the Lord appeared to Joseph
in a dream and said, "Get up! Take the Child and His mother and flee to Egypt,
and remain there until I tell you; for Herod is going to search for the Child to
destroy Him." So Joseph got up and took the Child and His mother while it
was still night, and left for Egypt. He remained there until the death of Herod.
This was to fulfill what had been spoken by the Lord through the prophet:
"Out of Egypt I called My Son."* —Matt. 2:13–15

In spite of her spiritual unfaithfulness and lawlessness, God has always
promised to restore Israel. Through the prophet Hosea, God reminded
Israel of His undying love for her: "When Israel was a youth I loved
him, and out of Egypt I called My son" (Hos. 11:1). Here Matthew applies the last part of that verse to Christ. Though Hosea did not know-
ingly predict Messiah's exile in Egypt, Matthew indicates that Israel's
earlier call from Egypt pictures Jesus' return from that country. As God
had once called His people out of Egypt to be His chosen nation, He now
would call His greater Son from there to be Israel's Messiah.

This is a type, a nonverbal prediction from the Old Testament that
illustrates something about Christ without specifically describing it.
However, we can't credibly label a person or event a genuine Old Testament type except as Scripture itself informs us of it. Therefore, because
Matthew makes the association here, Israel's exodus from Egypt is a type
of Jesus' return from Egypt as a young child.

In a more profound sense, Christ exited Egypt with Israel under
Moses. The Lord descended from Abraham and the royal line of David.
Had the Israelites died in Egypt or the wilderness, Messiah Himself could
not have come out of Egypt or even been born.

ASK YOURSELF

The uniting threads of God's bigger picture are comforting to read and
ponder. They soothe our inborn need for security and protection,
surrounding us with the sure embrace of His eternal plans and purposes.
How does this assurance speak to your life specifically right now?

TRAGEDY IN BETHLEHEM

*Then when Herod saw that he had been tricked by the magi, he became
very enraged, and sent and slew all the male children who were in Bethlehem
and all its vicinity, from two years old and under, according to the time which
he had determined from the magi. Then what had been spoken through
Jeremiah the prophet was fulfilled: "A voice was heard in Ramah, weeping
and great mourning, Rachel weeping for her children; and she refused
to be comforted, because they were no more."* —MATT. 2:16–18

Matthew provides a sobering synopsis of Herod's slaughter of the in-
nocents to portray the rejection of Christ by the Jewish leaders and their
representatives. The chief priests, scribes, and Pharisees must have heard
something about Jesus' birth, but they had no true interest in finding
Him or worshiping Him. Herod had only a hypocritical concern for the
Child. In reality, Herod's sadistic brutality against the male infants
around Jerusalem reflected his own and the Jewish leaders' unrelenting
rejection of Jesus. Those little ones were the first casualties in the re-
intensified spiritual warfare between the kingdom of this world and the
kingdom of heaven.

"Rachel weeping for her children" represents the grieving of all
Jewish mothers over Israel's distress during the days of Jeremiah (see
Jer. 31). In this gospel we see it as a type and prefigurement of the Beth-
lehem mothers crying over the massacre of their sons by Herod. While
Christ was still an infant, Rachel had cause to weep again, even as Jesus
Himself would later weep over Jerusalem because the Jews largely re-
jected Him and would therefore face many afflictions (Luke 19:41–44).
Before the day when God will save the Jews and cleanse their sins (Rom.
11:26–27), continued disobedience and tragedy will dog them.

ASK YOURSELF

We never wish for days of sorrow, but they come nonetheless—grievous
realities of our fallen world. What have you learned from times of
anguish and despair? How has God met you in the midst of them and
pulled you through? Who could use your comfort, even today?

JESUS THE NAZARENE

*He [Joseph] left for the regions of Galilee, and came and lived in a city
called Nazareth. This was to fulfill what was spoken through the prophets:
"He [Jesus] shall be called a Nazarene." —*MATT. 2:22b–23

The prophecy that Jesus would be a Nazarene—not specifically
recorded in the Old Testament—is said by Matthew to be fulfilled when
Joseph and Mary took Him to Nazareth. Whoever the prophets were
who had made the Nazarene prediction, this was probably common
knowledge among Matthew's original Jewish readers. For us it is enough
that we believe the apostle's Spirit-inspired words on this matter.

Nazareth, a town located fifty-five miles north of Jerusalem on an
elevated Galilean basin, contained a populace mainly noted for its crude
and violent ways. *Nazarene* had long been a term of derision, describing
anyone plain and rugged. That's why Nathanael asked Philip, "Can any
good thing come out of Nazareth?" (John 1:46). Nathanael would not
have been one to malign his neighbors (v. 47), but he was stunned that
the Christ could actually come from a place like Nazareth.

Early Jewish opponents of Christianity spoke disparagingly of Paul
as "a ringleader of the sect of the Nazarenes" (Acts 24:5). Church father
Jerome reported that other Jews cursed Christians as Nazarenes and
prayed that they be removed from the Book of Life (cf. Ps. 69:28). Thus
"Jesus the Nazarene" became a title of reproach, fulfilling the prophecies
that Messiah would be "despised and forsaken of men" (Isa. 53:3; cf. 49:7;
Pss. 22:6–8; 69:20–21). The Gospels also affirm this fact (Matt. 12:24;
Luke 23:4; John 9:22, 29).

It was thus in much-maligned Nazareth that the royal Son of God
lived for thirty years.

ASK YOURSELF

What does it mean to you that God would choose for His Son to be associ-
ated with people from the "wrong side of the tracks," those who were
looked down upon and disrespected? How does this change your attitude
and approach toward those who live today in derision or invisibility?

The Baptist's Believable Testimony, Part 1

There came a man sent from God, whose name was John. He came as a witness, to testify about the Light, so that all might believe through him. He was not the Light, but he came to testify about the Light. —JOHN 1:6–8

The phrase "sent from God" indicates John the Baptist's role as Christ's herald in five ways. First, John fulfilled Old Testament prophecies concerning Christ's forerunner (Mal. 3:1; 4:5–6; cf. Isa. 40:3). The angel told John's father that Malachi's prophecy of an Elijah-like prophet (Mal. 3:1; 4:5–6) referred to the Baptist (Luke 1:17). Second, God uniquely sent John, because his conception and birth were miraculous (Luke 1:7, 36–37). Third, the angel elaborated on details of John's birth and life as herald (Luke 1:8–17). Fourth, Zacharias prophesied by the Holy Spirit concerning John (Luke 1:67–79). Fifth, God sent the Baptist at exactly the right time to begin his public ministry (1:80).

As Jesus proclaimed, John was truly the greatest human being who'd ever lived up to his time: "Truly I say to you, among those born of women there has not arisen anyone greater than John the Baptist!" (Matt. 11:11). The reason he was the greatest is that the Father chose him for the most crucial task to that point in history—to announce the coming of His Son, Jesus Christ. John made the first public announcement that Christ was the Redeemer (John 1:29). But all of that did not remove the Baptist's humility, as John professed Jesus' superiority: "This was He of whom I said, 'He who comes after me has a higher rank than I, for He existed before me'" (John 1:15).

ASK YOURSELF

We have been placed here at this time and location with meaning, intention, and purpose. John grew into this awareness, as we all do. But from where you sit today, are you seeing glimpses of your reason for being here? Does your chosen lifestyle compete with this purpose?

THE BAPTIST'S BELIEVABLE TESTIMONY, PART 2

There came a man sent from God, whose name was John. He came as a witness, to testify about the Light, so that all might believe through him. He was not the Light, but he came to testify about the Light. —JOHN 1:6–8

The Baptist's ministry generated much excitement among the people (Matt. 3:5–6), but also caused no small amount of confusion regarding his identity (Luke 3:15). In fact, he had to clarify matters with some of his followers:

> You yourselves are my witnesses that I said, "I am not the Christ," but, "I have been sent ahead of Him." He who has the bride is the bridegroom; but the friend of the bridegroom, who stands and hears him, rejoices greatly because of the bridegroom's voice. So this joy of mine has been made full. He must increase, but I must decrease. (John 3:28–30)

John's mission was not to promote himself, but to be "a witness" on behalf of Christ and "to testify about the Light." The terms "witness" and "testify" relate to legal facts, as those provided in courtroom testimony. They carry far more weight than mere opinions.

It's appropriate to call John "the Baptist" because the Lord sent him to baptize repentant sinners in preparation for the Savior's arrival (John 1:31). Yet his main purpose was to bear witness to Jesus (1:15, 29; 5:33, 36). People like us believe in Christ (1:12–13; 3:18) through the testimony of witnesses like John. They are agents pointing to the message of saving faith; though Jesus, of course, is the object of that faith.

ASK YOURSELF

Though some are more naturally gifted and comfortable in engaging others in conversation, is there any doubt that we have each been called to share with others what we have experienced with Christ? In what ways could you testify and bear witness of your Lord?

UNBELIEVERS REJECT JESUS, PART 1

There was the true Light which, coming into the world, enlightens
every man. He was in the world, and the world was made through Him,
and the world did not know Him. He came to His own, and those
who were His own did not receive Him. —JOHN 1:9–11

The need for John the Baptist to point out the "true Light" vividly illustrates the world's spiritual blindness, because only blind people are unable to see light. This is true of unbelievers because "the god of this world has blinded the minds of the unbelieving so that they might not see the light of the gospel of the glory of Christ, who is the image of God" (2 Cor. 4:4).

Through His "coming into the world" Jesus "enlightens every man" (cf. Isa. 49:6), which makes the world's unbelieving blindness so inexcusable. Those who never believe the gospel are still accountable for the knowledge of God and His light revealed in Christ. Although everyone is at one time spiritually dead and blind (Eph. 2:1–3), they are accountable for what God has revealed about Himself in creation and conscience (Rom. 2:14–15) and for rejecting the "Light of the world" (John 8:12):

This is the judgment, that the Light has come into the world, and men loved the darkness rather than the Light, for their deeds were evil. For everyone who does evil hates the Light, and does not come to the Light for fear that his deeds will be exposed. (John 3:19–20)

People refuse to come to Jesus' light because they love their sin and don't want it exposed. But despite this terrible rejection of Him, unbelievers will still be forced one day to acknowledge Jesus as Lord (Phil. 2:9–11) and as judge (John 5:22, 27).

ASK YOURSELF

Is there anything in your life that you are restricting to the darkness, any part of your actions and behaviors that would shame you if they were exposed? Let your acceptance of Jesus' light permeate beyond saving faith and into sanctified living. Why live with less of His warmth?

UNBELIEVERS REJECT JESUS, PART 2

There was the true Light which, coming into the world, enlightens every man.
He was in the world, and the world was made through Him, and the world
did not know Him. He came to His own, and those who were
His own did not receive Him. —JOHN 1:9–11

Jesus came to God's land, the city of David, the temple, and ministered among the Jews. Yet, tragically, those who had waited through the centuries for their Messiah and Savior for the most part "did not receive Him" when He did come.

Like their ancestors, the Jews during Jesus' time stiffened their necks (Deut. 10:16; Jer. 7:26) and rejected Him in spite of clear Old Testament witness to Him (John 5:39). Rather than repenting of sin and believing that Jesus was Messiah, they eventually screamed, "Crucify Him! . . . His blood shall be on us and on our children!" (Matt. 27:23, 25). This rejection was later a theme in the apostles' preaching, as Peter's sermon shows:

> Men of Israel, listen to these words: Jesus the Nazarene, a man attested to you by God with miracles and wonders and signs which God performed through Him in your midst, just as you yourselves know—this Man, delivered over by the predetermined plan and foreknowledge of God, you nailed to a cross by the hands of godless men and put Him to death....Therefore let all the house of Israel know for certain that God has made Him both Lord and Christ—this Jesus whom you crucified. (Acts 2:22–23, 36)

This reminder of the Jews' role in Jesus' death is a sobering one. But it is also a reminder of God's sovereign work in the crucifixion and an exhortation for all who still reject Christ to accept by faith His atoning work.

ASK YOURSELF

What areas of cynicism and faithlessness exist in your family background? Do any of these natural reactions still play through your head when faced with whether to live by faith or not? How have you been able to experience victory over these spiritual stumbling blocks?

BELIEVING TESTIMONY

But as many as received Him, to them He gave the right to become children of God, even to those who believe in His name, who were born, not of blood nor of the will of the flesh nor of the will of man, but of God. —JOHN 1:12–13

Even though there is much hatred of God and unbelief directed toward Jesus Christ, there will be many who receive Jesus. People whom God wills for salvation from eternity past (Eph. 1:4; 2 Tim. 1:9) will embrace His Son by faith. This is the great truth of sovereign, electing grace, which the apostle John introduces here (cf. 6:37).

Believing in His name refers to trusting in the totality of Christ's being—all that He is and does. Therefore, we must not separate His deity from His humanity, His being Savior from His being Lord, or His person from His redemptive work. Saving faith accepts all that the Bible reveals concerning Him.

We can't be saved unless we of our volition embrace by faith the Lord Jesus. But salvation is nonetheless God's sovereign work. Thus John says no individuals would come to saving faith unless God granted them "the right to become the children of God." We are saved entirely by "grace . . . through faith; and that not of [ourselves], it is the gift of God; not as a result of works, so that no one may boast" (Eph. 2:8–9), because "God has chosen [us] from the beginning for salvation" (2 Thess. 2:13).

Since all humanity bears the guilt of unbelief and rebellion, John's little phrase "but of God" means that saving belief in Jesus is impossible by sinful persons alone. The Holy Spirit must give us the power to believe and with it divine life and light rather than spiritual death and darkness.

ASK YOURSELF

This doctrine obviously touches on issues that have caused misunderstanding and division over the years. But can we all not agree that God's Word is truth? Do any of us want to limit His power and influence over our lives? Will we accept His Word even when it challenges us?

PETER: THE RIGHT RAW MATERIAL

Now the names of the twelve apostles are these:
The first, Simon, who is called Peter. —MATT. 10:2a

Peter possessed the right raw material from which Jesus could fashion the sort of leader of the apostles He intended him to be. One such qualification was that Peter constantly asked Jesus questions. Many were superficial and immature, though they reflected a real concern for Christ and His work (e.g., Matt. 15:11, 15; 19:27; Mark 11:21; 13:4; John 21:21). Peter's questions, self-centered and off the mark as many were, still gave Jesus opportunity to train him in leadership.

Secondly, Peter showed initiative, usually being the first disciple to respond to Jesus' questions (cf. Matt. 16:15–16). Although his actions could be impulsive (John 18:10), Peter was ready to respond in Jesus' favor.

Third, Peter naturally thrusted himself into the middle of the action. Even when he denied Christ, he was in close proximity to Him, whereas the other apostles had fled. When hearing of the Lord's resurrection, Peter was one of the first disciples to reach the tomb (he arrived second only because John was a faster runner, John 20:4). Peter was always there.

Peter's very names reveal something of his character. He was naturally unstable, so when Jesus changed Simon to Peter ("stone," Matt. 16:18), the other disciples likely had reservations. But the new name was a reminder of the kind of resolute man Christ wanted him to be.

ASK YOURSELF

Does any of your dissatisfaction with yourself and your walk with Christ come from being unwilling to take risks? Does your inability to maintain perfect consistency in all matters deter you from striving to be as fully submitted as possible, or from getting up again after failure?

PETER: THE RIGHT EXPERIENCES, PART 1

Now the names of the twelve apostles are these:
*The first, Simon, who is called Peter. —*MATT. 10:2a

Another valuable characteristic for good leadership is having the right experiences. Jesus gave enough of those to Peter to develop his leadership.

Jesus first of all gave Peter wondrous revelations. After Peter confessed that Jesus was the Son of God, Christ explained, "Blessed are you, Simon Barjona, because flesh and blood did not reveal this to you, but My Father who is in heaven" (Matt. 16:17). When many other followers forsook Christ over the cost of discipleship, Peter's response to also leaving was divinely insightful: "Lord, to whom shall we go? You have words of eternal life" (John 6:68). In later days the Spirit of God allowed Peter to record His revelations in the form of two New Testament letters.

Second, Peter experienced great honor and reward from Christ. Right after explaining the source of his great confession, Jesus told him, "You are Peter, and upon this rock I will build My church; and the gates of Hades will not overpower it. I will give you the keys of the kingdom of heaven; and whatever you bind on earth shall have been bound in heaven, and whatever you loose on earth shall have been loosed in heaven" (Matt. 16:18–19). The Lord also used Peter to preach to Jews from all over the world at Pentecost and to bring the gospel to Cornelius, the first Gentile convert. Peter thus unlocked the door of salvation to both Jews and Gentiles.

ASK YOURSELF

What are some of the defining experiences of your life, events that have profoundly shaped the person you are and the attributes you possess? If not for being used by God, what damage could these occurrences have caused, or how might they have led you away from Christ?

PETER: THE RIGHT EXPERIENCES, PART 2

Now the names of the twelve apostles are these:
The first, Simon, who is called Peter. —MATT. 10:2a

Continuing from yesterday's theme, we find three more experiences Peter had with the Lord. First he experienced great rebuke. After Peter rebuked Christ concerning His predicted death (Matt. 16:21–22), Jesus had to reprimand Peter: "Get behind Me, Satan! You are a stumbling block to Me; for you are not setting your mind on God's interests, but man's" (v. 23). When Peter began elevating his own position and understanding—relying on his own strength and wisdom to lead—he began serving Satan rather than God.

Second, Peter experienced temporary but great rejection of Jesus. When He predicted that all the apostles would desert Him after His arrest, Peter contradicted the Lord: "Even though all may fall away because of You, I will never fall away" (Matt. 26:33). Peter protested even more strongly against the notion that he would three times deny Jesus that very night (vv. 34–35). But Jesus was proved correct and Peter wrong (vv. 69–75).

Third, Peter experienced a great recommissioning (John 21:15–23). Christ confronted him about his lack of love, and Peter three times assured Jesus that he did indeed love Him. So the Lord reinstated Peter three times, charging him each time to care for His sheep. Jesus did not give up on Peter but reassured him that his divine calling was still valid. The imperative to "Follow Me!" was always applicable for Peter and is for us.

ASK YOURSELF

What does the challenge to "Follow Me" entail in your current set of circumstances and decisions? What will be the costs involved? How will you face resistance from others? What perhaps seems attractive or safer about not following Him? How do you propose to handle this tension?

PETER: THE RIGHT ATTITUDES, PART 1

Now the names of the twelve apostles are these:
The first, Simon, who is called Peter. —MATT. 10:2a

If Peter was going to be a good leader, Jesus knew he also needed to have right attitudes. First, he would need to learn submission because leaders can become domineering. When tax agents demanded a two-drachma temple tax from the Lord, He ordered Peter to catch a fish that would have a stater coin—exactly enough to pay the taxes for both Jesus and Peter (see Matt. 17:14–27). From this Peter learned to submit to both secular and divine authority: "Submit yourselves for the Lord's sake to every human institution, whether to a king as the one in authority, or to governors as sent by him for the punishment of evildoers and the praise of those who do right. For such is the will of God that by doing right you may silence the ignorance of foolish men. . . . Honor all people, love the brotherhood, fear God, honor the king" (1 Peter 2:13–15, 17).

Peter also needed to demonstrate restraint. When the crowd arrived in the garden to arrest Jesus, Peter drew his sword and began to resist. Jesus promptly told him to stop and allow God's plan to work (John 18:10–11).

Third, Peter needed a large portion of humility. Shortly after he boasted that his loyalty would never waver (Matt. 26:33), Peter denied Christ three times (vv. 69–75). Years later he had learned the lesson about pride and humility: "Clothe yourselves with humility toward one another, for God is opposed to the proud, but gives grace to the humble" (1 Peter 5:5).

ASK YOURSELF

Age and experience can put many things into spiritual perspective. What are some of the ways your reactions and responses have changed over the years? How has God grown wisdom into you? Can you think of some effective ways for passing these truths along to others?

Peter: The Right Attitudes, Part 2

Now the names of the twelve apostles are these:
The first, Simon, who is called Peter. —MATT. 10:2a

Our Lord had several more crucial attitudes for Peter to embrace. First was that of sacrifice. When Peter worried that his sacrifice (his death) might be greater than John's (John 21:18–19), Jesus said, "If I want him to remain until I come, what is that to you? You follow Me!" (v. 22). From then on Peter obeyed and trusted God for the outcome: "Those also who suffer according to the will of God shall entrust their souls to a faithful Creator in doing what is right" (1 Peter 4:19).

Second, Peter needed to learn love. Jesus showed him truly humble love when He washed the disciples' feet (John 13:1–20). And Peter again recorded the lesson learned: "Keep fervent in your love for one another, because love covers a multitude of sins" (1 Peter 4:8).

Finally, Peter needed a courageous attitude, and through the Holy Spirit he was able to embrace it. Acts 4:8–10 attests to this:

> Then Peter, filled with the Holy Spirit, said to them, "Rulers and elders of the people, if we are on trial today for a benefit done to a sick man, as to how this man has been made well, let it be known to all of you and to all the people of Israel, that by the name of Jesus Christ the Nazarene, whom you crucified, whom God raised from the dead—by this name this man stands here before you in good health."

Peter was no longer the fearful coward he was when he betrayed Jesus.

ASK YOURSELF

What are some of the specific things you have learned from the Lord lately? In what situations do you find that you are most receptive to the influence of His Word and truth? What are some things you still need to learn? Ask Him to keep your heart open and teachable.

PETER: THE RIGHT ATTITUDES, PART 3

Now the names of the twelve apostles are these:
The first, Simon, who is called Peter. —MATT. 10:2a

The New Testament contains many examples of how Peter applied his divinely acquired right attitudes to effective ministry for Christ. Among the apostles, he initiated the replacement for Judas (Acts 1:15–17), became the early church's first preacher (2:14), gave the first gospel defense before the council (4:8), first administered church discipline (5:3–9), confronted Simon the magician (8:18–23), healed Aeneas and raised Dorcas from the dead (9:34, 40), first took the gospel to the Gentiles (chap. 10), and penned two letters bearing his name and including the lessons Christ had taught him.

The Father and the Son were very gracious to Peter. As a "wandering heart" God sovereignly drew to Himself, the apostle could have readily sung the familiar words of Robert Robinson:

> Let Thy goodness, like a fetter,
> Bind my wandering heart to Thee.
> Prone to wander, Lord I feel it,
> Prone to leave the God I love;
> Take my heart, O take and seal it,
> Seal it for Thy courts above.

We can summarize Peter's life in his own words, at the end of his second letter: "Grow in the grace and knowledge of our Lord and Savior Jesus Christ. To Him be the glory, both now and to the day of eternity. Amen" (2 Peter 3:18).

ASK YOURSELF

Spend a few moments meditating on the familiar words of this closing verse. As a theme applicable to any believer's life, how do these thoughts and expressions mirror your true desires as a Christian? How can you align yourself more squarely within these noble goals and ideals?

JAMES: SON OF ZEBEDEE

. . . James the son of Zebedee. —MATT. 10:2c

During the three years Jesus trained the apostles, James is always portrayed in the Gospels with his brother John. Being mentioned first, James was probably the older and more dynamic of the two. In their secular vocation they were partners with their dad, Zebedee, in his prosperous fishing business.

Not a lot is written of James in Scripture, thus he appears more as a silhouette than a detailed portrait. From Jesus' reference to him and his brother as "Boanerges, which means, 'Sons of Thunder'" (Mark 3:17), we can infer that James was zealous, fervent, and passionate regarding his convictions.

Jesus once sent messengers ahead to make arrangements for lodging in Samaria, but the Samaritans refused Him. Hearing this, James and John wanted permission to destroy the Samaritans (Luke 9:52–54). However, Jesus rebuked their intolerant and vengeful reaction: "You do not know what kind of spirit you are of; for the Son of Man did not come to destroy men's lives, but to save them" (Luke 9:55–56). It is good for believers to become righteously indignant when the Lord is dishonored, but Jesus does not want us to return evil for evil (Matt. 5:38–42).

Christ bridled James's zeal and directed his energy into fruitful ministry. James did drink of the Master's cup (Acts 12:20, just as He had predicted; see Matt. 20:23). James's ministry was a short, bright flame that culminated in martyrdom. All the Lord's followers should be willing for such a fate.

ASK YOURSELF

Have you ever become so indignant about a particular conviction that you lost all perspective of what you were really saying? Does winning your point become more important to you than the people involved? When is "thunder" helpful, and when does it cause more harm than good?

John: Brother of James, Part 1

. . . James the son of Zebedee, and John his brother. —Matt. 10:2*d*

John, the brother of James, is one of Christ's leading apostles in the New Testament. He was one of the three closest disciples to Jesus, and he wrote one gospel, three letters, and the book of Revelation.

Because at the end of his life he was so meek and self-effacing, we tend to think of John as being naturally that way his entire life. But when he was young he was as much a "Son of Thunder" as his brother James. John stood with James in wanting to destroy the unbelieving Samaritans (Luke 9:52–54). On another occasion John told Jesus, "Teacher, we saw someone casting out demons in Your name, and we tried to prevent him because he was not following us" (Mark 9:38). The Lord then had to rebuke him because of his prejudice and sectarianism (vv. 39–41).

John was always uncompromising in doctrine and morality, but the Holy Spirit also shaped in him a strong facility for love—so much so that people called him the apostle of love. Jesus knew that the disciple who became the strongest advocate for love would also need to remain a teacher of uncompromising truth so that his love would not become mere sentimentality.

In John's inspired writings he used forms of the term *love* eighty times, and he used *witness* or its synonyms seventy times. Truth guarded his love, and love surrounded his truth.

ASK YOURSELF

John did show signs of change and refined perspective over the course of his life. How do you hope to see your own heart change as you grow older? What kind of person do you truly want to be? And what needs to start happening now in order to make those desires reality?

JOHN: BROTHER OF JAMES, PART 2

. . . James the son of Zebedee, and John his brother. —MATT. 10:2d

John revealed a heart of love and compassion throughout his teaching of truth. The apostle continually took in Jesus' love and continually gave it out. John was so identified with Christ's love that he called himself the disciple "whom Jesus loved" (John 13:23; cf. 19:26; 20:2; 21:7, 20). There was no greater honor John could have claimed for himself.

According to tradition, John didn't leave Jerusalem until Jesus' mother, Mary, had died. That's based on Christ's first entrusting Mary into the apostle's care (John 19:26). Jesus knew that John's special and sincere kind of love would cause him to treat Mary as his own mother.

Ten truths contained in John's sacred writings best summarize his teaching on love: God is love (1 John 4:8), God loves His Son (John 3:35), Christ loves the Father (14:31), God loved the disciples (17:23), God loves all people (3:16), Christ loved the disciples (13:34), Christ loves all believers (1 John 3:1), Christ commands everyone to love Him (John 14:15), believers are to love one another (13:34), and love fulfills all the commandments (1 John 5:3).

In the end the authorities exiled John to the barren island of Patmos (cf. Rev. 1:9) off the west coast of Asia Minor. Those who knew John could not help but remember him best by his signature admonition, "My little children, love one another" (cf. 1 John 4:11).

ASK YOURSELF

The primacy of love is everywhere championed and proclaimed in the Scriptures. So why isn't it as evident as it should be among God's people? What areas of the church are in the most need of love in practice? What aspects of your own life need its warmth and strength?

PHILIP: A SEEKER

. . . Philip and Bartholomew. —MATT. 10:3*a*

Philip was the first person the Lord expressly commanded to "Follow Me" (John 1:43). No one wants to follow Christ unless the Father gives him the desire (cf. John 6:44), and God gave Philip the desire to find Messiah before Jesus called him.

From what he said to Nathanael (Bartholomew) in John 1:45, Philip was studying Scripture to learn God's plan regarding Messiah. God used His Word and prepared his heart so that Philip was ready to obey when Jesus instructed him to follow Him. Thus when he heard Jesus' call, he knew it was from God. The joy and excitement that filled his soul at this time must have been great.

The fact that Philip not only immediately embraced Christ by faith but also began to tell others of Him shows the genuineness of Philip's conversion. Right after Jesus called him, Philip went to his friend Nathanael and told him he had found the Messiah. Because Philip already knew and cared about Nathanael, it made sense that he shared this greatest discovery with his best friend. Philip and Nathanael are mentioned together in every list of the apostles, thus it's likely they were friends a long time before they met Jesus. Philip the seeker of the Lord became one who sought others for Him.

ASK YOURSELF

Do you have any close friends who are still unsaved and somewhat cynical or suspicious of Christ and His purposes? Make this a day to redouble your prayer efforts for them, and also to stay watchful and diligent in keeping the gospel an open topic of conversation between you and them.

PHILIP: PRACTICAL AND ANALYTICAL

. . . Philip and Bartholomew. —MATT. 10:3*a*

In addition to being a seeker, Philip also had a practical and analytical mind. When Jesus tested him and asked how they could feed the 5,000 (John 6:5), Philip thought only of the practical problems presented. But he should have realized that Jesus' question exceeded the practical and implied the impossible. After all, Philip had seen Jesus perform many miracles, including when He turned water into wine to meet the needs of people at a wedding (John 2:1–11).

Nonetheless, Philip gave an answer based solely on financial considerations: "Two hundred denarii worth of bread is not sufficient for them, for everyone to receive a little" (v. 7). This response was sincere but showed no consideration for Jesus' supernatural provision. Philip was face-to-face with the Son of God, but for this situation he saw only the inadequate, earthbound, human solution. In this way he lost sight of the unlimited potential of divine power.

An essential characteristic for good leadership is to have a broad sense of the possible. Like most people, however—and unfortunately perhaps many believers—Philip limited himself to a human-centered view of the impossible. His methodical, common-sense approach, helpful as that can be, was an obstacle to the greater virtue of trusting God for the impractical. Philip and his fellow apostles did not yet understand Jesus' teaching that "with people this is impossible, but with God all things are possible" (Matt. 19:26).

ASK YOURSELF

What "impossible" situation are you facing right now? How have you tried to manufacture your own solution or let the bleakness of the circumstances cause you to doubt God's interest, despairing of any good outcome? What limits have you mistakenly placed on Him?

BARTHOLOMEW: OVERCOMING PREJUDICE

. . . Philip and Bartholomew. —MATT. 10:3*a*

Bartholomew (or Nathanael, as he is called in John 1:45–51, the only passage that describes him in detail) came to Christ via his friend Philip, who "found Nathanael and said to him, 'We have found Him of whom Moses in the Law and also the Prophets wrote—Jesus of Nazareth, the Son of Joseph'" (John 1:45). Philip knew Nathanael would recognize these references to Messiah because they both loved God's truth and longed for the arrival of the Anointed One.

But Nathanael initially did not judge Jesus by what He did and taught, being prejudiced by His coming from Nazareth—an unrefined, rowdy town with an unsavory reputation. Nathanael's question, "Can any good thing come out of Nazareth?" (v. 46) was probably commonly asked among Galilean Jews.

Such prejudice is an unjustified generalization based on superior feelings, and it can be a real obstacle to truth. Prejudice wants to turn a deaf ear and blind eye to any information that doesn't fit cherished and preconceived notions. Satan often appeals to human prejudices and gets people to reject the gospel without even listening to what it really is. Man-made prejudices blinded many Jews of Jesus' day to the true teaching of their Scriptures and resulted in their rejection of Christ, even though He clearly fulfilled Old Testament prophecy.

Fortunately, Nathanael's genuine desire to find God's truth overcame his initial prejudice, and he went with Philip to see and trust Jesus for himself.

ASK YOURSELF

We tend to think that prejudice lost its grip on us and our culture following, for instance, civil rights legislation in America or the end of apartheid in South Africa. But can you truly declare yourself free from sizing people up by class, race, and background? In what ways does prejudice continue to dampen the effectiveness of the church?

BARTHOLOMEW: A GENUINE PERSON

. . . Philip and Bartholomew. —MATT. 10:3a

Nathanael was a true, spiritual Jew (Rom. 2:29) and a genuine person, "in whom there [was] no deceit!" (John 1:47c). Unlike many of his fellow Jews (e.g., the Pharisees), Nathanael was free from guile and phoniness.

Nathanael did not swell with pride at Jesus' commendation, but simply wondered how He could know about the inner life of someone He had not met before (v. 48a). In his genuineness and humility, Nathanael may have thought Jesus' assessment was mere flattery. But the Lord's next words removed all questions: "Before Philip called you, when you were under the fig tree, I saw you" (v. 48b). Nathanael now realized Jesus was omniscient and declared, "Rabbi, You are the Son of God; You are the King of Israel" (v. 49).

Jesus said to Nathanael, in effect, "I saw you in your private place of retreat, and I could see what was in your heart." God answered Nathanael's prayers and brought his search for the Messiah to a joyous conclusion. Because his heart was prepared to find Christ, he promptly embraced Him as soon as he encountered Him. Nathanael's tremendous faith caused Jesus to declare to him, "Because I said to you that I saw you under the fig tree, do you believe? You will see greater things than these" (v. 50).

Nathanael might have understood Jesus' glory as well or better than any of his fellow apostles. Thus we can reasonably deduce that he was one of Jesus' most teachable and dependable apostles.

ASK YOURSELF

How has Jesus surprised you lately—whether from a Scripture that suddenly sang with new meaning, or a miraculous turn of events He caused, or a deep awareness of His presence at a time when you really needed it. How do we keep ourselves able to be astounded by Jesus?

THOMAS: WILLINGNESS TO DIE

... Thomas and Matthew the tax collector. —MATT. 10:3*b*

Thomas was willing to die for Jesus (John 11:16) because he had complete faith in Him. Thomas had such an intense love for his Savior that he felt he could not live without Him. If Christ was willing to face certain death in Jerusalem (cf. vv. 7–9), so was Thomas. As Herbert Lockyer wrote, "Thomas, come life, come death, was resolved not to forsake his Lord, seeing he was bound to Him by a deep and enthusiastic love."

Thomas and the other disciples had virtually no comprehension of Jesus' death, resurrection, and ascension (cf. 14:1–5). Yet Thomas took the initiative to encourage all of them to go with Jesus to Jerusalem and face whatever awaited them there (11:16). As a pessimist, Thomas anticipated the worst results; yet he was willing to go with Jesus. His pessimism makes his words and subsequent actions all the more courageous.

Thomas had no illusions about coming events. He did not flinch in the face of potential danger, preferring death rather than disloyalty to Christ. What Thomas feared more than anything was a permanent separation from his Lord, and his love for Christ made that fear unbearable. Jesus understood Thomas's heartfelt concerns and therefore assured him—as well as all who would ever read these words—that He could be trusted for salvation: "I am the way, and the truth, and the life" (14:6).

ASK YOURSELF

Pessimists say they are actually just realists—that seeing the glass half empty is the only way to accurately describe it. If you're more of an optimist, what value could you glean from those more blunt? If a pessimist, what could you learn from those more hopeful?

THOMAS: HIS DOUBTS

. . . Thomas and Matthew the tax collector. —MATT. 10:3*b*

Thomas's notorious attitude of doubt concerning Jesus' resurrection (John 20:25) was essentially the same as the other apostles when they first heard He had risen (Luke 24:11; cf. v. 25; John 20:9–10). When Jesus appeared to the ten behind closed doors, they weren't sure He had physically come to them until "He showed them both His hands and His side" (John 20:20). With the exception of John (v. 8), none of the apostles believed Jesus had risen until they saw Him in person.

The Lord allowed Thomas, who had been absent, to remain in doubt another eight days after the appearance to his colleagues. The next time He came to the disciples (20:26), Jesus singled out Thomas: "Reach here with your finger, and see My hands; and reach here your hand and put it into My side; and do not be unbelieving, but believing" (v. 27). Thomas responded with one of the greatest professions of faith ever uttered: "My Lord and my God!" (v. 28).

After that, Thomas's doubt was gone and he believed with certainty that the Lord Jesus was God's Son and truly alive, having been raised from the dead. Christ's gentle rebuke of Thomas (vv. 28–29) does not really detract from his position of faith because his doubts, although more openly declared, were really just the same as the other apostles' private ones.

Tradition holds that Thomas was faithful to evangelize as far east as India. One church in southwest India bears his name and traces its origins to him.

ASK YOURSELF

So Thomas gets a bad rap for being one of many with reasonable doubts about the news they were hearing. When have you been misunderstood or had a certain statement or action blown out of proportion? How can we keep from passing such quick, sweeping judgment on others?

MATTHEW: ACCEPTING TRUE DISCIPLESHIP

... Thomas and Matthew the tax collector. —MATT. 10:3*b*

Prior to his salvation and service with Jesus, Matthew was a hated tax collector (Matt. 9:9). This job had a stigma most would want to bury, yet Matthew here still humbly refers to it. He also shows humility in his low-profile role in his own gospel. Mark 2:15 and Luke 5:29 tell us that Jesus' banquet with "many tax collectors and sinners" was in Matthew's house. Matthew's own Gospel merely implies that he hosted the event (9:10). He was eager to introduce those he knew to Christ, but he wanted to downplay his personal role.

Matthew's humility perhaps stemmed from his great sense of unworthiness in the face of God's superabundant saving grace. He was the silent apostle until the Holy Spirit prompted him to write the opening book of the New Testament—twenty-eight chapters on the ministry of Jesus Christ.

It's likely that Matthew sensed the sinfulness of his former life as none of the other disciples did. He had been willingly involved in extortion, deception, graft, and no doubt various forms of immorality. However, like the woman caught in adultery (Luke 7:36–50), the Lord forgave Matthew much and thus he loved Him much (see vv. 42–43). He proved his love by his desire to tell his friends and others through the centuries (by his gospel) the good news of Jesus' salvation.

ASK YOURSELF

How wonderful that the past sins designed by our enemy to cause us shame have been transformed by Christ into instruments of grace and gratitude—living examples of what He can forgive on His way to reclaiming lost souls. Is Satan still trying to keep old sins hung around your neck?

JAMES THE SON OF ALPHAEUS:
AN ORDINARY DISCIPLE

. . . James the son of Alphaeus, and Thaddaeus. —MATT. 10:3c

This James was considerably less influential than James the son of Zebedee. That the son of Alphaeus is called "James the Less" in Mark 15:40 could also mean that he was smaller or younger than the more famous James.

Matthew's father was also named Alphaeus (Mark 2:14), which means this apostle could have been a brother to Matthew. Also, Mark 15:40 says James the Less's mother, along with other women, was present at the crucifixion. John 19:25 refers to her as the wife of Clopas, a form of the name Alphaeus, a fact further indicating that James and Matthew could have been brothers.

We can assume this James faithfully served Christ while an earthly apostle, and we know he is in heaven with the other apostles (cf. Matt. 19:28). But he was not a gifted leader endowed with outstanding ability or achievement. Rather he was an ordinary man used in ordinary ways to help accomplish the extraordinary mission of advancing the Lord's kingdom into the entire world.

To this day James the son of Alphaeus remains largely unknown from among the apostles of Jesus. None of his words or deeds is recorded in Scripture. Some of the church fathers claimed James preached in the area that is now Iran and that people there martyred him because of the gospel. How different world history might have been had they been more receptive to the good news!

ASK YOURSELF

Perhaps you are one whose role in the church or at work or in other places is a lesser-known, less glamorous, less recognizable position. How do you keep yourself uplifted while often going unnoticed? How can you keep from being envious of those with more public exposure?

THADDAEUS (JUDAS THE SON OF JAMES)

. . . James the son of Alphaeus, and Thaddaeus. —MATT. 10:3c

Two verses (Luke 6:16; Acts 1:13) tell us that Thaddaeus was also known as "Judas the son of James." Most likely Judas was his actual name and Thaddaeus a nickname. This nickname literally means "breast child" and was a common colloquialism for the last family member to be nursed.

In the Upper Room the night before Jesus' arrest, we read of this exchange between Jesus and Thaddaeus:

> "He who has My commandments and keeps them is the one who loves Me; and he who loves Me will be loved by My Father, and I will love him and will disclose Myself to him." Judas (not Iscariot) said to Him, "Lord, what then has happened that You are going to disclose Yourself to us and not to the world?" (John 14:21–22)

The apostle focused on a visible manifestation and wondered how Christ could reveal Himself only to His disciples and not to everyone else as well.

In light of Jewish misunderstandings about the kingdom, Christ did not reprove Thaddaeus's sincere misapprehension. The question was legitimate and gave our Lord further opportunity to explain His teaching: "If anyone loves Me, he will keep My word; and My Father will love him, and We will come to him and make Our abode with him. He who does not love Me does not keep My words; and the word which you hear is not Mine, but the Father's who sent Me" (vv. 23–24).

Only those whom God purifies by love and who obey His Word perceive the fullness of Christ. Thaddaeus was such a person.

ASK YOURSELF

Do you have some questions for the Lord that continue to exceed your ability to understand? Obviously from this example, He is open to hearing His people ask. But if He decides the answers are more than you need to know or can handle, can you live faithfully with that?

JUDAS ISCARIOT: HIS CALL

. . . and Judas Iscariot, the one who betrayed Him. —MATT. 10:4*b*

Judas never had a saving faith in Jesus, and from the start believed he could have clout within a political and religious enterprise Jesus would establish. In spite of such selfish motives, Judas followed Christ half-heartedly until disillusioned about the real nature of the kingdom.

Jesus chose Judas very purposefully: "For Jesus knew from the beginning who they were who did not believe, and who it was that would betray Him" (John 6:64). The Lord made a further reference to Judas after the false disciples at Capernaum turned away: "'Did I Myself not choose you, the twelve, and yet one of you is a devil?' Now He meant Judas the son of Simon Iscariot, for he, one of the twelve, was going to betray Him" (vv. 70–71).

Before His death, Jesus made additional mentions of Judas's unique situation among the Twelve: "But behold, the hand of the one betraying Me is with Mine on the table. For indeed, the Son of Man is going as it has been determined; but woe to that man by whom He is betrayed!" (Luke 22:21–22; cf. John 17:12).

Although our minds can't understand it, God had predetermined Judas's betrayal of Jesus. At the same time, however, God held him completely accountable for his sin because he acted by his own will. Those seemingly contradictory truths are ultimately resolved only in the mind of God. And we must recognize this as we seek to comprehend other similarly difficult scriptural truths.

ASK YOURSELF

Most every unbeliever thinks their good works or good intentions will be enough to earn them a measure of clout and understanding with God. What keeps this fatal hope alive in a human heart? What can we say in response to those who are so sure about life but so risky about death?

JUDAS ISCARIOT: HIS CHARACTER

. . . and Judas Iscariot, the one who betrayed Him. —MATT. 10:4*b*

Judas possessed many of the same character traits as his fellow apostles, having no less common decency or more innate sinfulness. However, the same sun melts the wax and hardens the clay, and Judas became increasingly fixed in his resistance to Jesus' teachings (cf. John 12:5–6).

Judas was likely one of the youngest apostles and outwardly probably had an acceptable personality and exhibited appropriate Jewish devotion and patriotism. Though not a Zealot, he was eager to remove Roman control from Israel and thought Jesus' messianic kingdom would help accomplish that.

Judas was primarily a materialist who wanted the benefits of a restored Jewish kingdom but had no interest in regeneration or personal holiness. The Lord gave him many opportunities to turn from this temporal, self-centered approach, but Judas did not respond. He would have heard Jesus' parables of the unjust steward, the wedding garments, the rich fool, and other warnings, but he was not really listening or obeying. In this respect Judas must have been a remarkable hypocrite. Unlike Peter and some of the others, he rarely argued with Christ and in all likelihood superficially seemed to agree with Him on most matters.

Judas was part of the group of four disciples that was least intimate with Jesus. Even from that group he operated from the sideline fringe, seldom participating with the other apostles and not being close to any of them. Judas was the ultimate loner and outsider—surely not a character model for any who would follow Jesus Christ.

ASK YOURSELF

There are certain risks and vulnerabilities involved in being engaged with others—in working together and interacting. But what are the greatest dangers of isolating yourself, doing things your own way, resisting or resenting others' influence? Why is this a problematic sign?

JUDAS ISCARIOT: HIS REJECTION OF JESUS

. . . and Judas Iscariot, the one who betrayed Him. —MATT. 10:4*b*

W hen Jesus, at His triumphal entry into Jerusalem, rejected the crowd's crown and instead taught even more fervently about His upcoming arrest and death, Judas knew that Jesus' plans had no relationship to his own motives and schemes. From then on Judas turned his back on Jesus and no longer restrained his sinful motives for self-glory and personal gain. Judas showed his true self when he expressed more concern for "wasted money" used to anoint Jesus (cf. John 12:1–8) than concern for His death.

Judas's interest in Jesus declined first to disappointment, then finally to hatred. He had never loved Jesus or the other disciples but only stole from them and took advantage of them. Now Judas turned completely against all of them.

In the Upper Room, as He began to wash the apostles' feet, Christ declared, "You are clean, but not all of you," referring to Judas (John 13:10). As the betrayal drew closer, Jesus "became troubled in spirit, and testified and said, 'Truly, truly, I say to you, that one of you will betray Me'" (v. 21). His own loss of life did not trouble Him—He willingly laid it down. But Jesus grieved over Judas's pending spiritual death (cf. 2 Peter 3:9), and likely was making one final appeal before it became forever too late (John 13:18).

Our Lord lamented for Judas as He lamented for Jerusalem: "How often I wanted to gather your children together, the way a hen gathers her chicks under her wings, and you were unwilling" (Matt. 23:37).

ASK YOURSELF

Surely you know someone who is undeniably heading down the wrong path in life, but no matter what you say, they will not listen, will not change, will not see the error of their ways or the inevitable end of their actions. What does Jesus' interaction with Judas teach us in this regard?

JUDAS ISCARIOT: HIS BETRAYAL OF JESUS

. . . and Judas Iscariot, the one who betrayed Him. —MATT. 10:4*b*

The incident of Mary's anointing Jesus with perfume (John 12:1–8) likely prompted Judas to initiate his plan to betray Him by receiving thirty pieces of silver (Matt. 26:14–16). Luke adds that Judas "began seeking a good opportunity to betray Him to them apart from the crowd" (22:6). Judas wanted no one to learn of his duplicity—certainly not a hostile crowd—because, like the Jewish leaders, he was a coward (Luke 22:2).

Judas's relatively small compensation for betraying Christ suggests he was willing to settle for any price and that the Jews had a degree of disdain for his treachery. Nevertheless, they pragmatically turned it to their own ends.

To identify Jesus in Gethsemane's darkness, Judas "had given them a signal, saying, 'Whomever I kiss, He is the one'" (Mark 14:44). When the fateful time came, Jesus knew what was happening and "went forth and said to them, 'Whom do you seek?'" (John 18:4). When the crowd formally stated it sought Jesus, He identified Himself (vv. 5–7), but Judas still kissed Him (Matt. 26:49). That was the height of hypocrisy, pretending to love Jesus by the cherished mark of the kiss while turning Him over to His enemies. Despite this evil, Jesus still called Judas "friend" (v. 50)—His love extended beyond Judas's apostasy.

Judas's betrayal against God's Son was most striking, but others have committed the same kind of profanity (Ezek. 13:19; Amos 2:6). Along with all other false apostles, however, Judas is especially guilty and worthy of total disdain.

ASK YOURSELF

It's hard to even begin relating to Judas, but are there any ways that we are routinely or even occasionally guilty of betraying Jesus for cheap alternatives? Do we ever act ashamed of being His follower or feel apologetic for His teachings in Scripture? May there be no Judas in us.

JUDAS ISCARIOT: LESSONS LEARNED FROM HIS LIFE

... and Judas Iscariot, the one who betrayed Him. —MATT. 10:4b

There is great profit from taking an extended look at Judas Iscariot's life. Even sin and tragedy can teach us important lessons.

First, Judas represents history's greatest example of lost opportunity. As one of the original twelve apostles, Judas didn't share his colleagues' receptivity to the gospel or their appreciation of Christ's obedience to it. The Lord gave Judas the most specific warning about sin and many opportunities to repent and believe—but he always refused such offers. Today many people hear the gospel and see real but imperfect examples of its transforming power in their believing friends or family, yet they also reject it.

Second, Judas illustrates wasted privilege. He foolishly bargained to exchange the riches of eternal life for the small value of temporary wealth. This incredible sin also shows the horrific results that can derive from the love of money (see 1 Tim. 6:10).

Third, Judas's life shows us how patient and forbearing God's love can be. Only God could have known Judas's dark heart and yet extended His offer of grace to the very end.

Judas's hypocritical life and treacherous betrayal had to bring much anguish to Jesus' heart. Through that and other earthly torments, God perfected His Son through suffering (Heb. 2:10). And thus He fully empathizes with our sufferings.

ASK YOURSELF

Like everything else in life, we must choose to let even the tragic life of Judas paint our God in broader, more awe-inspiring colors. After several days of examining Jesus' interactions with Judas, what have you seen that causes you to worship, honor, and adore Him even more?

The Apostles' Divine Commission, Part 1

These twelve Jesus sent out after instructing them. —Matt. 10:5a

According to the purpose for which Jesus had called each apostle to follow Him, He here sent each one out on an initial ministry assignment.

Our divine calling and sending is not so direct, but we can still know what it is and that it's come at Christ's command. Three criteria help us know if we are called into the Lord's service.

First, God's Word reveals a strong desire for service when we obey Him (cf. Ps. 37:4). If a godly man aspires to the office of elder, Paul writes, "it is a fine work he desires to do" (1 Tim. 3:1).

Second, there is the confirmation of the church. God uses other believers to confirm His call of persons to ministry and leadership. The qualifications by which the church should measure a believer's suitability for ministry reside in 1 Timothy 3 and Titus 1. Paul well summarized matters for Timothy: "Do not neglect the spiritual gift within you, which was bestowed on you through prophetic utterance with the laying on of hands by the presbytery [elders]" (1 Tim. 4:14).

Third, there is the criterion of opportunity. If and when we have the first two criteria in our lives, the Lord will open a clear door of service (cf. 1 Cor. 16:9).

ASK YOURSELF

If you don't feel confirmed in your calling for Christ, could it be that you've restricted Christian service to a small handful of spiritual vocations and activities? Are you perhaps withholding yourself from Him in some way? Could it be that He's wanting You to wait on Him?

The Apostles' Divine Commission, Part 2

These twelve Jesus sent out after instructing them. —Matt. 10:5a

When a Christian realizes his or her ministry call is of the Lord, he or she must respond as the apostles did, as a soldier does to his superior officer, as a courtroom official does to the judge. God does not call for innovation or creativity from us, but He does demand obedience and faithfulness (1 Cor. 4:2).

Believers, especially pastors and teachers who minister the Word, are not chefs but waiters. God has not called us to prepare the meal, which He has already done, but to serve the meal—the message—just as we have received it. Like Paul, any of us who are ministers are under divine compulsion and should remind ourselves, "I have nothing to boast of, for I am under compulsion; for woe is me if I do not preach the gospel" (1 Cor. 9:16).

Not all Christians are called to be preachers, missionaries, or teachers, but all (like the apostles) are called to be Christ's witnesses to the world. No true followers of Jesus Christ escape His command in the Great Commission to "make disciples of all the nations" (Matt. 28:19). The primary, most crucial element for Christian service is the clear understanding that God's Spirit sovereignly calls, gifts, and empowers us to do His work in His way.

ASK YOURSELF

What frightens you, if anything, about the calling God has placed on your life? What does it demand of you that requires more than you can accomplish on your own? How does your calling square with the general call to all believers to bear witness of Him to "all the nations"?

APOSTLES FIRST CALLED TO ISRAEL

Do not go in the way of the Gentiles, and do not enter any city of the Samaritans;
but rather go to the lost sheep of the house of Israel. —MATT. 10:5b–6

Three main reasons explain why Jesus restricted the apostles' ministry at
this time to the Jews. First, the Jews occupied a special place in God's plan.
He chose them to be the people of His covenants, promises, and law. Jesus
and John the Baptist both began their ministries primarily to the Jews with
a call for repentance (Matt.3:1–2; 4:17; cf. John 4:22). Later, Israel was the
launching point for taking the gospel to the rest of the world (Acts 1:8).
Even Paul, the apostle to the Gentiles, first preached in the local synagogue whenever possible (e.g., Acts 9:20; 13:5; 18:4).

Second, the apostles were barely able to witness to their own people,
the Jews, much less to Gentile cultures they didn't understand and despised. Such prejudice for Peter was so strong that God had to persuade
him the gospel was also for Gentiles (Acts 10).

Third, Jesus likely limited the disciples' beginning ministry just to the
Jews for a practical reason. They needed a special field of attack— somewhere they could focus their fledgling outreach efforts. The effective
Christian worker devotes his or her energy and effort into the particular
task God has given. We should be concerned for all areas of Christian
ministry, but we should not feel we have to do it all ourselves.

Jesus' restricted command to the apostles was valid for that time in
redemptive history. And it illustrates a point that is valid for us: God
gives His children clear, specific objectives for ministry.

ASK YOURSELF

Has Jesus' calling on your life been redefined or recast at different points
through the years? Have you joined Him in a specific task for a season
of time, only to have Him shift your focus elsewhere upon its
accomplishment? What is the beauty of this kind of variety in our lives?

THE APOSTLES' CLEAR MESSAGE

And as you go, preach, saying,
*"The kingdom of heaven is at hand." —*MATT. 10:7

Many of the lost fail to embrace the gospel because no one has presented it clearly to them. That's because many Christians communicate a muddled gospel that emphasizes lots of secondary issues, thanks in many respects to their leaders' digressing from the genuine message. A sure way for Satan to weaken the gospel is simply to prevent its clear and accurate presentation.

The heart of the gospel message Jesus gave the apostles was clear: "The kingdom of heaven is at hand." These men were essentially to expound this one foundational, incontrovertible truth, which reveals itself in three aspects. First, the kingdom reveals itself in conversion. That's when someone enters it by trusting Christ for salvation. Second, the kingdom reveals itself in believers' consecration, as they obediently live out principles in God's Word (cf. Rom. 14:17). Third, the kingdom will in the future reveal itself as the millennial kingdom when Jesus returns to earth and rules for a thousand years and then makes the transition to the eternal kingdom (Matt. 25:31; Rev. 11:15; 20:4).

The essence of a kingdom is not its geographical area but the actual ruling of its king. Such is true of the kingdom of heaven; it is the domain of divine lordship in which God rules His subjects by His sovereign will. All of Jesus Christ's earthly teaching pointed to the truths and principles of life in God's kingdom—now and for eternity.

ASK YOURSELF

What are a few of the side issues that often get interjected—either by you or by others—into your spiritual conversations? What are some good ways to keep from getting distracted by such goose chases and rabbit trails? Remind yourself of the essentials of Christian faith.

THE APOSTLES' CREDENTIALS: HEALING AND RAISING THE DEAD

Heal the sick, raise the dead, cleanse the lepers, cast out demons. —MATT. 10:8a

"The signs of a true apostle," Paul wrote, are "signs and wonders and miracles" (2 Cor. 12:12). It was with such confirming credentials that Christ empowered the apostles for their first ministry. Such phenomena did not occur merely to demonstrate raw supernatural power. Instead, the miracles created profound wonder for eyewitnesses and displayed God's character and kingdom. The healing miracles pointed to His compassion and mercy and His care for the suffering and needy. The future earthly kingdom will bring the removal of disease and the restoration of broken bodies; thus the apostles' works previewed the millennium (cf. Isa. 29:18; 35:5–6; 42:7).

Though signs and wonders ceased at the end of the apostolic age, true Christian ministers still serve the sick, suffering, downtrodden, and needy. The spiritual leader who devotes all his efforts to the healthy and well-off is not really from God or is not completely faithful to his call. Everyone needs the gospel and every believer needs continued divine provision, but the Lord has compassion especially for those in greatest need (see Pss. 35:10; 140:12; Isa. 41:17).

The power to raise the dead and cast out demons was also an apostolic credential from the Lord Jesus. By this the apostles could show God's power even by bringing the dead back to life and conquering the invisible kingdom of Satan.

The mark of God's power still validates the ministries of all those who are sent out to further His kingdom. Such endeavors result in redeemed lives, the granting of spiritual understanding, and the sanctification of Christ's church.

ASK YOURSELF

Be in prayer for those you know who are in serious need. Write a note, place a call, or make a visit to encourage someone who is caught in suffering and seeking relief.

THE APOSTLES' CREDENTIALS: UNSELFISHNESS

Freely you received, freely give. —MATT. 10:8*b*

The apostles' miraculous powers were God's, not theirs, and they were to use them for God's glory, with no thoughts for personal prosperity or advantage. Adopting this same attitude, the faithful servant of Christ today should likewise manifest unselfishness.

The apostles could have become wealthy had they charged for healings, raisings of the dead, and exorcisms. For example, when Simon the magician saw Philip performing dramatic miracles in Samaria, he envisioned much potential income. When he witnessed Peter and John laying hands on believers to confer the Holy Spirit on them, Simon offered those apostles money that he might obtain the same authority. But Peter rebuked him, "May your silver perish with you, because you thought you could obtain the gift of God with money!" (Acts 8:20; see also vv. 18–19).

False teachers typically put a price on their ministries because they are self-serving, not really interested in serving the Lord or people in need. About such "ministers" Peter wrote, "In their greed they will exploit you with false words; their judgment from long ago is not idle, and their destruction is not asleep" (2 Peter 2:3; cf. Isa. 56:11).

Peter also recognized that a primary qualification for elders is that they "shepherd the flock of God . . . not under compulsion, but voluntarily, according to the will of God; and not for sordid gain" (1 Peter 5:2; cf. 1 Tim. 3:3; Titus 1:7). The pastor or teacher who does ministry only for a payment prices himself outside of God's blessing.

ASK YOURSELF

Why are even the talents required to do God's work and to do good for others subject to being pride inducers? What does the enemy stand to gain by encouraging us to be enamored with ourselves and seekers of compliments? What do we stand to lose by letting this happen?

THE APOSTLES' CONFIDENT FAITH

Do not acquire gold, or silver, or copper for your money belts,
or a bag for your journey, or even two coats, or sandals, or a staff;
for the worker is worthy of his support. —MATT. 10:9–10

Jesus commanded the apostles not only to refrain from charging fees for their services, but also not to amass a great amount of wealth in advance of their mission. They were to proceed with empty money belts and were not even to take a bag or sack for food.

The apostles were also to go forth with a minimum of other provisions. That meant leaving behind extra clothing ("coats"), footwear ("sandals"), and protective equipment ("staff"). They were simply to trust their Lord for the provision of whatever else was needed. He established the principle that "the worker is worthy of his support" and that He would and always will be sure to fulfill it.

The rabbis had followed this principle for centuries, and the apostle Paul built upon it when he exhorted Timothy, "The elders who rule well are to be considered worthy of double honor, especially those who work hard at preaching and teaching. For the Scripture says, 'You shall not muzzle the ox while he is threshing,' and 'The laborer is worthy of his wages'" (1 Tim. 5:17–18; cf. 1 Cor. 9:14). We are to do more than merely provide for our pastors' bare needs. If they are faithfully proclaiming God's Word, we are to honor them with generosity.

ASK YOURSELF

Money becomes such an issue when we consider pastors and church leaders. The abuses are well documented and hard to digest. But how can we help safeguard our pastors and staff members from letting financial matters infringe upon their ability to lead and serve?

THE APOSTLES' SETTLED COMMITMENT

And whatever city or village you enter, inquire who is worthy in it,
and stay at his house until you leave that city. —MATT. 10:11

Jesus taught the apostles the ministry principle of settled commitment, which again applies to all who minister. First, God's servant is to find a proper place of lodging while ministering in a particular locale. Second, he should be satisfied to remain there until his work is done.

Wherever the apostles journeyed on their itinerary, they were to find someone to stay with who was recognized as godly, one whose integrity and lifestyle were unquestionably good. And still today, ungodly associations will damage the minister's own spirituality and the effectiveness of his testimony.

After securing adequate accommodations, the servant of Christ should stay there until completing his ministry. He is not to be keeping an eye out for something better, not even a voluntary, unsolicited offer of better lodging. The focus must remain on ministry. His contentment with his guest situation in the community will itself be a testimony. Such humble contentment also benefits the minister's own spirituality because "godliness actually is a means of great gain when accompanied by contentment" (1 Tim. 6:6). Paul mastered these principles well:

> Not that I speak from want, for I have learned to be content in whatever circumstances I am. I know how to get along with humble means, and I also know how to live in prosperity; in any and every circumstance I have learned the secret of being filled and going hungry, both of having abundance and suffering need. (Phil. 4:11–12)

ASK YOURSELF

Can anything truly threaten your contentment if you're committed to maintaining it? Imagine the freedom of feeling settled, even in your current circumstances, not comparing it with others but merely being thankful for what God has given. How could this attitude change your life?

CONCENTRATING ON THE RECEPTIVE

As you enter the house, give it your greeting. If the house is worthy,
give it your blessing of peace. —MATT. 10:12–13a

Jesus wanted the apostles to concentrate their ministry efforts on people most receptive to the gospel. The "worthy" house is representative of the various houses where listeners would appreciate and accept the truth the apostles proclaimed.

Households that positively embraced the gospel message would also receive the blessing of peace. "Peace" in Jesus' day signified much more than simply an absence of strife or war. It also meant total well-being— wholeness of body, mind, and spirit. The further implication for the disciples is that their receptive hearers would receive the fullest possible ministry and God's richest blessing. The Lord later elaborated: "He who receives a prophet in the name of a prophet shall receive a prophet's reward; and he who receives a righteous man in the name of a righteous man shall receive a righteous man's reward" (Matt. 10:41).

Those who would minister for Christ should not necessarily expect to serve *only* where people eagerly receive divine teaching. Many potential areas of mission are exceedingly resistant to sound teaching. The primary focal point under the given circumstances, however, should be the most receptive groups in a particular region. Jesus promised genuine spiritual satisfaction to all who hunger and thirst for righteousness (Matt. 5:6); therefore the faithful witness and teacher should devote himself fully and freely to those who most want the Word of God.

ASK YOURSELF

Does this instruction of Jesus strike you as being non-inclusive and restrictive? Or does it rather speak to the fact that God is also practical, teaching us to operate in ways that make the best use of our time and resources? As always, He never ceases to amaze, even in His simplicity.

THE APOSTLES REJECT THE CONTEMPTUOUS

But if it is not worthy, take back your blessing of peace. Whoever does not receive you, nor heed your words, as you go out of that house or that city, shake the dust off your feet. Truly I say to you, it will be more tolerable for the land of Sodom and Gomorrah in the day of judgment than for that city. —MATT. 10:13b–15

Today's ministry principle is the flip side of yesterday's, namely that the apostles or any ministers of the Word should not spend undue time trying to teach those who persist in rejecting the truth. The offer of peace that our audience stubbornly refuses must be withdrawn after a time. In a related way, this principle applies to how we respond to false teachers. The apostle John says, "If anyone comes to you and does not bring this teaching [Christ's incarnation], do not receive him into your house, and do not give him a greeting; for the one who gives him a greeting participates in his evil deeds" (2 John 10–11).

Jesus is not teaching that we should forsake people who don't immediately come to saving faith. Certainly not everyone who now believes came to that saving recognition right away. So there is a place for patience and perseverance in giving forth the gospel, as Paul urged those Corinthians yet unsaved, "Be reconciled to God" (2 Cor. 5:20). God Himself is extremely patient with sinners, "not wishing for any to perish but for all to come to repentance" (2 Peter 3:9).

The Lord's principle of rejecting the contemptuous states what we must do regarding those who hear the gospel clearly, see dramatic and undeniable evidence of its transforming power, and yet adamantly persist in opposing and refusing it. When a person's mind is so firmly set against the truth, we should not hesitate to turn our ministry efforts to others.

ASK YOURSELF

What are the main reasons that people reject the clear claims and eternal blessings of the gospel? How does being aware of these common obstacles benefit your witnessing efforts? Concentrate on just one of those obstacles today, and consider some biblical ways to refute that objection.

SHEEP AMONG WOLVES

Behold, I send you out as sheep in the midst of wolves. —MATT. 10:16a

The apostles and all of us who follow Jesus until He returns were and are the sheep of God. By this, Jesus vividly highlights the tensions between the believer's vulnerability and his invincibility—between our weakness in ourselves and our strength in Him.

Normally the danger for a flock of sheep is that wolves and other predators come in among the members. But here Christ calls for His apostles (and by extension all His other servants) to go straight into the jaws of their enemies. As the perfect Good Shepherd, He divinely loves and protects His sheep, knows them and is known by them, and even lays down His life for them (see John 10:11–15). But here Jesus begins to illustrate the sheep's rejection and persecution they will face from a God-hating world (the wolves) because of Him. Just as He Himself did not escape opposition and persecution, neither would the apostles nor any believers (cf. vv. 18–27; 16:33). Paul also envisioned that the world and false teachers (wolves) would invade the church (sheep): "I know that after my departure savage wolves will come in among you, not sparing the flock" (Acts 20:29; cf. 8:36; Matt. 7:15).

It is not natural for shepherds to send their sheep into places of certain peril, but that is what the Good Shepherd did with the apostles and does with all disciples. He sends us into a hostile world of ungodly people because that's where we can best serve Him and win others to Him.

ASK YOURSELF

What are some of the most prevalent hostilities you face in the world—differences of opinion, attitude, and lifestyle that make it hard for you to maintain stalwart allegiance to your Savior in public situations? How do you handle one of those hostilities when it rears its head?

COUNTING THE COST

Behold, I send you out as sheep in the midst of wolves. —MATT. 10:16a

Today's evangelism doesn't often declare the sinner's need to count the cost of salvation by repenting of sin and embracing the lordship of Jesus Christ. Nor does today's preaching emphasize the need to come to Christ humbly through the narrow gate as one hungers and thirsts for righteousness and then walks the narrow road of sanctification. How often do we hear calls for believers to take up their crosses, follow Christ, and go into the world as sheep led to slaughter? The popular appeal is a disingenuous call to ease, riches, and ambition—as an enticement for unbelievers to accept Christ and a motivation for believers to follow Jesus. But He made no such offers, promising instead hardship, suffering, and death for His disciples.

In other words, our Lord does not send forth His followers without warning us about the demands and dangers of discipleship. And the apostles certainly did not mislead the early church about the true cost of discipleship. The apostle Paul, Timothy's father in the faith, cautioned him that "all who desire to live godly in Christ Jesus will be persecuted" (2 Tim. 3:12). This does not mean that the unbelieving world will continuously inflict suffering and hardship onto Christians. Even the lives of Christ and the apostles were not marked by uninterrupted persecution. But faithfulness to God guarantees that Satan and the world will at different times and in varying degrees require believers to pay a price for obedience to His Word.

ASK YOURSELF

How do these unpopular teachings of Jesus affect you? Do they make you cringe under the weight of unwelcome realities? Or do they make you own your faith even more determinedly, ready to face whatever the Lord allows as a fitting backdrop for His grace and power?

HAVING AN INNOCENT ATTITUDE, PART 1

So be shrewd as serpents and innocent as doves. —MATT. 10:16*b*

Those who serve Jesus Christ are to be shrewd (as symbolized in ancient lore by serpents) when dealing with the unbelieving world. Paul instructed the Colossian believers, "Conduct yourselves with wisdom toward outsiders, making the most of the opportunity" (Col. 4:5).

Both Jesus and the apostle taught that saying the right thing at the right place and time is vital. This includes having a sense of propriety and seeking the best means to win others. It is always wrong to be needlessly inflammatory. When the Pharisees tried to trap Jesus concerning paying taxes to Rome, He neither condemned the government nor condoned its wicked activities. He simply told them, "Render to Caesar the things that are Caesar's; and to God the things that are God's" (Matt. 22:21).

In complementary fashion, Jesus cited the gentle dove as a representative of innocence, another character trait Christians must possess. Being accurate and uncompromising for the gospel does not mean we should be abrasive or without tact. No servant of Christ was more unswerving for the gospel than Paul, yet he wrote,

> To the Jews I became as a Jew, so that I might win Jews; to those who are under the Law, as under the Law though not being myself under the Law, so that I might win those who are under the Law... I have become all things to all men, so that I may by all means save some. (1 Cor. 9:20, 22*b*)

ASK YOURSELF

Which of these do you find the most difficult or unnatural to practice—discerning wisdom, or gracious tact? Do you view one or the other as being unnecessary or not worth aspiring to? How have you ever seen these seemingly contradictory skills at work in one person?

Having an Innocent Attitude, Part 2

So be shrewd as serpents and innocent as doves. —Matt. 10:16*b*

An innocent attitude is more than avoiding negative approaches. It also includes the positive attribute of purity. Nothing that is impure, untruthful, or unethical can make the gospel witness more effective. Paul assured his Thessalonian brethren that his ministry did "not come from error or impurity or by way of deceit" (1 Thess. 2:3).

Believers must be like their Lord Himself—their great "high priest, holy, innocent, undefiled" (Heb. 7:26). In further following Christ's and the apostles' examples, "when we are reviled, we bless; when we are persecuted, we endure; when we are slandered, we try to conciliate" (1 Cor. 4:12–13; cf. Luke 6:27; 1 Peter 2:23).

When some bystanders at the Jerusalem Sanhedrin rebuked Paul for reviling the high priest (Acts 23:3–4), he apologized: "I was not aware, brethren, that he was high priest; for it is written, 'You shall not speak evil of a ruler of your people'" (v. 5). Paul knew that what he said, although correct, was inappropriate and unwise because he uttered it against a leader and in defensive anger.

Integrity and humble purity are practical marks of truthfulness for the minister of Christ, without which an otherwise biblical gospel presentation is distorted and less effective.

ASK YOURSELF

Have you ever approached Christian witnessing as a contact sport, feeling the need to sneak and connive to set up an evangelistic encounter? How could you infuse your sharing about Christ with more compassion for the hearer, with more respectful kindness and consideration?

THE CONCEPT OF PERSECUTION

But beware of men, for they will hand you over to the courts and scourge you in their synagogues; and you will even be brought before governors and kings for My sake, as a testimony to them and to the Gentiles. —MATT. 10:17–18

The devil persecutes the church of Jesus Christ through men—men who are wolves that slander, oppress, imprison, torture, and kill believers.

The Lord warns us to be on guard and discerning in relation to these enemies. Many Christians insist on putting the best spin on every evil. This does not show love, however, but rather foolishness and self-deception. It's one thing to love our enemies and not return evil for evil, but to deny they are our enemies is something else.

Jesus had already promised blessing for those who are persecuted (Matt. 5:10–11). Here He promises the actual persecution that brings blessing. The Lord's purpose was not to frighten the disciples and make them suspicious of every nonbeliever. Their mission was to reach the unsaved and see them transformed from the kingdom of darkness to the kingdom of light. But the apostles needed to realize, as we do, that the world usually will not receive the gospel and its messengers with open arms.

We must also remember that the ultimate enemies who seek to persecute us are Satan and his demons, those described by Paul as "the rulers . . . powers . . . world forces of this darkness . . . the spiritual forces of wickedness in the heavenly places" (Eph. 6:12). Satan will enlist as many unbelievers as possible in his battle against God's kingdom, and we, with the Lord's help, must be prepared for the struggle.

ASK YOURSELF

How have unrealistic expectations affected your faithfulness to Christ and His calling? How dependent are you upon certain levels of ease, acceptance, and approval—without which you tend to doubt the goodness of God or withdraw from active ministry and service?

PERSECUTION BY RELIGION

For they will hand you over to the courts and scourge you in their synagogues.
—MATT. 10:17*b*

In advance of the apostles' going forth in Jesus' name, He told them it was certain that one day the authorities would punish them in Jewish religious courts. Paul as the unconverted Saul of Tarsus participated in such persecution. Years later as an apostle and persecuted believer, he recalled his confession before God "that in one synagogue after another I used to imprison and beat those who believed in You" (Acts 22:19). But eventually the weapon of persecution relentlessly turned on him, and the Jews scourged him at least five times (2 Cor. 11:24), probably always in a synagogue.

Over the centuries since Paul's day, many religious groups—some even using the name of Christ—have and will yet persecute millions of believers by harassment, oppression, imprisonment, torture, and killing. Before the apostolic era was over, persecution by religion had already started against the church. Local silversmiths and pagan idol makers in Ephesus strongly opposed Paul because his gospel preaching had sharply cut into their sale of idols and the income of the tradesmen (Acts 19:24–29).

The final persecution of Christ's followers will come from the worldwide religious system called "Babylon the great, the mother of harlots and of the abominations of the earth" that will become "drunk with the blood of the saints, and with the blood of the witnesses of Jesus" (Rev. 17:5–6). Humanity's religions have always opposed the true church, and they will fight against Christ and His people right to the end, but the Lord will prevail (Rev. 18:21–19:21; 20:7–10).

ASK YOURSELF

How frustrated are you by the harsh criticism and misunderstanding you and your church sometimes face from other religious groups, even from other Christian denominations? Why is this kind of persecution so hard to deal with? What does it distract us from?

MARCH 5

PERSECUTION BY GOVERNMENT

You will even be brought before governors and kings for My sake,
as a testimony to them and to the Gentiles. —MATT. 10:18

Throughout church history many governments have engaged in the persecution of Christians. Not long after the drama of Pentecost, the first Herod Agrippa "laid hands on some who belonged to the church in order to mistreat them. And he had James the brother of John put to death with a sword. When he saw that it pleased the Jews, he proceeded to arrest Peter also" (Acts 12:1–3). Herod's incentive in these actions, though involving the Jews, was more personal and political than religious.

As Christianity spread throughout the Roman Empire, Rome viewed it as a threat to its entire social and economic system. As a result, the government frequently leveled false charges against believers. Officials accused them of cannibalism regarding the Lord's Supper (partaking of the body and blood of Christ), immorality at love feasts, and rebellion for teaching Christ's return to establish a kingdom. In more modern times, totalitarian governments have killed millions of Christians and persecuted and imprisoned many others.

God established government to preserve social order (Rom. 13:1–7); Satan has also used it to promote his work and oppose God's. When government's citizens abandon God and His standards, even the most democratic countries, such as in North America and western Europe, will come to obstruct and shackle the free expression and practice of Christianity. Therefore we must never take for granted the present freedoms we have to worship and minister.

ASK YOURSELF

How have you felt the opposition of government to your freedom of religious practice and public expression? What is the best reaction to these kinds of threats and restraints? How would your life be affected if some of these lifelong liberties were further curtailed?

MINISTRY PROVISION

When they hand you over, do not worry about how or what you are to say; for it will be given you in that hour what you are to say. For it is not you who speak, but it is the Spirit of your Father who speaks in you. —MATT. 10:19–20

Whenever the threat of persecution is present, it is very difficult not to worry about what we will say. When falsely charged with wrongdoing or unfairly treated, it is only natural to speak out in our own defense and try to convince our accusers of our innocence. The apostle Paul, however, admonished us to "be anxious for nothing, but in everything by prayer and supplication with thanksgiving let your requests be made known to God" (Phil. 4:6). And in the event we would ever be hauled before a religious or civil court, Jesus gave us the added promise that "it will be given [us] in that hour what [we] are to say." If we suffer for Christ, He will surely support us and defend us.

Many of the great martyrs of the church spoke their most powerful and memorable testimonies just as their persecutors were putting them to death. Undoubtedly the Lord gave such martyrs a special presence of mind and clarity of utterance they would otherwise not have been able to have.

For the apostles, Jesus' promise of ministry provision included the all-important one of divine inspiration. "For it is not you who speak," He assured the twelve, "but it is the Spirit of your Father who speaks in you." Had God not fulfilled this promise we would not have had the New Testament and would have been left adrift without a most crucial component of daily ministry provision.

ASK YOURSELF

Do you suffer from insecurity at times because the practice of Christian faith rarely comes with specific instructions? How do you deal with the risks of vulnerability in the context of total confidence in Christ? Simply put, what are you most afraid of in living for Him?

Some Believers Hated by Family

Brother will betray brother to death, and a father his child; and children will rise up against parents and cause them to be put to death. —MATT. 10:21

This is a sobering promise from our Lord that some Christians may be persecuted even by their own families. Later on during this same time of teaching, Jesus told the disciples, "I came to set a man against his father, and a daughter against her mother, and a daughter-in-law against her mother-in-law." Then, quoting Micah 7:6, He cautioned that "a man's enemies will be the members of his household" (Matt. 10:35–36; cf. Mark 13:12).

In the Roman persecutions during the early centuries of the church, numerous parents, siblings, and children betrayed an untold number of Christians from their own families to the authorities. Enemies of Christianity have repeated that insidious practice thousands of times over the centuries, and it is not unknown in our day, especially in totalitarian countries or areas dominated by false religion (e.g., radical Islam or Hinduism).

Families in certain religious cultures will hold a "funeral service" for a family member who converts to Christianity. In the eyes of his or her relatives, this person is no longer considered truly alive or a legitimate member of the family. One observation says that only two things are more powerful than natural love within families—first, God's love that makes one willing to put Him before family; and second, Satan's hatred that will persecute those who desert him.

ASK YOURSELF

How have you experienced derision or disloyalty from your family because of your Christian beliefs—or if not your overarching beliefs, at least the way they impact your decisions, your child rearing, your priorities, and your lifestyle? How do you respond to this kind of criticism?

ALL BELIEVERS HATED BY SOCIETY

You will be hated by all because of My name, but it is the one
who has endured to the end who will be saved. —MATT. 10:22

Every single unbeliever on earth does not necessarily hate Christians.
But history has shown that unbelievers of all classes, religions, and ethnic
groups have hated believers.

Society does not persecute some Christians simply because the world
does not notice their weak testimonies. But other believers are in frequent conflict with the culture because they will not compromise biblical
doctrine and standards to accommodate sinful human nature or society's
evils.

However, Paul confronted the world with this declaration: "The
wrath of God is revealed from heaven against all ungodliness and unrighteousness of men who suppress the truth in unrighteousness" (Rom.
1:18). This blunt and unpopular—but biblical—pronouncement will
guarantee society's opposition to the gospel and those who proclaim it.

Endurance under persecution identifies the genuine believer: "the
one who has endured to the end who will be saved." Salvation is totally
the work of God's grace, but endurance provides part of the proof that a
person is a child of God. The letter to the Hebrews sets forth the same
truth this way: "We have become partakers of Christ, if we hold fast the
beginning of our assurance firm until the end" (3:14). Theologians call
this endurance the perseverance of the saints (see John 8:31; Col. 1:21–
23; Heb. 10:39; 2 Peter 1:10). Therefore, nothing else matches the persecution of Christians in its purifying and strengthening effect (cf. James
1:12; Rev. 2:10*b*).

ASK YOURSELF

Since endurance is such a necessary ingredient to living the Christian life
over the long haul, how do we prepare ahead of time to be able to draw
it up when needed? Why is the Christian's endurance to be preferred
over the endurance required of all to navigate life's journey?

THE RIGHT RESPONSE TO PERSECUTION

Whenever they persecute you in one city, flee to the next; for truly I say to you, you will not finish going through the cities of Israel until the Son of Man comes.
—MATT. 10:23

We should never seek out persecution or want to endure it for its own sake—or even ostensibly for Jesus' sake. God never commanded believers to persist at ministering in a certain place of animosity and danger. Even the apostle Paul followed Jesus' exhortation of fleeing from one city to the next to get away from persecution. Paul did not try to test the limits of his opposition but endured fierce opposition as need be while he ministered. However, he departed from a city or region when his effectiveness there ended. Every faithful missionary and minister should follow that pattern until Christ returns.

Even though the apostles spent three years learning from Jesus, ministering with Him, and realizing He was the vine and they were the branches (John 15:5), when they realized He was finally going to leave them, they panicked (cf. 14:5, 8).

Jesus made it clear that if the world persecuted Him, it would persecute His servants also (15:20). But just as the Lord promised persecution, He also promised to send the Holy Spirit to indwell His followers (15:26–16:15). It was both necessary and advantageous for Jesus to leave following His death and resurrection, in order to make way for the Comforter to come and empower the apostles and all subsequent believers. Our Lord assures us, "These things I have spoken to you, so that in Me you may have peace. In the world you have tribulation, but take courage; I have overcome the world" (16:33).

ASK YOURSELF

Have you known individuals who seemed to glory in their persecutions? What are the deceptions involved in having this misplaced focus? If you are to endure your own particular persecutions as Jesus would desire, what needs to be firmed up in your heart right now?

EMULATING CHRIST, PART 1

*A disciple is not above his teacher, nor a slave above his master. It is enough for the disciple that he become like his teacher, and the slave like his master. If they have called the head of the house Beelzebul, how much more will they malign the members of his household! —*MATT. 10:24–25

It goes without saying that disciples and slaves should not—indeed cannot—place themselves above their teachers or masters. By definition, the disciple has less knowledge and wisdom than his teacher, and the slave stands at a lower socioeconomic level than his master.

Jesus here represents human volition by the figure of disciple and teacher, and he represents divine sovereignty by the figure of slave and master. The two illustrations serve together to underscore the most important principle of discipleship—submission.

Matthew and all the gospels present Jesus as King of kings, Messiah, and Son of God who redeemed all who believe, the One who will ultimately rule the world. As the only Savior and Lord, Christ demands that we who would follow Him do so with genuine submission and emulation.

After David became king of Israel, Abner, the commander of Saul's army, refused to recognize David. For about two years Abner even managed to establish Saul's son Ish-bosheth as ruler over part of the kingdom. The commander soon realized how unqualified Saul's son was to rule and how foolish it had been to oppose David, God's chosen and anointed man, for leadership (see 2 Sam. 2:8–3:21).

The Lord Jesus, as it were, commands the Abners of this world to abandon all foolish allegiances to false masters and gods and to truly become slaves of Jesus Christ.

ASK YOURSELF

If you were being honest, would you be forced to admit that certain areas of your life are not submitted to Christ—perhaps not any more so than ever, perhaps even less than they once were? Confess this as folly today, bringing them not only under His rule but also His blessing.

Emulating Christ, Part 2

*A disciple is not above his teacher, nor a slave above his master. It is enough
for the disciple that he become like his teacher, and the slave like his master.
If they have called the head of the house Beelzebul, how much more will
they malign the members of his household!* —Matt. 10:24–25

We all ought to recognize that true disciples learn from their teachers
in order to be just like the teacher, and that faithful slaves work for their
masters to be just like the master. On another occasion, Jesus taught this:
"A pupil is not above his teacher; but everyone, after he has been fully
trained, will be like his teacher" (Luke 6:40). The disciple's overriding
purpose is to emulate his teacher—not only the teacher's wisdom and
character but also how the teacher treats others.

The Great Commission plainly states the function of Christian discipleship: "to observe all that I commanded you" (Matt. 28:20). A Christian becomes like the Teacher when he diligently absorbs and obeys
Scripture as that Word richly dwells within them every day (Col. 3:16).
The genuine disciple will continue to grow in Christlikeness and will
with other believers rejoice in the future day when "we will be like Him,
because we will see Him just as He is" (1 John 3:2*b*; cf. 2:6).

True disciples do not presume or demand to be loved and accepted by
the world. After all, Jesus was ultimately rejected and crucified by its cruel
and unbelieving forces. Paul understood that believers who knew Christ
and the power of His resurrection would embrace "the fellowship of His
sufferings, being conformed to His death" (Phil. 3:10*b*). That is certainly
what the apostle was committed to. And that is what any disciple of Christ
must be committed to as he faithfully emulates the Lord.

ASK YOURSELF

Think of any regular, ongoing strongholds in your life—particular
places where you find yourself resisting Christ's authority and
prevailing power. What would happen to those if you yielded them to
Jesus' control? What would becoming like Him look like in real life?

EMULATING CHRIST, PART 3

*A disciple is not above his teacher, nor a slave above his master. It is enough for the disciple that he become like his teacher, and the slave like his master. If they have called the head of the house Beelzebul, how much more will they malign the members of his household! —*MATT. 10:24–25

The logical result of becoming like Jesus Christ is to be treated like Him. Jesus here continues His teaching of that truth by switching from the disciple/teacher, slave/master figures to the household (family) head/members of the household figure. Family members who strive to emulate the family head should not expect they will receive better treatment than the head.

Jesus' point in referring to the name Beelzebul, one of pagan origin long used by the Jews as an epithet for Satan, was that if people called Him Satan they would also call His followers the same.

Jesus in effect repeated this warning to the apostles on other occasions. Right before His death He told them, "If the world hates you, you know that it has hated Me before it hated you. If you were of the world, the world would love its own; but because you are not of the world, but I chose you out of the world, because of this the world hates you" (John 15:18–19). The enemies of Christ persecuted Him and the apostles and now His present-day disciples "because they have not known the Father" or the Son (16:3).

Christ's traits of love, joy, peace, and kindness, when displayed by believers, can attract unbelievers to Him. But saints can also become more and more unattractive to the lost. Because unbelievers know nothing of the Lord, many will want nothing of us even though we emulate Him.

ASK YOURSELF

Boil it all down, and what could anyone find not to like about a person who consistently represents Christ in his or her actions and attitudes? What are the underlying points of resistance to an authentic Christian witness? How and what does it threaten in others?

DO NOT FEAR THE WORLD

Therefore do not fear them, for there is nothing concealed that will not be revealed, or hidden that will not be known. —MATT. 10:26

The writer of Proverbs 29:25 admonished us that "the fear of man brings a snare." Fear of how people will react has strangled many Christian testimonies and hindered many examples of potential service that believers would otherwise want to give for the Lord Jesus. We naturally don't want others to scorn or mistreat us, and our human nature does not readily look forward to trials, suffering, or death. We tend to fear entanglement in problems or conflicts. All of these considerations, fostered by society's emphasis on comfort zones and self-preservation, have made Christians increasingly reluctant to confront their culture with gospel demands and standards.

Professed believers who continually refuse to confront the world with Scripture's truths fairly suggest to others that they might not belong to Christ at all. The apostle John gives us clear warning of loving the world more than the things of God: "Do not love the world nor the things in the world. If anyone loves the world, the love of the Father is not in him. For all that is in the world, the lust of the flesh and the lust of the eyes and the boastful pride of life, is not from the Father, but is from the world" (1 John 2:15–16).

Knowing that fierce opposition would often confront the apostles, Jesus comforted them and all believers with these words: "Peace I leave with you. . . . Do not let your heart be troubled, nor let it be fearful" (John 14:27).

ASK YOURSELF

Realizing that being contentious shouldn't be our full-time occupation, how do you determine when a matter is worthy of being confronted—whether in business, within your family, or within your church? What are some issues around you that have already risen to that level?

GOD VINDICATES BELIEVERS, PART 1

*Therefore do not fear them, for there is nothing concealed that will
not be revealed, or hidden that will not be known. What I tell you
in the darkness, speak in the light; and what you hear whispered
in your ear, proclaim upon the housetops.* —MATT. 10:26–27

What the world says now about us is not important; but what God says
about us in the end is of infinite importance. When Christ returns, He
"will both bring to light the things hidden in the darkness and disclose
the motives of men's hearts; and then each man's praise will come to him
from God" (1 Cor. 4:5). God's final vindication of all things should be
the source of our greatest motive as believers to serve Him faithfully as
we fearlessly face the world. Paul further calls this great future reality
"the revealing of the sons of God" (Rom. 8:19) and "the freedom of the
glory of the children of God" (v. 21).

Since Christ has given us a message of truth to declare, we must
make it our business to declare it, not to hide it. Jesus clearly taught this
in His parable of the lamp: "No one after lighting a lamp covers it over
with a container, or puts it under a bed; but he puts it on a lampstand, so
that those who come in may see the light" (Luke 8:16).

When Jesus in today's passage decrees "there is nothing concealed
that will not be revealed, or hidden that will not be known," we can be
sure God will show the world's unrighteousness for what it is, and the
believer's righteousness for what it truly is. Therefore it is sinful to cover
up His light now in order to avoid persecution or criticism. God has
promised to vindicate His children.

ASK YOURSELF

When have you seen God's vindication come to pass in real time, not
waiting for eternity to declare Himself but revealing truth and perspective
to someone who doubted God's faithfulness and questioned your
allegiance to Him? How did this encourage you and change the situation?

GOD VINDICATES BELIEVERS, PART 2

*Therefore do not fear them, for there is nothing concealed that will
not be revealed, or hidden that will not be known. What I tell you
in the darkness, speak in the light; and what you hear whispered
in your ear, proclaim upon the housetops.* —MATT. 10:26–27

In Jesus' day, shouts from a housetop—which could be heard for great
distances—publicized personal as well as official announcements. This
method often achieved its objective of having as many people as possible
hear the particular news. Rabbis would blow trumpets from housetops to
signal the start of religious holidays.

Making God's truth known from *modern* housetops, as it were, involves
teaching the hard sayings of Christ and the apostles. We must not be unnec-
essarily offensive in what we say or how we say it. However, when we declare "the whole purpose of God," it will invariably offend unsaved people
because they will stand accused. Lost people do not like to hear they are lost;
sinful people don't want to face the reality that they are sinful; rebellious
people do not want to be indicted as enemies of the Lord. As a result of
Jesus and His apostles boldly teaching such truths, the world largely rejected
their message and persecuted them as offensive messengers.

In these matters the disciple's perspective has to be the same as
God's, realizing that His eternal view now sees the final outcome of
every human life. The world sees certain people (unbelievers and sinners) today as winners, but unless they repent they will be ultimate losers. At the same time those who now seem to be losers (Christians) will
in the final day be winners. Thus we must remain faithful to teach the
unpopular as well as the popular truths of passages such as John 3:16–18.

ASK YOURSELF

In a culture in which churches are increasingly intent on making
Christianity appear cool and accommodating, what teachings are rarely
heard from their pulpits? How would some of their leaders probably
respond to this charge? How should we in turn respond to them?

Believers Venerate God, Part 1

Do not fear those who kill the body but are unable to kill the soul; but rather
fear Him who is able to destroy both soul and body in hell. —Matt. 10:28

The harm the opponents of God's truth can do to saints is only temporary and limited. Therefore we should not fear (be afraid with terror of) them but instead fear (have awe and veneration of) God, who alone "is able to destroy both soul and body in hell."

When the apostle Paul's friends heard that he would be arrested by the Jews and turned over to the Romans (Acts 21:10–11), they began crying. Paul then remonstrated with them, "What are you doing, weeping and breaking my heart? For I am ready not only to be bound, but even to die at Jerusalem for the name of the Lord Jesus" (v. 13). Paul was not afraid of those who could kill just the physical body: "I do not consider my life of any account as dear to myself" (Acts 20:24).

The point of the Lord's statement here is that His disciples should fear no one but God, who is the only one who can send someone to spiritual death, eternally separated from Him. God will cast even Satan himself finally into hell, a domain ultimately under His control, not the devil's.

Our fear is to be one of reverential awe and honor toward God, not one of terror or fright that we might be damned. That's because the Christian's eternal destiny is sealed in heaven. Jesus mentions God's ability to impose eternal loss and ruin on people to contrast the Father's unlimited, permanent power with Satan's limited, temporary power. That being true, we have all the reason we need to venerate God now and for all eternity.

ASK YOURSELF

The fear of the Lord (the Proverbs say—1:7; 9:10) is the beginning of wisdom and knowledge. What would change about your attitudes and behavior if this became your starting point for dealing with temptation, handling relationships, approaching worries—everything?

BELIEVERS VENERATE GOD, PART 2

Do not fear those who kill the body but are unable to kill the soul; but rather fear Him who is able to destroy both soul and body in hell. —MATT. 10:28

Reverence of God in His sovereign majesty is a powerful motivation for believers to fearlessly minister for Him during their earthly sojourns. Human threats are so weak compared to the power of God's promises.

When Englishman Hugh Latimer was preaching before King Henry VIII in the sixteenth century, he reportedly told himself, "Latimer! Latimer! Remember that the king is here; be careful what you say." That was followed by the self admonishment, "Latimer! Latimer! Remember that the King of kings is here; be careful what you do not say." Enemies of the faith later burned Hugh Latimer at the stake for such unswerving faithfulness. Simply put, he feared failing God more than he feared offending men.

Throughout church history, millions have died for the sake and advancement of Christ's kingdom. Those martyrs feared human threats and opposition so little because they feared God so much.

The faithful disciple values his or her soul so much more than they value their body, and they will gladly sacrifice the physical and corruptible for the spiritual and incorruptible. Jim Elliot, the missionary who was martyred in 1956 along with several colleagues in the most prime years of their lives in the jungles of Ecuador, wrote in his diary, "He is no fool who gives up what he cannot keep to gain what he cannot lose."

ASK YOURSELF

We truly do live in troubling times, though in many respects they are no more frightful (perhaps even less so) than some earlier generations. What are the common experiences of our day that cause you the most fear and uneasiness? How would a proper fear of God affect that?

GOD VALUES DISCIPLES

*Are not two sparrows sold for a cent? And yet not one of them will fall to the
ground apart from your Father. But the very hairs of your head are all numbered.
So do not fear; you are more valuable than many sparrows.* —MATT. 10:29–31

With this down-to-earth illustration Jesus assured the apostles and
everyone who would ever believe in and follow Him through the centuries that He loves and values them more than anything. Consequently,
the Lord will not allow any permanent harm to befall them.

One cent, the coin of least value in Jesus' day, could buy two sparrows, which were as common and of low value then as now. Yet the most
insignificant of those small birds can't fall without God's knowledge.

Christ, who knows everything about every person, illustrates His
omniscience by the spiritually inconsequential fact regarding the number
of hairs on our heads. If Jesus notices such trivial things, He will be all
the more concerned about much more important spiritual matters.

Our Lord's obvious understatement that believers "are more valuable
than many sparrows" points up how infinitely valuable His disciples are to
Him. In the Sermon on the Mount, Jesus persuasively argues, "If God so
clothes the grass of the field, which is alive today and tomorrow is thrown
into the furnace, will He not much more clothe you? You of little faith!"
(Matt. 6:30). Knowing that God values us in such a practical and loving
manner, there is no way you or I should ever be afraid or anxious.

ASK YOURSELF

How often do you experience the crippling effect of worry? Which
situations are the most conducive to sending you reeling under waves of
anxiety? Do you ever feel that worry is a protective measure you can't
afford to let go of? What do you fear would happen if you did?

THE DISCIPLE CONFESSES CHRIST, PART 1

Everyone who confesses Me before men, I will also confess him before
My Father who is in heaven. But whoever denies Me before men,
I will also deny him before My Father who is in heaven. —MATT. 10:32–33

Jesus here warns everyone who would be a follower of His to carefully examine themselves concerning their willingness to confess Him to others. Such willingness determines Christ's own readiness to confess those people before the Father. Paul best exemplified this willingness to identify with Jesus Christ and His gospel: "I am not ashamed of the gospel, for it is the power of God for salvation to everyone who believes, to the Jew first and also to the Greek" (Rom. 1:16). Thousands of other believers throughout history—through preaching, teaching, personal witnessing, and martyrdom—have confessed Christ boldly to the lost and have thus been the most faithful disciples and effective disciple makers.

The word translated "confess" means not only to recognize a truth but to identify with it. Even the demons concede that God made the universe (cf. James 2:19), but as His enemies they do not embrace the truths of His kingdom. Paul instructs us how every person must receive Christ as both Savior and Lord: "If you confess with your mouth Jesus as Lord, and believe in your heart that God raised Him from the dead, you will be saved; for with the heart a person believes, resulting in righteousness, and with the mouth he confesses, resulting in salvation" (Rom. 10:9–10). Outward, oral confession is evidence of inward, genuine belief in the heart.

ASK YOURSELF

Perhaps you're not regularly asked to defend your technical belief that God exists or that Jesus is His Son. But in what other ways does your trust and faith in Him come into question as you interact with others? How have you confessed Him during one of those encounters?

THE DISCIPLE CONFESSES CHRIST, PART 2

Everyone who confesses Me before men, I will also confess him before
My Father who is in heaven. But whoever denies Me before men,
I will also deny him before My Father who is in heaven. —MATT. 10:32–33

Every Christian has occasional lapses from being faithful, which is why the divine promise in 1 John 1:9 is so precious: "If we confess our sins, He is faithful and righteous to forgive us our sins and to cleanse us from all unrighteousness." Peter denied the Lord but afterward wept bitterly in sincere repentance because he had so terribly grieved his Master (Luke 22:54–62). Timothy was like Paul's son in the faith, yet after he had become a church leader, Timothy evidently became hesitant enough about proclaiming the gospel that Paul had to admonish him: "Do not be ashamed of the testimony of our Lord" (2 Tim. 1:8). But feeling shame concerning Christ or His gospel was not the normal attitude for those servants, and it should not be for us either, or for any genuine disciple.

The negative side of Christ's warning is quite sobering: "Whoever denies Me before men, I will also deny him before My Father who is in heaven." This refers to anyone who once confessed Jesus but later renounces Him and proves never to have known Him.

Believers can deny Christ by their actions, by sometimes living by the standards and values of the rest of the world. Those who would follow Jesus can also deny Him by words, using worldly profanity, vulgarity, and blasphemy. But such sins will not be continual patterns for the true disciple. Such men and women earnestly strive to openly confess their Lord wherever they are, whether it's with other believers, a group of serious inquirers, or a hostile group of unbelievers.

ASK YOURSELF

Do you know someone who has backed away from his or her Christian faith, even going so far as to vocally renounce their former beliefs? What have been some of the main contributors to this change of heart? How are you praying for them as the Lord brings them to mind?

THE DISCIPLE'S WILLINGNESS TO FORSAKE FAMILY

He who loves father or mother more than Me is not worthy of Me; and he who loves son or daughter more than Me is not worthy of Me. —MATT. 10:37

Sometimes the gap between Christians and their unbelieving relatives can't be closed and even lasts a lifetime. Nevertheless, real disciples must be willing to pay that price. At least two would-be disciples were not willing to pay that price and follow Jesus wherever He commanded. One wanted to wait for his family inheritance, and the other wanted to wait until he had settled all matters with his family. Of such divided commitment Jesus said, "No one, after putting his hand to the plow and looking back, is fit for the kingdom of God" (Luke 9:62; cf. vv. 57–61).

Sometimes people will not come to Christ because they fear that commitment will cause separation from their spouse. Likewise, a parent might not come because he or she doesn't want to offend their children, or vice versa. But sometimes one family member's coming to faith results in the salvation of the entire family. Thus no one should presume that his conversion and resolve to follow Jesus will automatically have adverse effects within his family. Concern for your salvation and discipleship must have the top priority in your life, no matter what the cost in relationships might be.

God commands Christians to love their families with a self-sacrificing love. But believers' commitment to Jesus Christ is the most important one in all the world, and anything—even family ties—that threatens their commitment must be sacrificed, if necessary.

ASK YOURSELF

We often mistakenly perceive sincere Christian belief as something that should logically earn us approval and respect from others. Why is this a deceptive expectation, and what would be different about your daily practice of faith if you didn't think of it as a way to get acceptance?

THE DISCIPLE'S WILLINGNESS TO DIE FOR CHRIST

He who does not take his cross and follow after Me is not worthy of Me. He who has found his life will lose it, and he who has lost his life for My sake will find it.
—MATT. 10:38–39

Love of one's life can greatly hinder the disciple's dedication to Jesus Christ. The cross represented both excruciating pain and heartless cruelty; but above all it was a symbol of death. The apostles knew that Jesus' command to take up their crosses and follow Him meant they must unreservedly abandon themselves to His lordship, even if that resulted in death.

Contrary to popular belief, the crosses Jesus refers to do not equal life's hardships or tragedies that so often affect us. Nor do they signify some kind of spiritual or mystical identification with Jesus' cross or some sort of radical approach to sanctification ("the crucified life").

No sacrifice for Christ compares with what we receive from Him as a result of our willingness to die in His service. Anyone who thinks he can hold on to his life through the things of the world will lose his life anyway. Earthly life is merely temporary, and anyone who hangs on to it as his or her greatest priority is only clutching something they will invariably lose in the end. In so doing they forfeit the eternal life Christ offers, which is incapable of loss to those who truly embrace it by faith.

Jesus is not singling out martyrdom as a means of salvation, because redemption is all of grace, not works. But the willingness to give up everything, including life itself if necessary, for our Lord's sake reveals the spirit of genuine discipleship and thus the character of one who truly belongs to Christ.

ASK YOURSELF

What are some of the things Christianity has cost you? How would you answer someone who surmised that you have made a bad exchange, that you have sacrificed more than you've received? What assurance has God already given you that His way brings blessed rewards?

THE DISCIPLE'S REWARD

He who receives you receives Me, and he who receives Me receives Him who sent
Me. He who receives a prophet in the name of a prophet shall receive a prophet's
reward; and he who receives a righteous man in the name of a righteous man shall
receive a righteous man's reward. And whoever in the name of a disciple gives to
one of these little ones even a cup of cold water to drink, truly I say to you, he
shall not lose his reward. —MATT. 10:40–42

The disciple's spiritual reward is generally not experienced in this life,
except by faith and hope—God has reserved its primary enjoyment for
heaven.

Those who believe the gospel message will accept the one who
brings it to them. Not even the apostles could forgive sin or reconcile
people to God, but every believer whose witness helps bring someone to
Christ is God's agent of salvation. In that sense Jesus declares here, "He
who receives you receives Me."

In His infinite grace God not only rewards a prophet for his faithfulness but also rewards anyone who receives a prophet in a prophet's
name. In a way that's impossible to fathom, God rewards every person
who receives His people (the righteous) with the same kind of reward
that the righteous get because such persons demonstrate that they also
are righteous (believers).

"Little ones" represent Christians who appear inconsequential and
less important (cf. Matt. 25:31–46). They might be new believers, un-
taught and immature; or they could be seasoned believers who served the
Lord for years behind the scenes and unnoticed. Jesus' point is clear: the
Father will notice and reward even the simplest ministry.

ASK YOURSELF

Who brought the gospel to you, and how have you (or how did you) thank
them for it? Who continues to deliver gospel truth and biblical counsel to
you on a regular basis? Think of some very tangible, very personal ways
you can show your appreciation and encourage their hearts.

JESUS HEALS A SEVERELY IMPAIRED MAN

Then a demon-possessed man who was blind and mute was brought to Jesus, and He healed him, so that the mute man spoke and saw. —MATT. 12:22

Jesus had healed probably thousands of people like the man in this verse. But this healing was a key event in the culmination of Jewish rejection of Him. And it was a gateway to our Lord's teaching some of His most profound spiritual principles.

As with other healings, this one proved Christ's dominion over demons and disease, yet most of the sin-blinded witnesses remained ambivalent about His identity and the source of His power. They knew the Messiah would be a miracle worker, but they also expected Him to display royal fanfare and demonstrate military prowess. By contrast, the Jews saw that Jesus was a Man of compassion, gentleness, and humility, followed by twelve unimpressive apostles and thousands of other ragtag, would-be disciples. The former portrait of Messiah was easy for the Jews to accept; the latter picture was not.

The Jewish leaders for some time had been convinced Jesus was an enemy of Judaism. They were no longer simply skeptical of His ministry and envious of His popularity—now they were committed to His elimination. The religious leaders, along with the Herodians, had decided to kill Jesus more than a year before His crucifixion (cf. Matt. 12:14; Mark 3:6).

The Lord thus likely performed this particular miracle to force the scribes and Pharisees to publicly reveal their verdict against Him. Jesus dramatically delivered the impaired man of three great afflictions. The healed man stood as an incontestable example of the positive effects of Christ's divine, healing power. The miracle showed once again that Jesus was the true God-Man and Savior of sinners.

ASK YOURSELF

Those who say they'd believe in Jesus if they could see Him, or if He'd perform some kind of unquestioned miracle—this account proves just the opposite. But when life gets more complicated than their questions (which it always does), how can you be there to show them Jesus?

AN ABSURD ACCUSATION

*But when the Pharisees heard this, they said, "This man casts out demons only by Beelzebul the ruler of the demons." And knowing their thoughts Jesus said to them, "Any kingdom divided against itself is laid waste; and any city or house divided against itself will not stand. If Satan casts out Satan, he is divided against himself; how then will his kingdom stand?" —*MATT. 12:24–26

The accusation of Jesus' enemies that He cast out demons by the power of Satan was a logical absurdity. It is a truism that any nation, empire, corporate entity, or even household divided against itself will eventually self-destruct. The axiom is just as applicable in the spiritual realm; thus Jesus declared that if the devil were divided against himself, his kingdom wouldn't remain standing for long. Since other than the Godhead, Satan is the universe's most intelligent being, he would not command his forces to fight each other and destroy his own program from within.

Evil such as that directed by Satan is often destructive, including self-destruction. Because the evil one is the author of lies and hatred, confusion and inconsistency often mark his domain. Whereas God rules with order and harmony, Satan and his demons operate by disorder and chaos.

Furthermore, Satan often poses as an angel of light (2 Cor. 11:14), and thus could pretend to cast out a demon simply to give people the impression of a cleansing. He has worked such deception through the ministries of cultists, phony healers, and supposed exorcists for centuries.

In spite of appearances to the contrary, Satan's kingdom is not divided against itself, and he tolerates no disobedience from demons who carry out his agenda. It is therefore absurd for anyone to claim that Jesus Christ did His healings by the power of Satan.

ASK YOURSELF

This well-known statement of Jesus about a "house divided" is proven true every day in our world. How are you perhaps experiencing division today—in your home, in your church, in any of your other relationships? How could you work to restore peace in these places?

A Prejudiced Accusation

If I by Beelzebul cast out demons, by whom do your sons cast them out?
For this reason they will be your judges. —Matt. 12:27

Here Jesus demonstrates the Pharisees' prejudice against Him, revealed in their accusation's wicked, heartfelt bias. "Sons" is a synonym for disciples or followers, such as "sons of the prophets" (e.g., 2 Kings 2:3), and refers to certain followers of the Pharisees who conducted exorcisms. (The Jewish historian Josephus writes that such men used many esoteric incantations and cultic formulas in their rites; cf. Acts 19:13–16. This reality supports those exorcists' basic magical orientation, one far removed from Christ's method of operation.)

The Lord notes how extreme their prejudice against Him was by pointing out that the Pharisees approved the exorcisms attempted by members of their establishment. Not even in their wildest fantasies would they have called those activities ungodly or satanic. Yet when Jesus cast out all kinds of demons and healed every disease, they recklessly accused Him of working for the devil.

The Pharisees' response illustrates the response of every unbelieving individual who prejudicially rebuffs Christ and His message. The Jewish leaders' rejection derived not from lack of evidence but from a fundamental bias against the Messiah. Their deeds and thoughts were sinful and they could not tolerate the intimidating reality of Jesus' light and righteousness (John 3:19). As with all unrepentant sinners, they did not seek truth but rather ways to justify their sin and destroy anyone who exposed them.

ASK YOURSELF

Are you guilty of any prejudices in your attitudes, beliefs, and reactions? Are you aware of any double standards in your heart—things you approve of in yourself but not in others?

A REBELLIOUS ACCUSATION

But if I cast out demons by the Spirit of God, then the kingdom of God has come upon you. Or how can anyone enter the strong man's house and carry off his property, unless he first binds the strong man? And then he will plunder his house. He who is not with Me is against Me; and he who does not gather with Me scatters.
—MATT. 12:28–30

With the Pharisees' foolish charge dispelled that Jesus worked under Satan's power, the only remaining explanation for His work was that He "cast out demons by the Spirit of God." If that were true, then His healing miracles were of God and He had to be the Messiah (12:23; cf. Isa. 29:18; 35:5–6). The leaders also knew Messiah would be Israel's ultimate King (Zech. 9:9). Therefore Jesus' indication that He was the Christ and coming King had to mean God's kingdom had come upon the Pharisees, a notion they vigorously resisted.

The rebellious Jews surely saw that each of Jesus' miracles was opposed to Satan. The Lord healed impairments and diseases, raised people from death, cast out demons, and forgave sins. All of those evils Jesus counteracted were brought on and promoted by Satan, which further showed He could not have been working for the devil. Jesus' works corresponded in the smallest detail with everything the Old Testament taught, and the Pharisees could never convict Him of doing any sin or teaching any error (cf. John 8:46).

Jesus made clear to His supposedly sophisticated but rebellious critics that a relationship with Him includes no neutral ground: "He who does not gather with Me scatters." It is not necessary to overtly oppose or actively interfere with the Lord's ministry to be His enemy. Even the most passive unbeliever is the rebellious enemy of God (cf. Rom. 5:10).

ASK YOURSELF

Confess today any neutrality that exists in your heart—any signal of doubt or unbelief, any apathy or indifference toward the Scriptures, any silent resistance to Christ's claims on your lifestyle and behavior. How can you move from these feelings to active, living faith and obedience?

God Can Forgive Blasphemy

Therefore I say to you, any sin and blasphemy shall be forgiven people. . . .
Whoever speaks a word against the Son of Man, it shall be forgiven him.
—Matt. 12:31, 32

"Sin" here encompasses the complete range of immoral and ungodly thoughts and actions. "Blasphemy," however, is the worst sort of sin, denoting someone's conscious denouncing and mocking of God (cf. Mark 2:7). God's original penalty for it was death by stoning (Lev. 24:16). In the last days, blasphemy will be an outstanding sin of all wicked unbelievers (Rev. 13:5–6).

Yet just as He forgives any other sin when it's confessed and repented of, God will forgive blasphemy. Paul reported that "even though I was formerly a blasphemer and a persecutor and a violent aggressor . . . I was shown mercy because I acted ignorantly in unbelief; and the grace of our Lord was more than abundant, with the faith and love which are found in Christ Jesus" (1 Tim. 1:13–14). Peter blasphemed Jesus with curses (Mark 14:71), and yet His Lord forgave and restored him.

Similar to Peter, other believers can blaspheme, because any thought or word that defames God's name is blasphemy. Questioning His love, wisdom, faithfulness, goodness, and countless other traits—all of this equals blasphemy. Divine grace can forgive it all, however, as John reminds us, "If we confess our sins, He is faithful and righteous to forgive us our sins and to cleanse us from all unrighteousness" (1 John 1:9).

ASK YOURSELF

Forgiveness of sin is such a central, familiar part of the gospel message; its amazing wonder and relief is often lost on us over time. As you consider today the width and depth of this undeserved blessing, let His cleansing wash over you again. Give Him new thanks for the grace of forgiven sin.

BLASPHEMY AGAINST THE HOLY SPIRIT, PART 1

Blasphemy against the Spirit shall not be forgiven. —MATT. 12:31

"Blasphemy against the Spirit" is far more serious and irremediable than other sins, including speaking against the Son of Man, Jesus Christ. It reflects determined unbelief—stubborn refusal in the face of persuasive evidence that supports genuine faith—that will not even consider believing in Christ.

For the Pharisees, it was blasphemy against the deity of Jesus and the Holy Spirit who uniquely indwelt and empowered Him during His earthly ministry. It demonstrates such a permanent rejection of belief that the result is a loss of any opportunity ever to receive forgiveness, "either in this age or in the age to come" (v. 32). In the present age of human history, during which time such unbelief is inexcusable, as well as in the age of divine consummation, the result is the same—no forgiveness.

Many people had heard Jesus proclaim the gospel and God's truth as no teacher had ever taught before (Matt. 7:28–29), but they would not embrace Him. They had also seen Him perform nearly every kind of miracle and forgive every kind of sin, yet they said no to Him and even accused Him of falsehood and demonism. The Jewish leaders' rejection of Christ in the face of so much evidence meant God would do nothing more to reach them (cf. Isa. 5:1–6). Commentator William Hendriksen wrote this: "Their sin is unpardonable because they are unwilling to tread the path that leads to pardon. . . . When a man has become hardened, so that he has made up his mind not to pay any attention to the Spirit, he has placed himself on the road to perdition."

ASK YOURSELF

This is a hard teaching, of course—one that confuses and can run contrary to our human inclinations. How do you handle biblical instruction that either clashes with your feelings or creates more questions than answers within you? How do you think God expects us to react?

BLASPHEMY AGAINST THE HOLY SPIRIT, PART 2

Blasphemy against the Spirit shall not be forgiven. —MATT. 12:31

The serious consequences for the Jews of blaspheming the Spirit appeared not long after Jesus' time on earth. In AD 70, Roman troops destroyed Jerusalem and killed more than a million of its residents, along with destroying hundreds of other Judean towns. Until Christ returns and draws a remnant of the Jews to Himself, they remain (except for believing individuals) a nation completely apart from God.

The apostles ministered to the Israelite generation living after Jesus ascended. Those people received revelation and gospel proofs equivalent to what those who heard Jesus in person had received. But like the older generation, most later-first-century Jews did not believe. If they refused to believe in spite of a preponderance of evidence, there was nothing more God would do for them (cf. Heb. 2:3–4; 6:4–6). Whether they stubbornly refused to trust Christ or added blasphemy to their rebellion, both groups faced a future in hell.

People today can also disdain God's revelation and essentially place themselves into an apostate position, which permanently cuts them off from any further possibility of salvation. A time will come when God will no longer offer the light of the gospel, the Holy Spirit will no longer strive with people, and further opportunity for redemption is forever closed. That's why Paul exhorted the Corinthians and all who would read his words, "Behold, now is 'the acceptable time,' behold, now is 'the day of salvation'" (2 Cor. 6:2; cf. John 9:4).

ASK YOURSELF

It is clear that many maintain a resistance to Christ that will never change; they will die in their sins. But since we don't know who these are—since God alone is the One who judges—what should our actions be toward all men today? How are you proclaiming the salvation message?

ONE'S TRUE HEART: A PARABLE

*Either make the tree good and its fruit good, or make the tree bad
and its fruit bad; for the tree is known by its fruit.* —MATT. 12:33

Jesus' short parable illustrates the obvious maxim: a good tree produces
good fruit, and a bad one produces bad fruit (cf. Luke 6:43–44). The
Lord used the word translated "make" metaphorically to mean "consider,
evaluate, or judge"—we must make up our minds about the nature of
something and its products or results.

We might use our sanctified imaginations and paraphrase our Lord's
words as follows: "Make up your minds, friends, about Me and My ministry. I'm either evil and an evil doer, or good and one who does good.
But I can't be evil and a doer of good deeds, or vice versa. God would
enable Me to perform good works, and the devil would empower Me for
evil. These propositions would merely align with the logical workings of
God's universe, but only one can be true concerning Me."

Christ's more specific point is this: "Illness and death result from
sin, and demon possession is evil and from Satan. Therefore if I miraculously heal the sick, cast out demons, and raise the dead, these must be
good things because the result is a deliverance of people from the destroying power of sin. Anybody who accuses Me of doing good by
Satan's power, he attributes to Satan the work of the Holy Spirit. That is
the supreme and unforgivable blasphemy."

No matter what people like the Pharisees think of Jesus personally,
His works have always testified indisputably to His divine goodness and
power (cf. Matt. 11:4–5; John 5:36; 14:11).

ASK YOURSELF

Sometimes we're convinced that our defense of Christ, which seems so
easily defeated by a doubting skeptic, must therefore be in opposition to
logic and consistent thinking. Today's theme is one clear example of
how God's truth stacks up with common sense. What are others?

One's True Heart: Jesus Personalizes the Reality

You brood of vipers, how can you, being evil, speak what is good? —Matt. 12:34a

Jesus did not hesitate to personally condemn people, especially when, like the Pharisees, their sins were cruel, self-righteous, hypocritical, or blasphemous. He came to save sinners, not to confirm them in their evil ways or minimize their guilt. Christ was not engaged in a popularity contest or a campaign to win votes. He was concerned only to please His Father, not sinful people.

Calling the Pharisees a "brood of vipers" was a severe denunciation the people of Jesus' day understood. Because those poisonous snakes blend into surrounding rocks and wood debris, they can attack their victims with complete surprise, as one did to Paul on Malta (Acts 28:3, 6). The Pharisees' unscriptural traditions poisoned the minds of other Jews to the purity of God's Word, and their arrogant hypocrisy also drew others to that evil attitude.

Jesus knew that the Pharisees, "being evil," couldn't possibly "speak what is good." Thus He exposed their hearts' personal evil, which couldn't produce anything but ungodliness and blasphemy. Evil is the general legacy of fallen mankind, due to Adam's sin. As Paul expounds it, "Both Jews and Greeks are all under sin. . . . 'There is none righteous, not even one. . . . There is none who does good, there is not even one'. . . for all have sinned and fall short of the glory of God" (Rom. 3:9–10, 12, 23; cf. Eph. 2:1).

There is no escaping the real existence of humanity's evil heart— "the heart is more deceitful than all else and is desperately sick" (Jer. 17:9; cf. Ps. 51:5)—and the gospel is the only remedy.

ASK YOURSELF

How does a deep awareness of our fallenness and inadequacy benefit us as we seek to follow Christ? What kinds of traps are avoided when we know that nothing good can originate from our own initiative? How, though, can Satan twist this truth to continue defeating us?

THE PRINCIPLE OF THE TRUE HEART, PART 1

*For the mouth speaks out of that which fills the heart. The good man
brings out of his good treasure what is good; and the evil man
brings out of his evil treasure what is evil.* —MATT. 12:34b–35

The Lord here gives us one of the most basic principles concerning
mankind: what a person is internally, his or her mouth will sooner or
later reveal externally. In his letter, James takes this so far as to say that
one who did not sin with his mouth would be "a perfect man" (James
3:2). The Pharisees often spoke evil because their hearts contained much
evil. By their own words they condemned themselves, ironically even as
they tried to condemn Jesus.

In the Bible, "the heart" signifies the seat of human thought and
will—it represents the character of a person. Therefore when the mouth
speaks, it simply reproduces orally what is already in the heart and un-
veils what the person is really like. Using this same symbol of the human
heart, Jesus later explained that "the things that proceed out of the mouth
come from the heart, and those defile the man. For out of the heart come
evil thoughts, murders, adulteries, fornications, thefts, false witness, slanders" (Matt. 15:18–19).

A person who has animosity toward another will eventually express
those feelings. Someone who constantly entertains lustful thoughts will
someday express them by crude or suggestive remarks. The man or
woman who has an ongoing attitude of anger or hate will ultimately
transfer those feelings into words. Similarly, the faithful believer who is
truly loving, considerate, and gracious will express those heart attitudes
in words and deeds.

ASK YOURSELF

Life generally leads us to become more gentle and gracious, or to
become increasingly harsh and hard to live with. Knowing that these are
largely the result of how we live our early lives and the mind-sets we
adopt along the way, which direction would you say you're headed?

THE PRINCIPLE OF THE TRUE HEART, PART 2

For the mouth speaks out of that which fills the heart. The good man brings out of his good treasure what is good; and the evil man brings out of his evil treasure what is evil. —MATT. 12:34b–35

James understood Jesus' true heart principle, and his letter contains some powerful warnings about the tongue:

If anyone thinks himself to be religious, and yet does not bridle his tongue but deceives his own heart, this man's religion is worthless. (1:26)

No one can tame the tongue; it is a restless evil and full of deadly poison. (3:8)

The mouth is the ultimate expression of mankind's depraved heart (Rom. 3:13–14, cf. Prov. 23:7).

The heart is the vast and varied reservoir the mouth draws its expressions from. With that figure of speech Jesus again emphasizes the maxim that good produces good and bad produces bad: "The good man brings out of his good treasure what is good; and the evil man brings out of his evil treasure what is evil" (cf. James 3:11).

One of the earliest acronyms from the computer realm is GIGO, "garbage in, garbage out." If a programmer, or even an average user, inserts bad data or inaccurate information while running a certain computer application, that will affect the outcome negatively. By analogy, the good or bad content of one's heart determines what a person says, defining in a major way the principle of the true heart.

ASK YOURSELF

How would you measure the quality of what you're infusing into your heart on a regular basis? If you're not convinced that it's the best kind of content to be dwelling on, what changes could you make to your "diet"?

CONSEQUENCES FOR OUR WORDS, PART 1

But I tell you that every careless word that people speak, they shall give an accounting for it in the day of judgment. For by your words you will be justified, and by your words you will be condemned. —MATT. 12:36–37

Scriptures consistently teach that the only way of salvation is by God's grace received through man's faith. Christ's point here is not that our words bring salvation or condemnation, but that they indicate the presence of salvation. Pure, wholesome, praising speech that honors God reliably reveals a person's new heart.

Whereas we are not saved *by* good works, the apostle Paul says we are saved *for* "good works, which God prepared beforehand so that we would walk in them" (Eph. 2:10). Similarly, God saves all who believe so they may utter good words. "With the heart a person believes, resulting in righteousness, and with the mouth he confesses, resulting in salvation" (Rom. 10:10), which then leads to "obedience . . . by word and deed" (15:18). Because our words are so vitally linked to our salvation, there is a sense in which they have essential consequences, either for redemption or condemnation.

God will eternally condemn the unrepentant for their words. Such speech is not limited to profanities, obscenities, or blasphemies, but includes "every careless word" for which they will "have to give an accounting for" in the last day.

Believers, on the other hand, use words that reflect God's transforming work in their hearts. But because of their remaining sinful tendencies, they need to be diligent about what they say, as the psalmist prayed, "Set a guard, O Lord, over my mouth; keep watch over the door of my lips" (Ps. 141:3).

ASK YOURSELF

The careless use of our words can become one of Satan's most effective inroads into our hearts, causing us to feel condemned by our sinful speech habits and (of course) causing pain to others. What situations or environments put you most at risk to be unwise with your words?

Consequences for Our Words, Part 2

But I tell you that every careless word that people speak, they shall give an accounting for it in the day of judgment. For by your words you will be justified, and by your words you will be condemned. —Matt. 12:36–37

Jesus' words here apply to both the saved and the unsaved, but primarily to the unsaved, as illustrated in the extreme by the blaspheming Pharisees. Even the seemingly good words of unbelievers, although sincere, helpful, and comforting, are ultimately devoid of spiritual value because they come from an unredeemed heart. After all, Jesus has just noted that no good thing can come from a heart that is spiritually evil.

The ultimate "day of judgment" for unbelievers takes place at the great white throne judgment, when God will condemn them because of their sins (Rev. 20:12, 15). Christ's blood at Calvary, however, has already washed away believers' sins. Not that any believer after salvation has not sinned occasionally by his words; but God has forgiven those and all other sins through Jesus' atoning work. Unbelievers' evil words and sinful deeds, by contrast, will remain as evidence against them at the great white throne (cf. Luke 19:22).

Sound waves, according to scientists, never completely dissipate but simply fade beyond detection. With the right instruments, every word mankind has ever uttered could theoretically be retrieved. We can be all the more sure that an omnipotent, omniscient God can perfectly preserve every human word and deed, ready for unerring, complete retrieval for use as evidence in the day of judgment.

ASK YOURSELF

People are so sure that their good deeds, when weighed against the bad, will be enough to gain them entrance into heaven. In case the enormity of your salvation has been lost on you lately, just imagine the monstrous heap of sins that could so easily be used as evidence against you.

DEMANDING A SIGN

Then some of the scribes and Pharisees said to Him,
*"Teacher, we want to see a sign from You." —*MATT. 12:38

The scribes' and Pharisees' demand of Jesus—"We want to see a sign from You"—was really just an official insistence that He prove Himself to be the Messiah. Their use of "Teacher" was actually sarcastic because they considered Him a heretic and wanted to expose Him as a false teacher. It was also hypocritical because they desired to put Jesus off guard by flattering Him in front of the crowd.

Matthew 16:1, a parallel verse, tells us, "The Pharisees and Sadducees came up, and testing Jesus, they asked Him to show them a sign from heaven." Such a mark would be a large and spectacular one, which would be both from heaven and visible across the heavens, such as some unprecedented celestial occurrence or spectacular movement across the skies.

Although most of the Old Testament prophets did not perform miracles or signs but simply confirmed their divine messages by the messages' truthful content, the Jews had come to expect signs accompanying every man of God, especially Messiah (cf. 1 Cor. 1:22). Perhaps the Jewish leaders here thought Christ would fulfill Joel's prophecy of turning the moon into blood (Joel 2:31), or painting the heavens some other colors by a mere wave of His hand.

Actually the Jews did not think Jesus would perform any sort of miracle because their purpose was to discredit Him before the crowd, unmasking Him as one who could not do what they demanded. Such an arrogant demand really only disobeys Deuteronomy 6:16 (cf. Matt. 4:5–7) by putting God to the test and revealing one's unbelief.

ASK YOURSELF

As usual, the Pharisees' sarcasm and hypocrisy kept them from enjoying a blessed reality—the fact that God loves to reveal Himself and make His ways known to His people. How has He shown Himself strong, capable, and compassionate in your life lately?

JESUS ANSWERS THE JEWS

But He answered and said to them, "An evil and adulterous generation craves for a sign; and yet no sign will be given to it." —MATT. 12:39a

The very request the Jewish leaders disingenuously placed before Jesus represented the wicked expectation of most of the nation of Israel: "An evil and adulterous generation" that had strayed far from fellowship with God and from trust in His Word in favor of a superficial, self-righteous religion. This unbelieving generation was spiritually adulterous because it had violated its vows of unique covenant relationship to God, so often described in marriage terms (see Ps. 73:27; Jer. 3:6–10; Hos. 9:1).

Believing Jews who served the Father faithfully under the Mosaic covenant would accept His Son and the Messiah because anyone obedient to the Father would by faith recognize and embrace the Son—as did Simeon and Anna (Luke 2:25–38), John the Baptist (Matt. 3:14), and the apostles (except Judas Iscariot; Luke 5:27–28; John 1:41, 49). Because those godly people knew the Father, they did not need a sign to verify the Son's identity and believe in Him.

Because of their unbelief, Jesus told the scribes and Pharisees "no sign [would] be given" to them. He could not possibly perform the kind of miracle they wanted—not because He was powerless to do so, but because such a sign would be completely contrary to His moral nature and sovereign plan. God did not then and does not now bend Himself to please the whims of evil people who don't know Him.

ASK YOURSELF

How well do you deal with the silences of God, those times when in His wise Fatherhood He forces you to exercise your spiritual muscles of faith and perseverance? If you've been going through one of these seasons, be encouraged today that your unseen God is ever-present.

JESUS AND JONAH, PART 1

For just as Jonah was three days and three nights in the belly of the sea monster,
so will the Son of Man be three days and three nights in the heart of the earth.
—MATT. 12:40

There was one sign Jesus was willing to give the Jewish leaders—the sign of Jonah. The prophet Jonah disobeyed the divine call to preach to Nineveh and headed for Tarshish on a ship. God therefore sent a hurricane and had Jonah thrown into the sea to save the sailors on board. God then "appointed a great fish to swallow Jonah" (Jonah 1:17), and he remained in its stomach for three days and nights.

Based on Jesus' own words, the account of Jonah is a prophecy that typifies or foreshadows the person and work of Messiah. Rather than using specific words of prediction about Christ, Jonah pictures what would happen to Him. Jonah was buried in the sea; Jesus was buried in the earth. Jonah came out of the fish after three days; Jesus rose from the tomb after three days.

By comparing Jonah's experiences to Himself, Jesus verified the historicity and accuracy of the book of Jonah. The Savior trusted the biblical account. If Jonah had not been actually swallowed up and then delivered from harm, those occurrences could not have typified Christ's actual burial and resurrection. This demonstrates for us that our Lord looked to the Old Testament as a totally reliable and instructive divine record that pointed ahead to His earthly ministry and redemptive work.

ASK YOURSELF

Many would claim that the story of Jonah is merely that—a story, a fish tale. But what are the real, underlying reasons behind such attempts to deconstruct the reliability of the Bible? In what ways have you found yourself resisting His authority and questioning His ways?

JESUS AND JONAH, PART 2

For just as Jonah was three days and three nights in the belly of the sea monster,
so will the Son of Man be three days and three nights in the heart of the earth.
—MATT. 12:40

The Lord Jesus' resurrection after three days in the grave—analogous to Jonah's emergence from the great fish—was not the sort of sign from Him the religious leaders had in mind. However, it was infinitely more significant and miraculous than anything God did through the prophet. The resurrection was Jesus' final sign given directly to the world to authenticate his messianic credentials and saving power.

After He rose from the dead, He appeared in His glorified body to His disciples on various occasions (1 Cor. 15:4–7) and then spectacularly ascended into heaven as the eleven watched. After that, God performed other signs and miracles through the apostles to prove their unique authority to minister on behalf of the Son. Jesus told the skeptical Jewish leaders that His resurrection would be the only heavenly sign aimed directly at them.

Sadly, however, most of the Jews, whether leaders or people, did not accept the miracle of the resurrection—"If they [did] not listen to Moses and the Prophets, they will not be persuaded even if someone rises from the dead" (Luke 16:31; cf. Matt. 28:11–15).

What any person does with the facts of Jesus Christ's earthly ministry and the powerful truths of His atoning death and glorious resurrection determines that person's eternal destiny. To spurn those most convincing and gracious of divine signs is, like the scribes and Pharisees, to reveal yourself as the worst of sinners, no matter how outwardly moral and religious you might be.

ASK YOURSELF

We can hardly go wrong by focusing on the cross, the site of our forgiven sin. But we should be equally transfixed by the empty tomb, by which we are not only released from our guilt but are freed to live with all the glorious repercussions, now and forever. How are you experiencing that?

GENTILE FAITH VERSUS JEWISH UNBELIEF

The men of Nineveh will stand up with this generation at the judgment, and will condemn it because they repented at the preaching of Jonah; and behold, something greater than Jonah is here. The Queen of the South will rise up with this generation at the judgment and will condemn it. —MATT. 12:41–42a

The residents of Nineveh were not only Gentiles who lived outside of God's covenant and law, they were especially brutal pagans. But even apart from a previous knowledge of the true God and His will, they by faith repented of sin and embraced God, which gave them spiritual salvation and spared them physical destruction (Jonah 3:5–6). Jonah grudgingly preached a terse message of judgment to Nineveh (3:4) and did no miracles and made no promises of deliverance. Yet God could use that to cause the people to humbly grasp His mercy and receive salvation.

By sharp contrast, God's own people rejected the gospel, even when His Son preached to them, performed many miracles and signs, and graciously offered them eternal life. For that sin the Jews will hear words of condemnation from former pagans at the judgment.

"The Queen of the South" (from the prosperous country of the Sabeans) brought massive treasure to Solomon in gratitude and honor for his divinely wise teachings. Jesus again makes a telling comparison: A Gentile woman came on her own initiative to learn God's truth from Solomon. But the Jews, hearing Christ's offers of blessing and salvation, rejected Him and forfeited forgiveness and redemption. So one day the pagan queen, like the Ninevites, "will rise up with this generation at the judgment and will condemn it." What a tragic conclusion when One much greater than Jonah or Solomon willingly taught not only wisdom but salvation, only to have it largely rejected by His own people.

ASK YOURSELF

Think of the present-day factors that could lead men to repentance: unstable economic conditions, personal crises, health concerns, deteriorating relationships. How is God continuing to reach out to a fallen world, and how could He use you to help others see their need for Him?

The Danger of Moral Reform, Part 1

Now when the unclean spirit goes out of a man, it passes through waterless places seeking rest, and does not find it. Then it says, "I will return to my house from which I came"; and when it comes, it finds it unoccupied, swept, and put in order. Then it goes and takes along with it seven other spirits more wicked than itself.
—Matt. 12:43–45a

Here Jesus strikingly provides the picture of what happens when religious and moral reformation occurs apart from a right relationship to Him. The parable's main character is a demon whose specific evil characteristics are unidentified. For whatever reason and by whatever means, an unnamed man became free of this evil spirit. Perhaps the man morally renounced a sin and the demon temporarily lost control over him, or maybe Jesus cleansed the man of the demon but the man did not savingly embrace Jesus.

After a time, the unclean spirit decided to "return to [his] house from which [he] came," which indicates he still had a strong sense of ownership over the man. That the spirit was so easily able to reenter, along with other more evil spirits, proves the practical reality of his possessiveness. The unoccupied nature (by any other demons) of the house, along with its clean, orderly status, suggests that the human resident had engaged in some sort of real moral reformation. But such self-cleansing, no matter how complete and well-meaning, is never permanent.

If repentance from sin and trust in Christ do not deal with someone's basic sin nature, the removal of a sinful habit or demon leaves the person's spiritual house vulnerable to reoccupation and becoming worse than before. The self-righteous, self-reforming person is subject to Satan in a way an immoral person is not, because his or her morality blinds them to their fallen condition and need for redemption.

ASK YOURSELF

Have you tried to paper over certain pockets of rebellion in your life, not by genuine repentance, but by the establishment of daily disciplines and religious practices? What "results" have you seen?

THE DANGER OF MORAL REFORM, PART 2

Now when the unclean spirit goes out of a man, it passes through waterless places seeking rest, and does not find it. Then it says, "I will return to my house from which I came"; and when it comes, it finds it unoccupied, swept, and put in order. Then it goes and takes along with it seven other spirits more wicked than itself.
—MATT. 12:43–45a

A terrible aspect of formalistic, pharisaic religion is that it tends to get more ungodly over the generations. Jesus indicted the religious leaders: "Woe to you, scribes and Pharisees, hypocrites, because you travel around on sea and land to make one proselyte; and when he becomes one, you make him twice as much a son of hell as yourselves" (Matt. 23:15). One discipled into legalism often becomes more self-righteous than his or her discipler.

It is far easier to reach someone overwhelmed with a sense of sin and guilt than someone steeped in the false security of his own morality. That's why Jesus said, "I did not come to call the righteous, but sinners" (Matt. 9:13). Consider that it was not the common, unrighteous people of Israel who crucified Jesus but the arrogant religious leaders who were proud of their own goodness.

Many years later the apostle Peter also warned of the danger of personal reformation without true regeneration (2 Peter 2:20–22). Such an individual, who merely escapes the world's pollutions for a time, will eventually revert to sin just as the dog returns to its vomit or the sow to its mud—one's nature was not really changed. We can't emphasize enough that outer reformation without inner transformation does not bring justification for sins.

ASK YOURSELF

Are you ever tempted to think that you can manage just fine without God's help, or perhaps that God is fortunate to have someone of your high standards and character on board with Him? How do the vestiges of self-righteousness sneak into your manner of thinking and living?

THE IMPORTANCE OF RELATIONSHIP, PART 1

Stretching out His hand toward His disciples, He said, "Behold My mother and My brothers! For whoever does the will of My Father who is in heaven, he is My brother and sister and mother." —MATT. 12:49–50

When Jesus' family came looking for Him (Matt. 12:46–47), it gave Him the perfect opportunity to illustrate the necessity of a personal, saving relationship with Him.

During our Lord's earthly ministry, no evidence clearly revealed that any member of His family other than Mary trusted in Him as Savior and Messiah. His brothers did not believe (John 7:5)—although they did later (Acts 1:14)—and perhaps even Mary, despite divine revelations to her in Luke 1:26–2:38, had not at this time embraced Jesus as her Lord .

Scripture does not tell us precisely why Christ's earthly family members sought Him (cf. Mark 3:31–32; Luke 8:19–20), but likely they were very concerned about His safety and even joined friends from Nazareth in fearing He had "lost His senses" (Mark 3:21). The people probably already had passed rumors along of the Pharisees' plan to destroy Jesus. Thus His family likely wanted to dissuade Him from continued ministry and get Him to go into seclusion until the troubles passed.

Some public teachers would have been highly upset if their families did as Jesus' did, but the Lord was unperturbed. He loved His family (cf. John 19:26–27) and understood their concerns; but He used this occasion to declare a more transcendent truth: all genuine disciples constitute His spiritual family. Thus Jesus was not renouncing His physical family but teaching that anyone who believes can become an intimate member of His divine family, and that only God's family ultimately matters.

ASK YOURSELF

In what ways are your ties with brothers and sisters in Christ more intense and meaningful than even the ties of natural family relationships? How has God knit you together through shared experience and belief to form unbreakable bonds of unity, togetherness, and joy?

THE IMPORTANCE OF RELATIONSHIP, PART 2

Stretching out His hand toward His disciples, He said, "Behold My mother and My brothers! For whoever does the will of My Father who is in heaven, he is My brother and sister and mother." —MATT. 12:49–50

Being a member of Christ's human family did not by itself merit salvation. Any gospel invitation He ever gave implicitly included His relatives, because they too needed redemption from darkness to light. Anyone who faithfully obeys Jesus is a member of His spiritual family. Hence He tells us here, "Whoever does the will of My Father who is in heaven, he is My brother and sister and mother."

Jesus' use of "whoever" denotes the universality of His invitation (cf. Matt. 18:11–14; 1 Tim. 2:3–4; 2 Peter 3:9): no one who believes is excluded, and no one who does not believe is included. God's great desire for humanity is that people be well-pleased with His Son, just as He is (Matt. 3:17), and that they believe and obey the Savior (cf. John 6:29). Outside of such a relationship, God can't and won't render spiritual help, and a person can't truly serve Him.

Having a right relationship to Jesus, however, demands much more than a bare rhetorical statement of intellectual understanding or superficial loyalty (see Matt. 7:21–23). A true saving relationship results only when we humbly respond to the gospel of grace, as described at the birth of the church: "When they heard [Peter's sermon], they were pierced to the heart, and said . . . 'Brethren, what shall we do?' Peter said to them, 'Repent, and each of you be baptized in the name of Jesus Christ for the forgiveness of your sins; and you will receive the gift of the Holy Spirit'" (Acts 2:37–38).

ASK YOURSELF

How has God helped you overcome any doubts about the salvation you have received by His grace, through faith? What gives you confidence that your relationship with Him is not based on words or mental assent, but rather on His own sure promises and your genuine repentance?

Jesus Returns to Nazareth

He came to His hometown and began teaching them in their synagogue.
—Matt. 13:54*a*

Jesus returned to Nazareth following His baptism and temptations (Matt. 4:12–13), and Luke tells us the response to Him then was the same as on this occasion. Then Jesus had been gone just a short time and was still a familiar figure in the Nazareth synagogue. The devout Jews present on that particular Sabbath had attended services there for many years. They might have thought things would go on as always, but they would witness a fundamental change in Joseph's son. While away from town, Jesus began His ministry and became well known in the region: "News about Him spread through all the surrounding district . . . and [He] was praised by all" (Luke 4:14*b*–15*b*).

For that earlier Sabbath, Jesus stood and read the familiar messianic passage of Isaiah 61:1–2 (see Luke 4:16–22). Realizing that the people's initial response (4:22) derived merely from a faithless recognition of His popularity and power, Jesus exposed their real motives—wanting to see signs without having to believe. He reminded them of the drought and famine God had sent during the time of Elijah, the divine mercy shown to the Gentile widow of Zarephath, and how God had healed Naaman the Syrian of leprosy but no Israelites during Elisha's day (vv. 23–27). Jesus' point is clear: God accepts believing Gentiles, but not unbelieving Jews.

In their attempt to kill Christ (vv. 28–29), the Jews revealed their evil character. They selfishly wanted only entertainment and earthly benefits from a miracle worker, not forgiveness of sins and salvation from the Messiah.

ASK YOURSELF

We, too, can be guilty of wanting Jesus primarily for the things He can do for us, for the way He makes us feel, for the possibility of answers to our selfish prayers. What happens when these become the primary motives of faith? How have you experienced the disappointment?

UNBELIEF BLURS THE OBVIOUS, PART 1

They were astonished, and said, "Where did this man get
this wisdom and these miraculous powers?" —MATT. 13:54*b*

The Jews' unbelieving attitude against Jesus remained the same. Their skeptical question revealed again their refusal to recognize the obvious. We have to ask how they could for a second time reject their Messiah when it was obvious God had empowered Him. To this point, the Lord had taught the truth about everything pertaining to spiritual life and godliness (cf. 2 Peter 1:3), and demonstrated an unrivaled, omniscient, and omnipotent mastery over it all.

Our Lord did not study at an elite rabbinical school or have any more formal Bible training than the average layman. Thus when He taught the people at one Feast of Booths, the religious leaders marveled, "saying, 'How has this man become learned, having never been educated?'" (John 7:15). In spite of having no academic credentials, Jesus' spiritual and moral wisdom was so credible and profound that His critics could not refute Him.

Nicodemus immediately conceded that Christ had "come from God as a teacher; for no one can do these signs that You do unless God is with him" (John 3:2). Later Jesus urged a group of Jews who wanted to stone Him, "If I do not do the works of My Father, do not believe Me; but if I do them, though you do not believe Me, believe the works, so that you may know and understand that the Father is in Me, and I in the Father" (10:37–38).

How could the Jews not embrace the obvious that Jesus was God, when that was the only explanation for the extraordinariness of His ministry?

ASK YOURSELF

What continues to mystify you as to why people can't see the hand of God in creation, the hand of God in world events, the hand of God in people's lives who are so obviously changed by His presence in their hearts? How have you seen the hand of God on display in recent days?

UNBELIEF BLURS THE OBVIOUS, PART 2

They were astonished, and said, "Where did this man get this wisdom and these miraculous powers?" —MATT. 13:54*b*

Just as the religious leaders did, the people of Jesus' home synagogue allowed willful unbelief and prejudice to blur obvious truth about who He was. They refused to let the seed of the Father's Word and the Son's specific gospel message penetrate their sin-hardened hearts. This phenomenon happened and still does, in large measure because "men loved the darkness rather than the Light, for their deeds were evil" (John 3:19). Their stubborn refusal to believe their Messiah occurred in the face of overwhelming evidence, and because they wanted to keep their sin. The Jews preferred their way to Christ's words and way.

When people reject the Lord, even the most convincing evidence and arguments won't persuade them to turn from error to truth (cf. Luke 16:31). Adherents of sects and those who prefer liberal and postmodern theologies always seem to find countless arguments for not acknowledging who Jesus really is and for discounting the most obvious Scripture truths. They have an academic respect for the Bible but don't apply its precepts, and they want to honor Christ in a superficial way without embracing Him as Lord and Savior. To such people our Lord continues to say, "Not everyone who says to Me, 'Lord, Lord,' will enter the kingdom of heaven, but he who does the will of My Father who is in heaven will enter" (Matt. 7:21).

ASK YOURSELF

How deeply are you affected by the fact that people who reject the truth about Christ are dooming themselves to eternal damnation? How often is this heart's cry a part of your praying? How are you laboring to present authentic faith to those who are turning away to idols?

UNBELIEF FOCUSES ON THE IRRELEVANT

Is not this the carpenter's son? Is not His mother called Mary, and His brothers,
James and Joseph and Simon and Judas? And His sisters, are they not all with
*us? Where then did this man get all these things? —*MATT. 13:55–56

J esus was simply an average carpenter's son to those friends and relatives who knew Him while He grew up. This commonness of Jesus and
His family contributed to the peoples' stumbling over His true identity. It
was difficult for them to accept Him as a great teacher, much less as the
Messiah.

Like people throughout church history, residents of Nazareth found
many excuses and irrelevant facts to distract them from the real issues
and prevent them from believing. People today don't like the personality
of the evangelist, claim all church members are hypocrites, and dislike
the details and order of a worship service. There is always a rationaliza-
tion for them to rebuff the clear message of Jesus Christ. The genuine
seeker, on the other hand, may have a lot of questions about the Bible and
the gospel before turning in faith, but he or she proves their sincerity by
eventually accepting the truth.

True skeptics are easily offended by the most trivial things Christians do, and they often allow those matters to be all-important and the
center of their perspective. As for most citizens of Nazareth, they allowed pride, envy, resentment, embarrassment, and dozens of other sinful factors to fill their hearts and prevent them from coming to salvation.
We dare not do likewise, or allow others to hide behind irrelevant obstacles to saving faith.

ASK YOURSELF

Beyond the smokescreens that hinder people from receiving salvation,
we believers can still be quite adept at using all kinds of excuses to keep
us from taking Christ's claims seriously enough to live by them. What
are some reasons you're using to justify less-than-biblical living?

UNBELIEF IS BLIND TO THE TRUTH

And they took offense at Him. But Jesus said to them, "A prophet is not without honor except in his hometown and in his own household. " —MATT. 13:57

The people in Nazareth "took offense" (Greek, *skandalizo*, from which we get the English *scandalize*) at Jesus' claims, especially since they came from one so ordinary, with no formal theological education or official religious status.

The New Testament does not tell us exactly what Jesus taught on either appearance in the Nazareth synagogue. However, during both occasions, the Lord caused His hearers to stumble at what He declared. No doubt He exposed the hypocrisy of their wicked desire for Him to perform miracles for miracles' sake. He likely spoke to them as well about their sinfulness and need to repent. All in all the people were antagonistic toward Jesus because their firm unbelief made them blind to the truth. "While seeing they do not see, and while hearing they do not hear, nor do they understand" (Matt. 13:13; cf. 1 Cor. 1:23).

The gospel will offend a person until he allows God's truth to plow up the hard soil of his heart. Then that man or woman must confess sin and forsake it. The truth of the gospel will be hidden and the blessing of knowing Christ lost until a person faces his sin in genuine penitence.

ASK YOURSELF

You probably aren't offended by Jesus. You love Him. You've given your heart to Him. But are you offended by what life with Him costs at times? Offended by the fact that obedience doesn't always result in visible blessing? How should you deal with these pockets of disillusionment?

UNBELIEF BLOCKS THE SUPERNATURAL

*He did not do many miracles there because of their unbelief. —*MATT. 13:58

Jesus did His miracles to strengthen the faith of those who trusted Him. Although God could have worked through Him to perform miracles in the absence of faith, He chose not to do so when there was willful unbelief. The Lord possessed all His supernatural power at Nazareth, but the Jews' unbelief caused Him not to fully exercise that power (cf. Matt. 7:6). His signs were beneficial only as they led sinners to faith in Him or strengthened those who already believed. Miracles did not benefit those fixed in unbelief—miracles were not for entertaining the crowds or satisfying ungodly curiosity.

We ought to consider the case of the man born blind in John 9:

> As He passed by, He saw a man blind from birth. And His disciples asked Him, "Rabbi, who sinned, this man or his parents, that he would be born blind?" Jesus answered, "It was neither that this man sinned, nor his parents; but it was so that the works of God might be displayed in him." (vv. 1–3)

After Jesus restored the man's sight, he was brought before the Pharisees who debated Jesus' credibility in the miracle and interrogated the man. The man's favorable testimony of Jesus only served to harden the Pharisees in unbelief. But when the healed man realized Jesus was the Messiah, he turned to Him in saving faith.

The Pharisees' incredulity in John 9 illustrates that when unbelief meets Christ's miracles, it rejects them (see vv. 6–41). Unbelief rejects God's works because it rejects His truth.

ASK YOURSELF

You are within your rights and privileges as a follower of Christ to ask Him for miracles, to pray for seemingly impossible things. But how would a positive response from Him advance your faith or serve as a beacon of His power to others? These are important questions to answer.

HEROD'S REACTION TO JESUS

At that time Herod the tetrarch heard the news about Jesus, and said to his
servants, "This is John the Baptist; he has risen from the dead, and that
is why miraculous powers are at work in him." —MATT. 14:1–2

Although Jesus ministered in Galilee more than in any other locale, we don't know that He ever visited or passed through Tiberias, home of Herod the tetrarch's palace on the southwest shore of the Sea of Galilee. Had the Lord wanted to go there it would have been easy enough because it was within walking distance of Capernaum, Nazareth, Cana, and other more familiar places. Jesus might have avoided Tiberius so as not to prematurely arouse Herod's interest.

Herod was greatly distressed when he finally did hear about Jesus. Because of the guilt that nagged him for having murdered John the Baptist, Herod had the superstitious fear that John had returned from the dead to exact revenge on him. The speculative notion that John perhaps had risen from the grave did not originate with Herod, "because it was said by some that John had risen from the dead" (Luke 9:7). Thus Herod "kept trying to see Him [Jesus]" (v. 9), most likely due to a disproportionate sense of morbid curiosity. Herod's guilt-ridden mind had convinced him that Christ was none other than a reincarnated John the Baptist.

The angel told John's father, Zacharias, that John would "go as a forerunner before Him in the spirit and power of Elijah" (Luke 1:17). God had empowered Elijah with miracle-working capabilities and John might have done miracles we don't know of. Thus Herod was convinced that Jesus' miracles proved He was John returned from the dead—a wrong reason to seek Jesus, not based on faith but fear and misinformation.

ASK YOURSELF

How do you keep yourself seeking Christ for all the right reasons—
neither legalistically (trying to prove your self-worth) nor
superstitiously (trying to cover your bases)? What have been some of
the greatest blessings of seeking Him for His glory alone?

HEROD'S REASONS, PART 1

Although he was grieved, the king commanded it [John's head] to be given
because of his oaths, and because of his dinner guests. —MATT. 14:9

As yesterday's discussion revealed, Herod's reaction to Jesus stemmed from an irrational fear that He was actually John the Baptist come back to confront the tetrarch again. So Herod's wavering response to Christ directly flowed from his earlier feelings toward John.

Even as John the Baptist feared nothing and no person but God, Herod feared everything except the Father and His Son. In addition to John and the multitudes, Herod was paranoid of his family and friends and feared potential threats to his position by Rome and other nations.

Herod felt ambivalence toward John, being both fearful and fascinated—feelings he undoubtedly now had toward Jesus. Mark's gospel says, "Herod was afraid of John, knowing that he was a righteous and holy man, and he kept him safe. And when he heard him, he was very perplexed; but he used to enjoy listening to him" (6:20). From this and his being grieved about agreeing to the beheading of John, Herod seemed to have developed a fondness for the Baptist, or at least a more respectful fear—both of which he could have transferred to Jesus.

Although Herod "was grieved," such grief had nothing to do with sadness for sin or authentic repentance. Similar to Pilate, who should have released Jesus but caved in to Jewish intimidation (cf. Luke 23:22–25; John 19:12), Herod cowardly succumbed to the injustice and revenge favored by his wicked wife and stepdaughter and let an innocent man be executed. His foolish excesses and complicity in evil now haunted him and prompted a faithless interest in and faulty analysis of Jesus' works.

ASK YOURSELF

Do you operate with any irrational fears that motivate your decision-making and perhaps alter your ability to follow Christ as fully as you should? What are you doing to counteract them? How could you keep yourself more accountable to those who help you see life in perspective?

HEROD'S REASONS, PART 2

Although he was grieved, the king commanded it [John's head] to be given because of his oaths, and because of his dinner guests. —MATT. 14:9

Herod's morbid fascination with John the Baptist and Jesus was very sad. It had nothing to do with real faith and a seeking after truth and salvation. Rather it was the religious curiosity of unbelief that does not respond to God's grace, love, and truth.

After John's death Herod "kept trying to see Him [Jesus]" (Luke 9:9). But the Lord would not see him prior to the Father's perfect time. Jesus responded this way to a death threat from the tetrarch: "Go and tell that fox, 'Behold, I cast out demons and perform cures today and tomorrow, and the third day I reach My goal'" (Luke 13:32). So He stuck to the purposes of His earthly ministry, undeterred by Herod.

Finally, hours before His crucifixion, Jesus did meet Herod:

> Herod was very glad when he saw Jesus; for he had wanted to see Him for a long time, because he had been hearing about Him and was hoping to see some sign performed by Him. And he questioned Him at some length; but He answered him nothing. . . . Herod with his soldiers, after treating Him with contempt and mocking Him . . . sent Him back to Pilate. (Luke 23:8–9, 11)

For fear of losing his earthly reputation and power, and for pride in his own accomplishments—and for lack of fear toward God—Herod rejected Christ and doomed his soul forever.

ASK YOURSELF

Pride and preoccupation with one's veneer of self-reliance are such dangerous threats to a life of faith—we should guard against them with all diligence. How have these heart enemies curtailed your free experience of fellowship with Christ? What has helped you war against them?

JESUS' RESPONSE TO JOHN'S DEATH

His [John's] disciples came and took away the body and buried it; and they went and reported to Jesus. Now when Jesus heard about John, He withdrew from there in a boat to a secluded place by Himself; —MATT. 14:12–13a

John the Baptist's disciples must have experienced much pain and sadness when they carried away his decapitated body for burial. He was a great man, the forerunner of Messiah, who had been their loyal friend and faithful teacher. They had responded to his urgent preaching and taken his message of repentance to others.

Probably in accord with previous instruction, John's disciples told Jesus what had happened to John. Our Lord deeply loved John. And when He received the sobering news, He wanted to be alone, so "He withdrew from there . . . to a secluded place by Himself" with the apostles (see Mark 6:31–32).

Some suggest that Jesus left the area to avoid John's fate, but that makes no sense when Jesus knew that in the coming months He would willingly carry out the Father's plan to suffer an atoning death for sinners. Jesus avoided Herod only because it was not then in the Father's timetable for Him to meet the tetrarch.

John was the first martyr of the faith (even before Stephen), and Christ likely used this event to teach the apostles more about what lay ahead for them. Although most believers around the world today have freedom to practice their faith, some still suffer John's fate. Enemies of Christianity persecute believers and kill them; but like John, such martyrs would rather die than deny their Lord or the truth of His message.

ASK YOURSELF

Sometimes we overcompensate in reaction to life's heaviness by drowning ourselves in escapes, avoiding having to think about our own or others' pain. Could it be possible, in trying to keep ourselves upbeat, we lose some of the joy that comes from letting God dry our tears?

JESUS' GREAT COMPASSION

When He went ashore, He saw a large crowd, and felt
compassion for them and healed their sick. —MATT. 14:14

The normal, natural inclination for Jesus at this time would have been to ignore the crowd or to forthrightly dismiss the people and tell them he'd do no more miracles to help them. But Jesus, being God's Son, did not merely operate according to human emotions. Even though He was exhausted and in need of rest, the Lord "felt compassion for them," which drew Him to the people.

The word translated "compassion" means literally to be moved in one's bowels, which the ancients considered to be the seat of human emotions. Christ was far from detached and unfeeling regarding humanity's needs, but was deeply touched by fallen people's confusion, suffering, and spiritual lostness. No doubt He felt here much as He did when He approached Lazarus's grave and wept (John 11:35), or as He did when He wept for Jerusalem (Matt. 23:37; Luke 13:34–35; 19:41–42).

In His divine mercy, Jesus had compassion even on many shallow, self-centered thrill seekers in the crowds following Him. This displayed God's loving heart toward people who would not understand or believe the gospel, and would thus ultimately reject Him.

Jesus' compassion also derived from His perfect perspective of hell and the terrible consequences He foresaw for those who would not trust Him for salvation. As much as our Lord wanted to heal people's sick and injured bodies, He was infinitely more concerned about their sin-plagued souls. Physical bodies can become sick or injured again, but once Christ redeems a fallen soul it forever remains whole and free from sin's dominion.

ASK YOURSELF

Perhaps you struggle to sense or experience the love of your heavenly Father. But Jesus said, "He who has seen Me has seen the Father" (John 14:9). When you see the Son's heart bursting with compassion, do you realize you're also seeing the heart of your Father?

THE APOSTLES' DULL PERSPECTIVE

But Jesus said to them, "They do not need to go away; you give them something
to eat!" They said to Him, "We have here only five loaves and two fish."
—MATT. 14:16–17

Earlier on this day Jesus had brought up the matter of feeding the large
crowd (John 6:5–6), and the subject proved to be a test of faith for the
apostles. Would they look to Christ to meet this tremendous need, or
would they trust in earthly resources (see vv. 7–9)?

From our contemporary vantage point, with the benefit of hindsight,
it's difficult to understand why the concept of Jesus' feeding the people
miraculously did not sooner enter the apostles' minds. It would not have
required that much faith for them to have expected Jesus to feed the multitude. But instead they saw no further than their own meager resources:
"We have here only five loaves and two fish." The apostles' outlook was
much like someone standing near Niagara Falls and asking where he
could find water to use. They were face-to-face with God incarnate and
yet were spiritually blind to what He could do.

We might be tempted to presume that, had we been there with Jesus
and the crowd, we would have automatically asked Him to use His powers to feed the people. That would hardly have been a challenge for Him
who created the universe, walked on water, calmed the storm, and healed
hundreds of people, even raising some from the dead. But how many
times have believers today, including us, faced a seemingly insurmount-
able crisis and looked to ourselves first rather than exercising faith and
looking to God for the solution?

ASK YOURSELF

What are the reasons behind our frequent reluctance to look first to God
and His provision? Is it fear that He won't come through? Is it doubt
that He is able? Is it laziness, an unwillingness to persevere in prayer?
Whatever it is, it's keeping us from resting fully in His care.

JESUS FEEDS THE 5,000

*Ordering the people to sit down on the grass, He took the five loaves and the two fish, and looking up toward heaven, He blessed the food, and breaking the loaves He gave them to the disciples, and the disciples gave them to the crowds, and they all ate and were satisfied. —*MATT. 14:19–20a

The people who had been standing on the beautiful, grassy northeastern shore of the Sea of Galilee to better see and hear Jesus likely had little idea why He was now telling them to sit down in such carefully arranged groups. The apostles might have finally guessed that Jesus was going to feed the masses, but they still did not know exactly how.

The Lord's divinely backed methodology immediately became apparent to the twelve. After He blessed the food and gave thanks for it, Jesus broke the loaves, gave them to the apostles, and had His men distribute the bread to the people seated. The text does not tell us precisely when the miracle occurred. A continuous multiplication of the food evidently took place as the disciples distributed it among the people. The miracle was probably unnoticed at first, with no fanfare or dramatic change from little food to much. But the stunning magnitude of the miracle quickly became clear as the thousands of people all had food to eat.

Because God through His Son created the multiplied bread and fish, the crowd's eating satisfaction must have been the best the people ever experienced. Here Matthew uses the same word for satisfaction as Jesus used in the Beatitudes when He promised those who hunger and thirst for righteousness "shall be satisfied" (Matt. 5:6). All those who in faith partake of God's provision will never ultimately be dissatisfied.

ASK YOURSELF

Strange, isn't it, that even though we're all seeking the satisfaction of being filled and content, we so often seek it in ways that are incapable of providing it. Why do we expect fulfillment from anything other than ongoing fellowship with Christ? Why do we doubt we'll find it in Him?

LESSONS FROM THE FEEDING:
THE TWELVE ESTABLISHED, PART 1

Ordering the people to sit down on the grass, He took the five loaves and the two fish, and looking up toward heaven, He blessed the food, and breaking the loaves He gave them to the disciples, and the disciples gave them to the crowds, and they all ate and were satisfied. —MATT. 14:19–20a

The twelve apostles were always objects of Jesus' concern, training, and instruction. Just from this episode of the feeding of the 5,000, our Lord taught them a number of vital principles.

First, Christ demonstrated the principle of withdrawing from needless danger (Matt. 14:13). Martyrdom or any type of unnecessary suffering sought for the wrong motives (e.g., self-glory) has no place in the believer's life. Second, the Lord modeled the importance of rest and solitude, even when there is much ministry to do. We can't always realize such rest and refreshment just how and when we want it, but that does not mean we have to abandon it. Similarly, the apostles saw from Christ the need for occasional times of retreat with fellow laborers to support one another and share needs and feelings.

Further, Jesus confirmed the apostles' need to have compassion on the needy, even if those people seem fickle and undeserving. Christ generously met the physical needs of the crowd that day even though He knew most of the people would not follow Him to the end. Rest and leisure are important, but these must sometimes give way to service to others when that need is greater. Christians have no inalienable rights to personal prerogatives. Those must be expendable, along with all possessions, in service to others in the name of the Lord Jesus (see 1 Cor. 9).

ASK YOURSELF

If you struggle with allowing yourself to rest and retreat, think about what this is likely to cost you in the long run. How could you force yourself to take more seriously your own limitations and your need for recharging, being as driven to relax as you are to exert yourself?

LESSONS FROM THE FEEDING:
THE TWELVE ESTABLISHED, PART 2

Ordering the people to sit down on the grass, He took the five loaves and the two fish, and looking up toward heaven, He blessed the food, and breaking the loaves He gave them to the disciples, and the disciples gave them to the crowds, and they all ate and were satisfied. —MATT. 14:19–20a

Today we continue our look at how Jesus' feeding of the 5,000 established the apostles with some valuable lessons. Another such lesson is that He taught them to do things in an orderly and careful manner (1 Cor. 14:33, 40), which taught the twelve the importance of obeying Christ even when the reason is not clear. Only when the disciples went ahead and seated the people and began distributing the food did they see Jesus' miracle take effect.

Our ministry to others should always display an unreserved generosity that considers their needs before our own. Just as the food did not multiply until they obeyed, the apostles' own needs were not met until others were fully satisfied.

Supremely, Jesus' men learned they could trust God to supply the impossible. As we do today, the disciples at first looked everywhere but to Him for assistance. God can work without us, but He often chooses His servants and their small resources to magnify His goodness and power.

The Lord's redemptive plan entails the witness, work, and means of His followers, whether it's the apostles or us. He delights to show His power and abundance in the most "impossible" of situations (cf. 1 Cor. 1:26–29). At the feeding, Jesus truly taught the apostles the effectiveness of the humble over the grandiose—in this case a boy's lunch.

ASK YOURSELF

Where does your generosity usually start and stop? Have you seen it devalued into the mere giving of money without a corresponding compassion for others or a genuine desire to worship and glorify the Father? How could generosity begin to truly transform you?

LESSONS FROM THE FEEDING: FAITHFUL REMNANT CONFIRMED; UNFAITHFUL REJECTERS REVEALED

*Ordering the people to sit down on the grass, He took the five loaves and the two fish, and looking up toward heaven, He blessed the food, and breaking the loaves He gave them to the disciples, and the disciples gave them to the crowds, and they all ate and were satisfied. They picked up what was left over of the broken pieces, twelve full baskets. There were about five thousand men who ate, besides women and children. —*MATT. 14:19–21

The final two lessons of Jesus' miraculous feeding are of the utmost spiritual significance to us. The event confirmed the presence of a faithful remnant. A segment of the crowd already believed and followed Jesus to be blessed, and others followed so they might believe and join that saved group. The apostle John recorded their attitude: "'What shall we do, so that we may work the works of God?' . . . Then they said to Him, 'Lord, always give us this bread'" (John 6:28, 34). Those elect ones observed not only the multitude receiving abundant food from seemingly so little, but also a tremendous illustration of Jesus' compassion—and they praised and glorified Him for that. They saw a demonstration of the divine kingdom and the King Himself at work, and those faithful ones appreciated the Lord's integrity and stewardship. His miracle power was genuine unlike the histrionics of many charlatans and false prophets.

Sadly, the miraculous feeding also confirmed the presence of many unbelieving rejecters. Most in the crowd merely saw what to them was simply a fascinating work of magic. Thus the gospel significance of Jesus' miracle fell on hard soil—the unbelieving saw the human Jesus but completely missed the Son of God. Jesus met their physical hunger as never before, but spiritually they did not taste of the Bread of Life.

ASK YOURSELF

Ultimately, only these two groups determine who is inside or outside God's kingdom. Humbly examine yourself today and seek by faith to be among the faithful remnant.

A FICKLE CROWD SEEKS JESUS

After these things Jesus went away to the other side of the Sea of Galilee (or Tiberias). A large crowd followed Him, because they saw the signs which He was performing on those who were sick. Then Jesus went up on the mountain, and there He sat down with His disciples. Now the Passover, the feast of the Jews, was near.
—JOHN 6:1–4

Except for Jesus' resurrection, the feeding of the 5,000 is the only miracle recorded in John's gospel that also appears in each of the Synoptic Gospels (Matt. 14:13–20; Mark 6:30–44; Luke 9:10–17). That underscores the miracle's significance since most of John's gospel simply supplements the other gospels with additional material. John's account of the feeding also sets the stage for his record of the bread of life discourse (John 2:22ff.).

Today's passage indicates that Jesus and His apostles sought a place of seclusion, likely because they had been engaged in a period of busy ministry and now needed a time of rest and debriefing (Mark 6:7–13, 30–32; cf. Matt. 11:1). But it was soon apparent to them that they would not find the peace and quiet they desired. The multitude that awaited them near the mountain (a peak probably located in the area today called the Golan Heights, on the Israeli-Syrian border) was not motivated by genuine spiritual concerns. Instead, most of the people were there merely "because they saw the signs which He was performing on those who were sick." Those thrill seekers failed to understand the real meaning of Jesus' miracles (cf. John 6:26), which unquestionably pointed to Him as God's Son and the Messiah. The people were eager to have the benefits of the Lord's power in their physical lives, but they did not seek the faith, repentance, and love for Him they really needed.

ASK YOURSELF

If one of our favorite writers or celebrities or public figures gave us a brief moment of their time, we would be talking about it for years. How can we train ourselves to treasure the value of God's Word, His presence, and His listening ear—and let His simple nearness thrill us?

THE APOSTLES' FAITHLESS REMEDY, PART 1

Therefore Jesus, lifting up His eyes and seeing that a large crowd was coming to Him, said to Philip, "Where are we to buy bread, so that these may eat?" This He was saying to test him, for He Himself knew what He was intending to do. Philip answered Him, "Two hundred denarii worth of bread is not sufficient for them, for everyone to receive a little." —JOHN 6:5–7

Today's passage reveals in more detail how faithless two of the disciples were toward meeting a practical need. Philip and Andrew focused only on human solutions to the food necessity for 5,000 (cf. Matt. 14:15).

The Lord, however, would demonstrate a very different solution. First He asked Philip, "Where are we to buy bread, so that these may eat?" Jesus already knew what Philip was thinking. He didn't need his input to develop a feeding plan. By asking, Jesus simply articulated the impossibility of their finding any place to obtain enough food for the people.

Further, Jesus' question really had nothing to do with the specifics of buying bread. As He occasionally does with us, Jesus presented a dilemma so He could test and strengthen the apostles' faith. As James encourages us, "Consider it all joy, my brethren, when you encounter various trials, knowing that the testing of your faith produces endurance. And let endurance have its perfect result, so that you may be perfect and complete, lacking in nothing" (James 1:2–4). Peter similarly states the challenge, "In this you greatly rejoice, even though now for a little while, if necessary, you have been distressed by various trials, so that the proof of your faith . . . may be found to result in praise and glory and honor at the revelation of Jesus Christ" (1 Peter 1:6–7).

ASK YOURSELF

Can you look back at a recent event (or perhaps a presently occurring one) and see that what appeared to be just a hard problem may very well have been a test from your Father, trying to mature and develop your faith? How can we make the most of these opportunities?

THE APOSTLES' FAITHLESS REMEDY, PART 2

*Philip answered Him, "Two hundred denarii worth of bread is not sufficient for them, for everyone to receive a little." One of His disciples, Andrew, Simon Peter's brother, said to Him, "There is a lad here who has five barley loaves and two fish, but what are these for so many people?" —*JOHN 6:7–9

It seemed pointless to Philip to even discuss where the apostles might have obtained bread. They plainly didn't have sufficient cash to buy bread even if they could find it. Philip's answer emphasized from his view the impossibility of the situation and further showed his insufficient faith. He had witnessed other miracles by Jesus—including the changing of water into wine (John 2:1–11)—and would have known of God's various miraculous provisions of food in Old Testament times (see Num. 11:31–32; 1 Kings 17:9–16; 2 Kings 4:1–7). Yet Philip's mind focused only on the bottom-line considerations of buying enough food to give everyone a little.

Andrew also focused on the human side of the equation, although he was not quite as pessimistic as Philip. Jesus told the apostles to find out how much food the crowd had, and Andrew likely reported their findings. That report simply confirmed the discouraging nature of the situation when it looked toward the boy with a meager "five barley loaves and two fish." We can easily summarize Andrew's faithless response with his own words: "But what are these for so many people?"

Philip and Andrew and the other apostles failed Jesus' test of faith for them. None responded by affirming His power to provide the food.

ASK YOURSELF

Have you experienced a time when you settled for less from God, not stepping back to consider that He might have more to accomplish through you than seemed practical or most obvious? What have been some of the biggest costs from living inside the safe and the known?

A FULFILLING DINNER FOR 5,000

*He distributed to those who were seated; likewise also of the fish as much as they
wanted. When they were filled, He said to His disciples, "Gather up the leftover
fragments so that nothing will be lost." —JOHN 6:11–12*

W hen feeding the 5,000, Jesus simply and without fanfare continually
"broke the loaves and . . . kept giving them to the disciples to set before
them; and . . . divided up the two fish among them all" (Mark 6:41). Contrary to what we might have expected, our Lord did not create a large
amount of food all at once; but the crowd that partook of the meal was
truly astonished—those present had witnessed the Creator God at work.

Although Jesus chose to use the apostles to distribute the food, He
could have just as easily used some supernatural means to dispense the
meal. For His own glorious purposes, God often works through weak
and fallible human beings. Paul reminds the Corinthians and us that
"God has chosen the foolish things of the world to shame the wise, and
. . . the weak things of the world to shame the things which are strong"
(1 Cor. 1:27; cf. Num. 12:3; Judg. 6:15).

Christ does not minister to people in a halfway manner. In this instance everyone ate "as much as they wanted," so that "they were filled."
Such abundant and divine provision offered no excuse for wasting the
leftovers (cf. Prov. 25:16). Therefore the Lord ordered the apostles to
collect the fragments of bread and fish, and these were enough to fill
twelve baskets. Some theorize that the baskets represent the twelve tribes
of Israel, but more simply Jesus provided twelve baskets because the
twelve apostles each needed one to collect the remaining food. Amaz-
ingly, the food more than satisfied the crowd *and* provided for another
day's meal.

ASK YOURSELF

What could be the most likely reasons for feeling less than full in
relationship with Jesus Christ? Are there seasons when fullness is more
than we should expect from Him? Or does emptiness and leanness of
spirit almost always represent a resistance to His plenty on our part?

MISGUIDED CORONATION ATTEMPT

Therefore when the people saw the sign which He had performed, they said, "This is truly the Prophet who is to come into the world." So Jesus, perceiving that they were intending to come and take Him by force to make Him king, withdrew again to the mountain by Himself alone. —JOHN 6:14–15

The crowd's assertion that Jesus was "the Prophet" offers us a solid clue regarding what the masses really wanted in a messiah. They sought an earthly deliverer who could meet all their physical needs, especially those related to food and health, and deliver them from the hated Roman oppression. Having identified Jesus as their ideal messiah, they likely would have forced Him to lead a march on Jerusalem to overthrow the Romans and usher in the ultimate social welfare state. But the Lord was not about to yield to their selfish and sinful demands.

Jesus does not yield to human fancies or come to anyone on that person's terms. Some contemporary preachers and evangelists, however, present Christ to unbelievers in "seeker sensitive" terms as the quick-fix answer to all their felt needs. But that turns the gospel on its head and makes it no more than a superficial marketing ploy.

People must abandon thoughts of falsely crowning Jesus on their terms and instead come to Him on His terms. He calls for sinners to mourn over their sin (Matt. 5:4), repent (4:17), and accept Him as sovereign Lord (Rom. 10:9). Our Lord then grants such believers a rich legacy of joy (John 15:11), peace (14:27), and comfort (2 Cor. 1:3–7). All the while they understand that they owe Him complete obedience in everything (John 14:15, 21; 1 John 5:3).

ASK YOURSELF

What would your life have become if God had been willing to let you alone determine the way He should work in your circumstances? What would you have never learned? How would you have lost ground and failed to grow? What would your desires have done to you?

MAY 6

JESUS' DIVINE AUTHORITY OVER THE TWELVE

Immediately He made the disciples get into the boat and go ahead of Him to the other side, while He sent the crowds away. After He had sent the crowds away, He went up on the mountain by Himself to pray; and when it was evening, He was there alone. —MATT. 14:22–23

With the crowd's ill-informed attempt to crown Jesus king, the apostles very likely rejoiced that Jesus was at last being recognized as the promised king who would overthrow tyranny and reestablish Israel's kingdom. Christ Himself had taught them to pray for the coming kingdom (Matt. 6:10), thus they reasoned this was an opportune moment to fulfill that promise. Certainly the ambitious, reprobate Judas Iscariot would have strongly encouraged such thinking among his colleagues.

But Jesus knew the apostles' thoughts and the almost sure potential for the crowd to persuade them. Thus He commanded them to "get into the boat and go ahead of Him to the other side." The Lord did not want them to be swept up by the ill-conceived political plans of the people.

It is fair to infer that the apostles probably resisted departing from Jesus and the crowd, both because of the crowd's enthusiasm for Jesus and because they wanted to be with Him always. In spite of their sin and weakness, the apostles were devoted to their Lord and felt vulnerable when apart from Him. No matter what the reasons for their reluctance, however, the twelve disciples entered their boat and headed for the other side of the lake. Jesus' firm word of authority was enough for them—He did not have to resort to supernatural force to compel their departure. As men under divine authority, it was a solid testimony that they obeyed.

ASK YOURSELF

When have you been most thankful that you put some time and space between yourself and an emotionally charged situation that had the potential to sway your better judgment? What are some of the worst decisions you ever made by going along with the consensus of the crowd?

JESUS' DIVINE AUTHORITY OVER PEOPLE

*Immediately He made the disciples get into the boat and go ahead of Him to the
other side, while He sent the crowds away. After He had sent the crowds away, He
went up on the mountain by Himself to pray; and when it was evening, He was
there alone.* —MATT. 14:22–23

In spite of its great size (probably 25,000 or more, counting women and
children), the crowd could not force Jesus to do anything contrary to His
Father's will and plan. Many people in the crowd were determined to ele-
vate Him to a throne to further their own selfish, ambitious purposes—
but they were unable to do so. Instead, after the Lord sent the apostles on
their way, He simply, without many words or any formalities, dispersed
the crowd and let people bed down for the night wherever they could
find a place near Bethsaida Julias (a town a few miles from the lake's
northeastern shore).

Christ has the final authority over the destinies of all people, including their final judgment (John 5:22). The multitudes who heard His Sermon on the Mount recognized that "He was teaching them as one having
authority, and not as their scribes" (Matt. 7:29). In His Great Commission, Jesus reminded the apostles and believers of all eras, "All authority
has been given to Me in heaven and on earth" (Matt. 28:18). The apostle
Paul further reminds us of Jesus' ultimate authority over all people, a
truth that ought to bring us much comfort in these last days: "at the name
of Jesus every knee will bow, of those who are in heaven and on earth
and under the earth, and that every tongue will confess that Jesus Christ
is Lord, to the glory of God the Father" (Phil. 2:10–11).

ASK YOURSELF

Wonder what your unsaved friends, neighbors, and family members
would think if they knew their lives were under the ultimate authority of
the God they refuse to acknowledge as Lord and King? What are some
ways you see God working around them, even if they don't see it?

JESUS' PRAYER TIME UNDERGIRDS HIS AUTHORITY

*He went up on the mountain by Himself to pray; and when it was evening,
He was there alone.* —MATT. 14:23*b*

The three temptations Jesus faced after His baptism were not the only
ones He'd ever face during His earthly incarnation (cf. Luke 4:13). In
fact, the enthusiasm of the crowd—and by inference the Twelve—to
make Jesus king was much like the third temptation when the devil offered Him all the world's kingdoms (Matt. 4:8–9). We can imagine Satan
now saying, "This Passover season is a great time to establish my kingdom. I could march triumphantly into Jerusalem at the front of thousands of loyal and enthusiastic Jesus supporters." Satan undoubtedly
would have felt Jesus would attract many additional supporters along the
way, and His divine power would guarantee triumph over any opposition. Under this scenario, Jesus could be a king without having to endure
an unfair trial and crucifixion later.

In the face of such temptations, however, Jesus refused an enticement to sin, as He would always shun any evil or disobedience to the Father's plan. The only victory our Lord celebrated was in prayer on the
mountain—victory over temptation and the forces of darkness, not mere
earthly powers.

Much later Jesus assured Peter, "Satan has demanded permission to
sift you like wheat; but I have prayed for you, that your faith may not
fail" (Luke 22:31–32). No doubt the Lord prayed for all the apostles long
before His magnificent high priestly prayer (John 17:6–26). And it's
likely He prayed for them now with full confidence His prayers would be
effective, because He had all authority over everything in the universe.

ASK YOURSELF

Perhaps prayer has become a perfunctory appendage in your life lately—
something you do but not something you really depend on. What goes out
of your heart every time prayer becomes an activity you can take or leave?
What helps you keep prayer in its proper place of importance?

JESUS WALKS ON THE LAKE

Then, when they had rowed about three or four miles, they saw Jesus walking on the sea and drawing near to the boat; and they were frightened. —JOHN 6:19

After the apostles "had rowed about three or four miles" over a nine- to twelve-hour period, a sudden squall on the Sea of Galilee caught their boat. Their progress had been stressful, exhausting, and slow; thus they continued "straining at the oars" (Mark 6:48), desperately seeking the safety of the lake's western shore.

Ever the faithful Shepherd, Jesus while alone praying (6:15) had not forgotten the apostles. In His perfect timing He planned to come to their aid, reminding us that divine sovereignty, omnipotence, and omniscience are never in a hurry. After making little headway for hours, the apostles saw through the swirling storm a figure walking effortlessly on the water, into the powerful winds and waves. Because of the darkness and storm, the men did not immediately recognize that it was their Lord. Although as fishermen (as many as seven of them) most of them were used to such gales, they were still in no way accustomed to seeing a man walking on water. Thus "they were frightened" and thought they saw a ghost (Matt. 14:26; Mark 6:49).

Skeptics have long theorized that Jesus was really just walking along the lake's shoreline, and that the frightened apostles erroneously saw Him as walking on the water. But the boat was too far from land for them to have seen Him there. Such a suggestion is merely an attempt to explain away the supernatural. By suspending the laws of nature, Jesus here gave the apostles dramatic proof that He is the Creator and controller of the universe (Col. 1:16).

ASK YOURSELF

Never forget that as amazing as this miracle was, the fact that Jesus—with all He had to think about—would return to help His storm-tossed followers was equally astonishing. How does this encourage you today—with all you have to think about, with all you need Him for?

A DISPLAY OF DIVINE KNOWLEDGE, PART 1

But the boat was already a long distance from the land, battered by the waves; for the wind was contrary. And in the fourth watch of the night He came to them, walking on the sea. —MATT. 14:24–25

The apostles were very confused and disappointed that Christ had sent them to the other side of the lake. Why would He have required them to travel on the water now, when storms were a distinct possibility? Nevertheless they obeyed and persevered, striving to obey the Lord's command, even when they wished He were with them.

Jesus knew of His companions' situation long before it developed. Therefore when the storm arose He did not have to rush away from prayer in order to arrive in time to rescue the apostles. With His divine knowledge, our Lord knew precisely what He would do concerning the storm and for His friends.

Jesus waited awhile before going to the apostles, just as He waited several days after Lazarus's death before going to Bethany. In both cases He could have acted much sooner; or He could have performed a miraculous remedy from a distance, just as when He healed the centurion's son (Matt. 8:13). Of course, Jesus could have prevented Lazarus's death or the rising of the storm from even occurring. But Christ's omniscience allowed Mary and Martha and the disciples to sense extreme need before He came for assistance. He knew infinitely better than His servants what was best for their welfare and for the Father's glory.

ASK YOURSELF

Waiting is not something we want Jesus to do with us very often. "Right now" would always seem like a better time to come to our rescue. But how have you benefited from His sovereign timing? How has it gotten easier to trust Him, knowing that He will never be a moment too late?

A Display of Divine Knowledge, Part 2

*But the boat was already a long distance from the land, battered by the
waves; for the wind was contrary. And in the fourth watch of the night
He came to them, walking on the sea.* —MATT. 14:24–25

While in their storm-buffeted boat, the apostles should have taken joyous comfort in David's words: "If I ascend to heaven, You are there; if I make my bed in Sheol, behold, You are there. If I take the wings of the dawn, if I dwell in the remotest part of the sea, even there Your hand will lead me, and Your right hand will lay hold of me" (Ps. 139:8–10). They should also have recalled other promises from the psalmist, such as:

> The Lord also will be a stronghold for the oppressed, a stronghold in times of trouble. (9:9; cf. 23:4)

> The Lord is my rock and my fortress and my deliverer, my God, my rock, in whom I take refuge. (18:2)

However, in a time of emergency the apostles forgot those psalms and other Old Testament instances of God's mercies toward His people (e.g., Gen. 22:13; Ex. 3:7). As would soon be evident, they had no confidence that God would remember their plight, as He had numerous times for His people in the past. Jesus' men even forgot His words from the Sermon on the Mount that God knew all their needs before they asked (Matt. 6:32) and was concerned about life's smallest details (10:29–30).

But the Lord utilized the very danger that threatened the apostles when "He came to them, walking on the sea." He couldn't see them from the mountain or through the storm, but He knew right where they were. His divine awareness was more than sufficient (cf. Prov. 15:3; Heb. 4:13).

ASK YOURSELF

How tempting it can be to forgo our need for reading and study, for meditating and bathing in the Word. But how have the reminders of Scripture sustained you at times when you needed them most? And how else would you have known them if not from frequent exposure?

PROOF OF DIVINE PROTECTION, PART 1

*When the disciples saw Him walking on the sea, they were terrified, and said,
"It is a ghost!" And they cried out in fear. But immediately Jesus spoke to
them, saying, "Take courage, it is I; do not be afraid." —*MATT. 14:26–27

Because of the nighttime storm, their exhaustion from hours of rowing,
and their general fear of the wind and waves, the apostles did not initially
recognize Jesus on the water. Their fear soon turned to extreme terror
when Jesus' form appeared to be a ghost (the Greek word *phantasma* indicates an apparition or imaginary creature), come to add to their torments. In their human panic the disciples could not help but cry out in
fear.

Jesus was testing the apostles' faith, but He also understood their
weaknesses and wanted to protect them from harm. So His simple statement, "Take courage, it is I; do not be afraid," instantly calmed their
panic and caused them to recognize it was their Lord.

Jesus did not offer any lengthy explanation of what He was doing or
why He hadn't come sooner—and He wasn't walking on water to show
the apostles how to do that. His purpose was simply to show His loving
protection and willingness to do whatever necessary to rescue His followers. His miraculous walking on water was not essential to the rescue,
but it was a vivid lesson on the power and extent of divine protection and
a permanent reminder that Christ can and will act on behalf of His own.

ASK YOURSELF

You may be at a point where the assurance of God's care and protection
is exactly what you're needing to remember. How would this
encouragement change the way you deal with the uncertainties you're
facing? What causes you to forget that God is able to meet your need?

PROOF OF DIVINE PROTECTION, PART 2

When the disciples saw Him walking on the sea, they were terrified, and said, "It is a ghost!" And they cried out in fear. But immediately Jesus spoke to them, saying, "Take courage, it is I; do not be afraid." —MATT. 14:26–27

As believers, we will always be in a place where Jesus can find us and help us, no matter how difficult the circumstances or how severe the opposition (cf. Josh. 1:5; Heb. 13:5). The lesson for the apostles in the boat is the same one for us: there is no reason for the Lord's children to fear.

Consider Paul's experience on the ship taking him to Rome. A particularly violent hurricane slammed that vessel and threatened to sink it or run it aground. When everyone else on board had given up hope of surviving, an angel appeared to the apostle and told him everyone would survive although the ship would be lost. Even prior to that event, Paul confidently told his shipmates that God would work everything out (Acts 27:25). And that is what happened—the ship was wrecked on Malta, Paul and everyone made it safely to land, he ministered on Malta, and eventually he went on safely to Rome.

The disciples on the Sea of Galilee also learned the valuable lesson of God's protection. Even though they were reluctant to leave Jesus, they obeyed and rowed out into the path of the eventual storm—and the Lord honored their faithfulness. Thus all believers can know that the place of protection and security is not necessarily the place with the best situation, but it is the place of obedience to God's will.

ASK YOURSELF

How do you determine whether or not you're in the center of God's will? Why would it be unrealistic for Him to decree that certain situations were always indicative of being rightly positioned and in tune with His heart? What can you misjudge by judging your surroundings?

DIVINE LOVE: PETER AND JESUS, PART 1

*Peter said to Him, "Lord, if it is You, command me to come to You on the
water." And He said, "Come!" And Peter got out of the boat, and walked
on the water and came toward Jesus. But seeing the wind, he became
frightened, and beginning to sink, he cried out, "Lord, save me!"
Immediately Jesus stretched out His hand and took hold of him, and said
to him, "You of little faith, why did you doubt?"* —MATT. 14:28–31

Peter undoubtedly was overjoyed to see that the figure on the stormy
waters was actually Jesus. Although Peter knew Jesus could empower
him to walk on water, he did not want to presume such an attempt without Jesus' permission. Peter's request that Jesus allow him to walk on
water was an act of affection built on confident faith.

The ever-eager Peter could be faulted for everything from brashness to
cowardice, but he also did many things out of love, courage, and faith. At
the Transfiguration, this statement was imprudent, but prompted by Peter's
sincere devotion: "Lord, it is good for us to be here; if You wish, I will make
three tabernacles here, one for You, and one for Moses, and one for Elijah"
(Matt. 17:4). He truly loved Jesus and wanted to serve Him to the fullest. In
this episode on the stormy lake, Peter sensed the comfort and relief of Jesus'
presence, and he wanted to be as close as possible.

Peter's love for Jesus was imperfect, but it was genuine. Later on, Jesus
would not contradict Peter's threefold affirmation of love for Him, but simply charge him to shepherd the sheep of God and warn him of discipleship's
cost (John 21:15–18). According to tradition, Peter requested to be crucified
upside down because he felt unworthy to die as Jesus had.

ASK YOURSELF

Can you tell that God is calling you to risk the safety of your comfort
zone, perhaps in a business decision, or the possibility of a leadership
position, or the resolution of a family matter? What might your next
bold move need to look like, and how are you praying about it?

DIVINE LOVE: PETER AND JESUS, PART 2

Peter said to Him, "Lord, if it is You, command me to come to You on the water." And He said, "Come!" And Peter got out of the boat, and walked on the water and came toward Jesus. But seeing the wind, he became frightened, and beginning to sink, he cried out, "Lord, save me!" Immediately Jesus stretched out His hand and took hold of him, and said to him, "You of little faith, why did you doubt?" —MATT. 14:28–31

Our Lord, displaying the greatest of compassion, commanded Peter to come to Him on the water. Christ was greatly pleased that Peter wanted to join Him. Thus we can be certain that Jesus wasn't inviting Peter, much less commanding him, to do anything sinful, even though it involved something bold and unprecedented. Just as the Savior always accepts and builds upon a Christian's weak faith, He always accepts and nourishes imperfect love such as Peter's. With much patience and care He takes believers' love and, through sufferings and trials as well as blessings and triumphs, molds that love into more perfect conformity to the divine love.

Jesus' telling the leader of the apostles to "Come!" was surely a loving order. John declares, "We have come to know and have believed the love which God has for us. God is love" (1 John 4:16). It is God's nature to love His own with an infinite, unqualified, unchanging, and perfect love. And believers most fully reflect the love of God when they are loving, especially to one another. "If someone says, 'I love God,' and hates his brother," the apostle John instructs us, "he is a liar; for the one who does not love his brother whom he has seen, cannot love God whom he has not seen" (1 John 4:20).

ASK YOURSELF

Have you had any reason lately to question the love of God on your behalf? It is so like our enemy to use negative situations to assail the sure Word of God, misinterpreting hardship as grounds for doubting the Lord's faithful compassion. Stand on what you know to be true.

DIVINE LOVE: PETER AND JESUS, PART 3

Immediately Jesus stretched out His hand and took hold of him, and said to him, "You of little faith, why did you doubt?" —MATT. 14:31

Peter's love for his Lord was sincere, but he did not grasp the extremity of what he was about to attempt. Once he got onto the water, the situation changed radically, he took his eyes off Jesus, and he began to sink.

Peter then could think of nothing else but drowning, and Jesus had to reach out and pull him up. The Lord then rebuked him, "You of little faith, why did you doubt?" But that would have been obvious to Peter. He was weary from rowing all night, frightened by the storm and what he thought was a ghost, and now he'd almost drowned before reaching Jesus.

Peter's weak faith, bolstered by a genuine love for Christ, was better than no faith. At least he did not cower in the boat as did the others; rather he made an attempt to join his Master.

When we get frustrated, anxious, or frightened during trials, Satan tempts us to question God's providence in allowing such difficulties. And if we focus on our circumstances rather than God, we will begin to sink like Peter did. But our Lord's abundant resources are available to us, just as they were for Peter. Years later, he would write,

> In this you greatly rejoice, even though now for a little while . . . you have been distressed by various trials, so that the proof of your faith, being more precious than gold which is perishable, even though tested by fire, may be found to result in praise and glory and honor at the revelation of Jesus Christ. (1 Peter 1:6–7)

ASK YOURSELF

What advice do you often receive from those around you when life overwhelms you and the swimming is nearly impossible? If faithless people are too often in your ear, seek out those whose counsel and perspectives are laced with biblical principles. Keep your eyes on Jesus.

PROOF OF DIVINE POWER

When they got into the boat, the wind stopped. And those who were in the boat worshiped Him, saying, "You are certainly God's Son!" —MATT. 14:32–33

Jesus accomplished this spectacular miracle without uttering a word or raising either hand. It was as if the wind was merely waiting for the miracles on the lake to culminate. When the wind had served its purpose in these dramatic events, it just stopped.

Just as abruptly, "the boat was at the land to which they were going" (John 6:21). According to normal human experience, we should hardly be surprised that the apostles "were utterly astonished" (Mark 6:51). But because those men had witnessed many miraculous displays of Jesus' powers over the previous two years, the present events should not have been that astonishing to them. However, Mark explains why the disciples reacted with such amazement: "They had not gained any insight from the incident of the loaves, but their heart was hardened" (v. 52).

But now the Holy Spirit softened those same hearts and opened their eyes as never before. As a result, "those who were in the boat worshiped Him, saying, 'You are certainly God's Son!'" The Lord took them past mere amazement and prompted them to worship Him, which was the original purpose of His signs. Finally the disciples were beginning to see Christ's lofty role as Son of God and creator of the universe:

> He is the image of the invisible God, the firstborn of all creation. For by Him all things were created . . . visible and invisible, whether thrones or dominions or rulers or authorities—all things have been created through Him and for Him. He is before all things, and in Him all things hold together. (Col. 1:15–17)

ASK YOURSELF

What if you could condition yourself to see every twist and turn in life as a fresh opportunity to worship—whether to thank Him for His help, or to fall back into His strong arms, or to renew your trust in Him for obedience and resistance to temptation? Ask God to help you see things this way again.

TRUE AND FALSE DISCIPLES CONTRASTED

He said to them, "It is I; do not be afraid." So they were willing
to receive Him into the boat. —JOHN 6:20–21a

The apostles' worshipful reaction to Jesus' miracles on the lake and their willing reception of Him back into the boat—along with their obedience in heading for the other side of the lake—demonstrated their true discipleship. Their behavior showed they ultimately loved Christ more than anything else, even life itself (see Matt. 10:38–39; Luke 9:23–24; John 12:25). Only genuine disciples are willing to submit to Jesus Christ's lordship in everything—even if it means persecution, execution, or death in a storm on the Sea of Galilee.

On the other hand, false disciples by definition are not receptive to the demands of real discipleship that the Lord sets forth. And when "affliction or persecution arises because of the word," or "the worry of the world and the deceitfulness of wealth choke the word" (Matt. 13:21–22), such people reveal their true allegiances and forsake the Lord Jesus.

The accounts of Jesus walking on the water, rescuing Peter from drowning, and calming the storm, illustrate the final response true disciples will have toward their Lord. But as we will see in the coming days, false disciples do not pursue Christ with the goal of recognizing and obeying Him as their Lord and Savior. Rather, they think only of personal gain, and when they don't receive their selfish desires, they abandon Jesus altogether (see John 6:60, 66).

ASK YOURSELF

You may have already gone far with Jesus, clinging to Him steadfastly in difficult times, suffering ridicule and misunderstanding for bearing His name. But is there any line you're not sure you could cross? Ask God to keep your heart open and submissive, whatever the cost.

The Response of False Disciples, Part 1

Jesus answered them and said, "Truly, truly, I say to you, you seek Me, not because you saw signs, but because you ate of the loaves and were filled. Do not work for the food which perishes, but for the food which endures to eternal life, which the Son of Man will give to you, for on Him the Father, God, has set His seal."
—John 6:26–27

Jesus' answer here actually bypassed the crowd's irrelevant, superficial question concerning His arrival in Capernaum (v. 25) and probed the real issue of the people's sinful motives. Just the previous day they had wrongly attempted to make Him king after the miraculous feeding; telling them about the latest events on the lake would have only further incited their misguided messianic fervor. Jesus never did commit Himself to such thrill-seeking false disciples (cf. Ps. 25:14; Matt. 13:11; John 2:24).

Jesus' rebuke to the crowd for seeking Him merely because it enjoyed eating the bread and fish exposed the people's materialistic hearts. Although the people had seen the miraculous feeding of the large crowd (John 6:14), they did not understand the spiritual implications of that miracle or other signs.

Instead of pursuing perishable food as they did, Jesus urged them to seek "the food which endures to eternal life," which was none other than the Messiah Himself, the Bread of Life (vv. 35, 54). He certainly knew that people needed physical nourishment, but He was much more interested in their spiritual welfare (4:14; cf. Matt. 16:26; 2 Cor. 4:16). As God's beloved Son, only He has the authority and power to bestow genuine spiritual food from the Father that truly satisfies the hunger for righteousness (Matt. 5:6).

ASK YOURSELF

What are some of the throwaway, temporary delights you sometimes seek, mistakenly hoping they'll be enough to keep you satisfied on a daily basis? What are they missing that only Jesus can provide? What does He give you that none of us can do without?

THE RESPONSE OF FALSE DISCIPLES, PART 2

Therefore they said to Him, "What shall we do, so that we may work the works of God?" Jesus answered and said to them, "This is the work of God, that you believe in Him whom He has sent." —JOHN 6:28–29

People in the crowd processed Jesus' words through the grid of their sinful minds and concluded that the Lord wanted them to do something to obtain eternal life. This was parallel to the rich young man's question, "Teacher, what good thing shall I do that I may obtain eternal life?" (Matt. 19:16), or the lawyer who "stood up and put Him to the test, saying, 'Teacher, what shall I do to inherit eternal life?'" (Luke 10:25). Questions like these were fairly common for the Jews who pursued eternal life through the duties and rituals of their religion.

Of course, we know authentic salvation does not come through good works (Titus 3:5). Therefore Jesus told the people that the only work God accepted was for them to "believe in Him whom He has sent." Salvation comes by grace alone (Eph. 2:8–9), through faith alone (Rom. 3:28), in Christ alone (Acts 4:12), "because by the works of the Law no flesh will be justified in His sight" (Rom. 3:20; cf. Gal. 2:16). Salvation is truly a divine gift (John 4:10; Rom. 6:23), thus it does not come from any human striving or morality, but from a sincere faith that results in good works (Eph. 2:10; cf. Matt. 7:16–20; Luke 6:43–46). So-called faith, devoid of any spiritual fruit, is dead and was never biblical faith at all (James 2:14–26).

Unlike the apostles, who responded to Christ's power with faith, the crowd was initially curious but ultimately unwilling to repent and abandon its unrighteousness, proving they were never true disciples of Jesus.

ASK YOURSELF

It is hard for us to grasp that "where there is no law, there also is no violation" (Rom. 4:15), that "there is now no condemnation for those who are in Christ Jesus" (8:1). But it's true. How does this saving grace become the living grace that keeps us resting in His righteousness?

THE PEOPLE DEMAND A SIGN

So they said to Him, "What then do You do for a sign, so that we may see, and
believe You? What work do You perform? Our fathers ate the manna in the
wilderness; as it is written, 'He gave them bread out of heaven to eat.'"
—JOHN 6:30–31

The crowd's foolish and brazen demand that Jesus prove His credentials by further miraculous works revealed the people's selfish curiosity. It also revealed their unregenerate spiritual blindness, as John Calvin observes, "This wicked question clearly shows the truth of what is said elsewhere: 'A wicked and adulterous generation asks for a miraculous sign' (Matthew 12:39)."

The Lord had urgently pointed the people toward saving faith (John 6:29), but they merely asked for another sign (cf. 2:18). They wanted Him to repeat the miraculous feeding they had just experienced. Rather than worshiping Jesus as Lord and Savior, these skeptics wanted Jesus to constantly provide "them bread out of heaven to eat" with their mouths rather than their hearts. They recalled what occurred in Moses' day when God gave Israel "manna in the wilderness" for forty years (cf. Ex. 16:4, 15; Ps. 78:24). The people therefore challenged Jesus to prove His messiahship by giving them an endless food supply.

Stubborn unbelief will not change, no matter how much evidence for truth and Christ's deity God gives. Hardened unbelievers "will not be persuaded even if someone rises from the dead" (Luke 16:31; cf. Mark 15:32). Even when Jesus did rise from the dead—a much greater miracle than feeding the crowds—most Jews still refused to believe in Him (Matt. 28:11–15; Acts 4:1–3). No miraculous sign is adequate for some doubters.

ASK YOURSELF

Understanding that no miracle would ever be enough to satisfy the unbelieving curious, is it any wonder that God in His wisdom also chooses not to satisfy every prayerful whim of His believing children? We are welcome to ask, but always wise to do so according to His will.

MANNA COMPARED TO THE TRUE BREAD

*Jesus then said to them, "Truly, truly, I say to you, it is not Moses who has given you the bread out of heaven, but it is My Father who gives you the true bread out of heaven. For the bread of God is that which comes down out of heaven, and gives life to the world." —*JOHN 6:32–33

Our Lord proceeded to rebuke the people for their fourfold misunderstanding of manna as it related to the true bread.

First, the people did not realize that it was God rather than Moses who gave their forebears "the bread out of heaven." In Exodus 16:4 "the Lord said to Moses, 'Behold, I will rain bread from heaven for you.'" Moses simply told the Israelites God's instructions for the gathering of the manna (Ex. 16:15–30).

Second, the people did not understand that manna had not ultimately been the true bread from heaven. Jesus' words indicate that the true bread was not the manna of long ago but what God presently gives. The manna, though an actual physical bread from God, merely foreshadowed the ultimate true bread from God—His Son the Lord Jesus.

Third, the crowd did not discern the life-giving differences between manna, which gave physical life, and "the bread of God," which gives spiritual life. Manna provided temporal nourishment to sustain the people in the wilderness, but Jesus Christ is the one and only giver of spiritual and eternal life (5:29; 6:53; 10:10; 14:6).

Finally, the people did not grasp that whereas manna came only to Israel, the true bread from heaven comes to the world. Salvation through Christ's death is for all who believe (3:15–16, 18, 36; 5:24), regardless of national background (4:39–42; Rom. 1:5–6, 16). Thus Jesus is the true bread from God and infinitely superior to Moses.

ASK YOURSELF

We have a tendency to look to others for our feeding—to anyone who keeps us spiritually taught and encouraged. What are the dangers of putting unrealistic hope in the conduits of truth rather than its Source?

RECEIVING THE BREAD OF LIFE

*Then they said to Him, "Lord, always give us this bread." Jesus said
to them, "I am the bread of life; he who comes to Me will not hunger,
and he who believes in Me will never thirst." —*JOHN 6:34–35

The people's demand to have Jesus meet merely their physical needs
clearly reveals their ongoing spiritual blindness. Their dull-witted approach illustrated that "a natural man does not accept the things of the
Spirit of God, for they are foolishness to him; and he cannot understand
them, because they are spiritually appraised" (1 Cor. 2:14).

The crowd's utter lack of spiritual understanding led our Lord to declare forthrightly, "I am the bread of life." Obviously Jesus did not refer
to Himself as physical bread, but to the supreme spiritual bread from
heaven. No earthly food, not even manna or what Jesus had recently created for the feeding, could permanently relieve physical hunger. When
He said those who come to Him will never again hunger or thirst, Jesus
referred metaphorically to the soul's hungering and thirsting (cf. Pss.
42:1–2; 63:1; Matt. 5:6).

Humanity must come to Christ and believe in Him in order to have
salvation. Although John doesn't use the term "repentance," the concept
is implied in Jesus' words. Our Savior urged people to forsake sin and
embrace Him as Lord. Spurgeon says, "You and your sins must separate,
or you and your God will never come together." One who comes to
Christ trusts Him completely as the Lamb of God and Bread of Life who
gave Himself on the cross for sinners. To repent is to turn from sin; to
believe is to turn in faith to the only Savior—inseparable concepts, like
sides of the same coin.

ASK YOURSELF

The incompatibility of sin and pure relationship with Christ is so clear in
Scripture and so evident in our own experience, it's a wonder we
continue to feel drawn to disprove it. What makes us think that anything
can rival the blessings of conscience-free fellowship with Him?

JESUS REBUKES UNBELIEF

But I said to you that you have seen Me, and yet do not believe. —JOHN 6:36

After asserting that He was and is the Bread of Life, Jesus rebuked the people with this indictment for their unbelief. What specific past incident Jesus referred to is not clear, but it's certain that the crowd's unbelief flouted His self-revelation. Thus the people's persistent rejection was inexcusable.

There was a sharp contrast between the people's response to Him and the one Jesus desired (cf. Matt. 23:37). Although the crowd had seen Him and witnessed His miracles, it failed to grasp the significance of those signs, and missed the real implications of His teaching. Similar to the Israelites in the wilderness, "The word they heard did not profit them, because it was not united by faith in those who heard" (Heb. 4:2).

The miracles Jesus' countrymen saw only whetted their appetites for more signs. Jesus intrigued them by what He could do to ease the pain and difficulties of this present life, but they were unwilling to accept Him as their Messiah and Lord, or believe in Him as the Savior who could give eternal life. They needed to hear and believe the words the author of Hebrews later sent to his readers:

> Consider Jesus, the Apostle and High Priest of our confession; He was faithful to Him who appointed Him, as Moses also was in all His house. For He has been counted worthy of more glory than Moses, by just so much as the builder of the house has more honor than the house. (Heb. 3:1–3)

ASK YOURSELF

Try naming some of the things you've seen God do in your own life, in your family's life, in your church's life, in your friends' lives. We forget a lot of what we see. But even if He showed us nothing else, haven't we seen enough already to be convinced that He is faithful and true?

GOD'S SOVEREIGN WORK IN SALVATION, PART 1

*All that the Father gives Me will come to Me, and the one who comes
to Me I will certainly not cast out.* —JOHN 6:37

Jesus was not discouraged, even though the crowd responded negatively to Him. The all-powerful sovereignty of the Father anchored Jesus' confidence in His mission's success. He was certain that everyone whom His Father gave Him—the collective body chosen before the foundation of the world—would come to Him. The story of redemption is one of calling this bride (the church) for the Son as a love gift from the Father. Every soul given by God to Christ is an expression of the Father's irresistible love; thus everyone given "will come" to the Son.

From the perspective of human responsibility, "God is now declaring to men that all people everywhere should repent" (Acts 17:30; cf. Rom. 10:13). Yet salvation does not depend on "the will of man, but of God" (John 1:13; cf. Rom. 9:16). God is the One who grants both repentance (Acts 11:18) and faith (Eph. 2:8–9). If that were not so, nobody would come to Him, since "there is none who seeks for God" (Rom. 3:11; cf. Eph. 2:1–3).

God's sovereignty in salvation is foundational to Christianity:

When the Gentiles heard this, they began rejoicing and glorifying the word of the Lord; and as many as had been appointed to eternal life believed. (Acts 13:48)

[He] has saved us and called us with a holy calling, not according to our works, but according to His own purpose and grace which was granted us in Christ Jesus from all eternity. (2 Tim. 1:9; cf. John 6:44; Rom. 8:28–30)

ASK YOURSELF

"Cause Your face to shine upon us, and we will be saved" (Ps. 80:19).
O, the magnificent grace of God in rescuing us from ourselves and
our sin! How could you make this a day to really celebrate this
. . . in ever new ways and expressions of praise?

GOD'S SOVEREIGN WORK IN SALVATION, PART 2

The one who comes to Me I will certainly not cast out. For I have come down
from heaven, not to do My own will, but the will of Him who sent Me.
—JOHN 6:37b–38

Jesus describes the one whom the Father gives to Him as "the one who comes to Me." From God's view, He sovereignly gives us to the Son; from our view, we come to Christ. Jesus would never reject anyone who comes as a love gift from God, thus the words "I will certainly not cast [that one] out." True saving faith never works in vain because it is divinely prompted (cf. Eph. 2:4).

Though the concepts of divine sovereignty and human responsibility seem to us impossible to harmonize, there is no such conflict in the mind of God (cf. Deut. 29:29). For example, both are at work in the Christian's mission of evangelism (e.g., Matt. 24:14; 28:19; Acts 8:25; 14:15; 16:10).

The disunity within the Godhead of Christ's rejecting any part of God's gift to Him is inconceivable, as Jesus' statement "I have come down from heaven, not to do My own will, but the will of Him who sent Me" shows (cf. 4:34; 5:30; Matt. 26:39). In His High Priestly Prayer Jesus told the Father, "I glorified You on earth, having accomplished the work which You have given Me to do" (17:4; cf. 14:31). The truth that Jesus came to earth to fulfill the Father's purposes thus guarantees salvation for members of the elect and ensures their eternal security.

ASK YOURSELF

When you arrive at aspects of God's nature and purposes that defy your ability to understand, how do you react? What would be the restful result of just letting His Word ring true in your heart rather than wrestling to make it line up with what you've always thought?

GOD'S SOVEREIGN WORK IN SALVATION, PART 3

*This is the will of Him who sent Me, that of all that He has given
Me I lose nothing, but raise it up on the last day.* —JOHN 6:39

God's sovereign oversight in the entire salvation process is evident in
the promise that it's the Father's will "that of all that He has given" to the
Son, Christ will "lose nothing, but raise it up on the last day." It is a wonderful reality to know with absolute certainty, based on the infallible
promises of the Father (cf. 6:40, 44, 54), that no part of His chosen
group—which He assigned to Jesus Christ in eternity past and gives to
Him in historical time—will ever be lost. This is an ironclad guarantee to
all true believers that their salvation is eternally secure. Jesus repeated this
comforting promise in the strongest terms when He told the disciples,

> My sheep hear My voice, and I know them, and they follow Me; and
> I give eternal life to them, and they will never perish; and no one
> will snatch them out of My hand. My Father, who has given them to
> Me, is greater than all; and no one is able to snatch them out of the
> Father's hand. (John 10:27–29)

In His High Priestly Prayer, Jesus underscored the safety of His
own when He told His Father, "While I was with them, I was keeping
them in Your name which You have given Me; and I guarded them and
not one of them perished but the son of perdition [Judas Iscariot], so that
the Scripture would be fulfilled" (17:12).

ASK YOURSELF

Do you ever allow yourself to doubt the salvation Christ has bought and
paid for you? What usually precedes such instances? What hurdles of
assurance can you just not seem to overcome? Know that the work of
God will have its full effect, whether it always feels like it or not.

GOD'S SOVEREIGN WORK IN SALVATION, PART 4

For this is the will of My Father, that everyone who beholds the Son and believes in Him will have eternal life, and I Myself will raise him up on the last day.
—JOHN 6:40

The letters of the New Testament support Jesus' teaching on the perseverance and protection of believers. Paul instructed the Romans,

> For those whom He foreknew, He also predestined to become conformed to the image of His Son, so that He would be the firstborn among many brethren; and these whom He predestined, He also called; and these whom He called, He also justified; and these whom He justified, He also glorified. (Rom. 8:29–30)

This passage is called by some the "golden chain of salvation." The apostle adroitly connects the whole salvation process from eternity past to eternity future with a series of indestructible links of the divine chain. None whom God brings into His family will be lost along the way (cf. 8:31–39), but they will persevere until the day of Christ (Phil. 1:6; cf. Col. 3:3–4; Rev. 19:14).

Peter's first letter further elaborates on the theme:

> [Those] chosen according to the foreknowledge of God the Father, by the sanctifying work of the Spirit, to obey Jesus Christ and be sprinkled with His blood . . . [will] obtain an inheritance which is imperishable and undefiled and will not fade away, reserved in heaven for [them], [because they] are protected by the power of God through faith for a salvation ready to be revealed in the last time. (1 Peter 1:1–2, 4–5; cf. Jude 1, 24–25)

ASK YOURSELF

The vast sweep of salvation, so eloquently revealed in Scripture, shows us a God who is more than big and strong enough to stand behind His promises. "If it were not so, I would have told you," Jesus said (John 14:2). Does anything hold more assurance for us than that?

THE JEWS' UNBELIEVING COMPLAINT

Therefore the Jews were grumbling about Him, because He said, "I am the bread that came down out of heaven." They were saying, "Is not this Jesus, the son of Joseph, whose father and mother we know? How does He now say, 'I have come down out of heaven'?" —JOHN 6:41–42

"The Jews were grumbling about" Jesus, just as their ancestors had grumbled against God (Ex. 16:2, 8–9; Num. 11:4–6). First, they were upset about His claim to be the source of eternal life (John 6:35). Second, because they thought of Him only as a fellow Galilean, they were angry at Jesus' assertion that He came "down out of heaven." Similarly, they were also upset because He came from the scorned town of Nazareth (cf. 1:46).

God will oftentimes judicially harden the hearts of those who continually reject the truth. For instance, Jesus obscured the truth by means of parables for those who persistently disbelieved His teaching (Matt. 13:10–15). John elaborates further on this:

> But though He had performed so many signs before them, yet they were not believing in Him. This was to fulfill the word of Isaiah the prophet which he spoke: "Lord, who has believed our report? And to whom has the arm of the Lord been revealed?" For this reason they could not believe, for Isaiah said again, "He has blinded their eyes and He hardened their heart, so that they would not see with their eyes and perceive with their heart, and be converted and I heal them." (John 12:37–40)

Jesus had already done enough that if the Jews had been so inclined, they would have believed. Had He elaborated on His heavenly origin, the Jews' hard hearts would have simply rejected that truth once again.

ASK YOURSELF

How would Christ want us to respond to those in our lives who have never met a loophole they didn't like, who work harder at disproving what God has revealed than at simply believing Him? What have you learned from your dealings with such people?

SPIRITUAL INABILITY

No one can come to Me unless the Father who sent Me draws him;
and I will raise him up on the last day. —JOHN 6:44

These solemn words of Jesus underscore humanity's inability and utter helplessness to savingly respond to Him apart from God's sovereign call. If God through the Holy Spirit did not efficaciously draw sinners to Jesus Christ, no person would ever come to Christ on his own strength and will (cf. 6:37).

There are plenty of scriptural reasons for fallen mankind's complete inability to come to Jesus by human power or wisdom. The unregenerate are dead in sin (Eph. 2:1), slaves to unrighteousness (Rom. 6:6), alienated from God (Col. 1:21), hostile to Him (Rom. 8:7), spiritually blind (2 Cor. 4:4), trapped in Satan's kingdom (Col. 1:13), powerless to change their sinful natures (Jer. 13:23), unable to please God (Rom. 8:8), and incapable of understanding spiritual truth (1 Cor. 2:14).

The human will must be at work in someone's coming to Christ, because God does not save anyone apart from the person's believing the gospel (Mark 1:15; Rom. 1:16; 10:9–15). But sinners can't come to Jesus completely of their own free will; the Holy Spirit instead effectively draws to the Son only those whom God chose from eternity past (Eph. 1:4–5, 11).

Jesus here again repeats the marvelous promise that He will raise all the elect on the last day (cf. vv. 39–40, 54). As believers, we can know that as those who have come to Him, the Father will perfectly keep us. Not one of us will be lost.

ASK YOURSELF

"The last day" is no vague, amorphous concept. As sure as "there was evening and there was morning" (Gen. 1:5)—the first day—we are hurtling toward a divinely calculated "last day." How amazing does it feel to know that "the last day" is sure to find you safe in God's care?

ASSURANCES FOR THE ELECT

Truly, truly, I say to you, he who believes has eternal life. I am the bread of life.
Your fathers ate the manna in the wilderness, and they died. This is the bread
which comes down out of heaven, so that one may eat of it and not die.
—JOHN 6:47–50

Here Jesus paraphrases Isaiah 54:13 to state the truth of verse 44 in different words and emphasize consistency with the Old Testament. People who receive salvation (the elect) do so because God teaches them. Thus, drawing and teaching are simply different facets of the sovereign call to salvation. God teaches people through His Word, and that's what draws men and women to trust His Son (Rom. 10:14, 17). As a result, "everyone who has heard and learned from the Father, comes to" the Savior. Had the Jews of Jesus' day really understood the Old Testament, they would have believed in Him (John 5:39).

Jesus' sure promise that "he who believes [in Me] has eternal life" (cf. 3:16; 5:24) summarizes the significance of trusting the Father's self-revelation of His Son. Believers can both hope for eternal life in the future, and enjoy that life even now, as the present-tense "believes" denotes.

Jesus concludes this portion of His teaching by reminding us that He is truly the Bread of Life and thus infinitely superior to the manna the Israelites ate in the wilderness. That food came miraculously from heaven but only sustained the people in this life—they all eventually died (cf. Heb. 3:17; Jude 5). On the other hand, the Lord Jesus as the Bread of Life comes to us "so that one may eat of [Him] and not die." "Eat" is a metaphor for saving faith in Christ, which alone rescues sinners from spiritual and eternal death (cf. John 14:6).

ASK YOURSELF

We can never get enough teaching on the blessed promises of Christ's salvation, just as we can never offer enough worship and gratitude in response. What opportunities might be available to share this glorious reality with someone today, tomorrow, and later this week?

JUNE 1

APPROPRIATING THE BREAD OF LIFE

I am the living bread that came down out of heaven; if anyone eats
of this bread, he will live forever; and the bread also which I give
for the life of the world is My flesh. —JOHN 6:51

Here Jesus uses the simple analogy of daily eating to suggest five parallels to appropriating spiritual truth. First, like uneaten food, spiritual truth is useless if not internalized (cf. Heb. 4:2). Merely knowing truth without applying it is worse than not knowing it at all—in fact, it results in more severe judgment (Luke 12:47–48).

Second, those who are full are not interested in eating, even as those satiated with sin have no appetite for spiritual truth (cf. Luke 6:21). But when people realize they're lost, the desire for forgiveness, deliverance, and peace drives them to embrace the truth of the heavenly Bread.

Third, physical food becomes part of your body through the digestive process. Likewise, when a person appropriates Christ by faith, he or she becomes one with Him (Gal. 2:20; Eph. 3:17).

Fourth, the actual act of eating implies trust that the food is safe and edible. Similarly, eating the Bread of Life implies believing in Jesus.

Fifth and finally, there is no such thing as eating by proxy; neither is there salvation by proxy. Sinners must individually and personally take hold of the Bread of Life to obtain salvation (John 6:58; 8:51; Rom. 8:13). Psalm 49:7 says, "No man can by any means redeem his brother or give to God a ransom for him."

ASK YOURSELF

How often do you find yourself merely observing Jesus, merely talking about Jesus, merely referring to Jesus—but not participating with Jesus, not letting Him become part of your bone and marrow, your heart and soul, your reason for getting up in the morning?

THE BREAD OF LIFE IS FOR SINNERS

The bread also which I give for the life of the world is My flesh. —JOHN 6:51*b*

The New Testament repeatedly states the concept of Jesus sacrificing His flesh, the Bread of Life, for sinners (Matt. 20:28; Eph. 5:2, 25; 1 Tim. 2:6). Here He looks ahead to His death (2 Cor. 5:21; 1 Peter 2:24), one of many such predictions (Matt. 16:21; John 12:24; Mark 10:33–34; Luke 18:31–33).

So it was the Lord's flesh that purchased our redemption. It would have done us no good had He simply preached the Father's standards and left us to try and keep them to earn salvation. That's impossible for us. The only way for sinners like ourselves to be reconciled to a holy God was for Jesus to die "for sins once for all, the just for the unjust, so that He might bring us to God" (1 Peter 3:18; cf. Isa. 53:4–6; Rom. 3:21–26).

The epistles instruct us that "the wages of sin is death" (Rom. 6:23) and "without shedding of blood there is no forgiveness" (Heb. 9:22); therefore Jesus Christ became the ultimate sacrifice for sin, "the Lamb of God who takes away the sin of the world" (John 1:29). The Lord offering up His flesh, or the Bread of Life, equals full payment to God for sin—to the eternal benefit of all who truly believe (Rom. 4:25; 1 John 2:2). If we have repented of sin, trusted in Christ's sacrifice, and by faith appropriated His flesh, we can be confident of a complete pardon (Acts 13:38–39; Eph. 1:7; 1 John 1:9).

ASK YOURSELF

Imagine being in such grave danger that you would consider going to someone you know and, if it were possible, asking him or her to die in your place. How would you feel about that person for the rest of your life? What keeps us from always feeling that way about our Lord?

JUNE 3

CHRIST'S REAL SACRIFICE

The bread also which I give for the life of the world is My flesh. —JOHN 6:51*b*

Over the centuries many Christians, as well as those merely having an academic interest or curiosity in Christianity, have wrestled with the nature of Jesus' atonement. How definitive was it, and was His death an actual satisfaction of God's justice, accompanied by a real turning away of His wrath from specific sinners? We can answer resoundingly that Jesus, the Bread from heaven, offered a genuine payment and full atonement—not one that was conditional or potential—on behalf of God's chosen people.

God commands people everywhere to repent and believe the gospel. And they thus do have to exercise a certain amount of responsibility to obey that call. But redemption is ultimately the work of God, and Jesus died to accomplish it. His sacrifice on the cross did not merely make salvation possible and contingent on the sinner's eventual acceptance. Rather, our Lord's sacrifice actually paid the penalty for all who believe. Humans don't limit the atonement by their lack of faith; God determines its extent by His sovereign plan.

Jesus did not give His flesh only for Israel, but for people everywhere (John 10:16; 1 John 2:2). He died for them regardless of nationality, culture, or socioeconomic standing (cf. Isa. 45:22; Matt. 28:19; Gal. 3:28; Col. 3:11). Christ Himself preached, "As Moses lifted up the servant in the wilderness, even so must the Son of Man be lifted up; so that whoever believes will in Him have eternal life" (John 3:14–15; cf. 12:32). The Son is the only Savior for lost sinners throughout the world.

ASK YOURSELF

What would keep someone from being willing to accept that Jesus' death on the cross is sufficient to cover their every transgression and declare them righteous before the Father? Why do many insist on adding more to the gospel, infusing human will into the process?

WHAT ABOUT EATING JESUS' FLESH?

Then the Jews began to argue with one another, saying,
"How can this man give us His flesh to eat?" —JOHN 6:52

As we have already seen, Jesus used the Bread of Life and flesh as metaphors to illustrate a vital point. Simply stated, those who consumed the Bread, or His flesh, were those who savingly appropriated spiritual truth about Him. But because of the ignorance of their unbelief, the Jews totally missed the spiritual significance of Messiah's teaching (cf. 3:4, 9; 4:11–12).

Also, for many decades Catholics and other spiritual communities have misunderstood Jesus' teaching about receiving His flesh. Catholics point here to support their doctrine of transubstantiation, the false teaching that Christ's body and blood are literally present in the elements of Communion. But this verse does not even refer to Communion—Jesus used a different Greek word for "flesh" than the word He used for "body" in referring to Communion (Matt. 26:26; Mark 14:22).

Furthermore, two additional considerations tell us Jesus' words here don't refer to Communion. First, the Lord's Table had not yet been instituted; otherwise the people would have understood Jesus' meaning. Second, the Lord said anyone who partook of His flesh received eternal life, but we know He did not say the same regarding Communion. The Bible teaches that those who properly receive Communion are already believers (1 Cor. 11:27–32) and that salvation comes by faith alone (Eph. 2:8–9). When you eat bread at Communion, you solemnly *remember* Christ's flesh wounded for you.

ASK YOURSELF

What are the proper responses to the Communion table, and how has God met you with His grace and refreshment through the partaking of the elements? When we talk about "remembering" Christ's death, what are some of the most tender, worshipful ways to do that?

What about Drinking Jesus' Blood?

Jesus said to them, "Truly, truly, I say to you, unless you eat the flesh of the Son of Man and drink His blood, you have no life in yourselves." —John 6:53

As with eating His flesh, Jesus spoke symbolically regarding the drinking of His blood. The blood metaphor thus also speaks vividly of the necessity to personally embrace His atoning death. The New Testament often uses "blood" in reference to the final sacrifice of the cross (Matt. 26:28; Rom. 3:25; Eph. 1:7; Heb. 9:12, 14; 1 Peter 1:19; 1 John 1:7; Rev. 5:9).

The idea of a crucified Messiah was hard to accept for the Jews (John 12:32, 34; cf. 1 Cor. 1:23; Gal. 5:11). Jesus even rebuked the Emmaus disciples for their hesitancy: "O foolish men and slow of heart to believe in all that the prophets have spoken! Was it not necessary for the Christ to suffer these things and to enter into His glory?" (Luke 24:25–26). The apostle Paul's evangelism to the Thessalonian Jews focused on "explaining and giving evidence that the Christ had to suffer and rise again from the dead, and saying, 'This Jesus whom I am proclaiming to you is the Christ'" (Acts 17:3).

The verbs rendered "eat" and "drink" are both aorist tenses in the Greek, which denote onetime occurrences rather than the continuous action of the present tense. This clearly suggests the onetime, by-faith acceptance of salvation, not the continual, literal consumption of Jesus' body and blood, as portrayed by the Catholic Mass.

ASK YOURSELF

We are certainly affected by the sight of blood. It horrifies and disturbs us. But is it possible that we are not horrified enough by what Jesus endured to eradicate our guilt, nor by the sight of our own sin? Are we not squeamish enough to turn our face away and walk in obedience?

PROMISES TO THOSE WHO RECEIVE CHRIST, PART 1

Unless you eat the flesh of the Son of Man and drink His blood, you have no life in yourselves. He who eats My flesh and drinks My blood has eternal life, and I will raise him up on the last day. —JOHN 6:53b–54

Here Jesus begins mentioning several promises to those who spiritually appropriate His body and blood. First, those who reject Christ have no genuine spiritual life within themselves; therefore those who do receive Him by faith have such life. The Lord Himself guarantees them abundant life even now (John 5:24; 10:10).

Second, Jesus promises eternal life to all who receive Him (eat His flesh, drink His blood). Believers' present experience of abundant life does not end at death, but it simply expands into completeness and lasts forever. In 6:40, resurrection and eternal life result from beholding and believing in Jesus, and here the same blessings occur from spiritually eating His flesh and drinking His blood. Our Lord thus gives us a genuine parallel between these two expressions.

Third, the Son of God promises to "raise up on the last day" everyone who eats His flesh and drinks His blood. This resurrection to eternal life is the Christian's greatest hope (Acts 23:6, 24). It should be an unambiguous reminder to us that without resurrection, the gospel is meaningless. As Paul writes,

Now if Christ is preached, that He has been raised from the dead, how do some among you say that there is no resurrection of the dead? But if there is no resurrection of the dead, not even Christ has been raised; and if Christ has not been raised, then our preaching is vain, your faith also is vain. (1 Cor. 15:12–14)

ASK YOURSELF

The fullness of what Christ has won for us by conquering death and rising up to eternal life is often lost amid the whirl and hum of the average day. Stop today to meditate on the abundance He has bought for you. What are some of the blessings you most often overlook?

Promises to Those Who Receive Christ, Part 2

For My flesh is true food, and My blood is true drink. He who eats My flesh and drinks My blood abides in Me, and I in him. As the living Father sent Me, and I live because of the Father, so he who eats Me, he also will live because of Me.
—John 6:55–57

Here Jesus tells us that His flesh and blood are true food and drink—in other words, the spiritual sustenance that gives believers union with Him. Then He goes on to declare, "He who eats My flesh and drinks My blood abides in Me, and I in him." This fourth promise is one of the most precious of the New Testament. In the Upper Room Jesus assured the apostles, "I am the vine, you are the branches; he who abides in Me and I in him, he bears much fruit, for apart from Me you can do nothing" (John 15:5; cf. 14:20). John later bore further testimony to this: "We know that the Son of God has come, and has given us understanding so that we may know Him who is true; and we are in Him who is true, in His Son Jesus Christ. This is the true God and eternal life" (1 John 5:20; cf. 2:24; 4:13).

Paul's letters reiterate the believer's union with Christ:

If anyone is in Christ, he is a new creature; the old things passed away; behold, new things have come. (2 Cor. 5:17; cf. 13:5)

I have been crucified with Christ; and it is no longer I who live, but Christ lives in me; and the life which I now live in the flesh I live by faith in the Son of God, who loved me and gave Himself up for me. (Gal. 2:20; cf. Col. 1:27)

Of course, God is the source of such promises to believers. Jesus has life in Himself (John 5:26), thus Christians have life in Him.

ASK YOURSELF

If you are not experiencing the freedom that comes from being one with Christ, saved from both guilt and the needless, religious manipulations to gain His favor, what is it costing you in terms of the peace and contentment He is able to provide? How could you go about reclaiming it?

DEFINING FALSE DISCIPLES

Therefore many of His disciples, when they heard this said,
"This is a difficult statement; who can listen to it?" —JOHN 6:60

To be called a disciple doesn't necessarily mean that someone truly followed Christ. The "disciples" here were superficially attracted by divine miracles and hope for deliverance from Rome. But Jesus would soon reveal their real status. When hearing His demanding teaching about the Bread of Life and salvation residing only in Him, they were unwilling to commit to it. It finally dawned on them that following Jesus meant more than tagging along with Him as thrill seekers.

The people's reaction is typical of false disciples—as long as Jesus was just a source of various free entitlements, the selfish disciples thronged to the Lord. But when He pressed them about their sin, need for repentance, and necessity to follow Him wholeheartedly (Luke 9:23–25), they found His words objectionable and unacceptable.

False disciples are okay with Jesus as the Christmas baby, the moralistic reformer, or the ideal human role model, but they are unwilling to receive the biblical Jesus. This is the divine Son and Savior who warns sinners of hell and tells them salvation comes only through faith in Him (John 5:24). Those who reject Christ and His teachings fail Jesus' own test of genuine discipleship: "If you continue in My word, then you are truly disciples of Mine" (8:31; cf. 15:8). Regular obedience to the Lord's words always defines the true disciple (cf. 1 John 2:3–5).

ASK YOURSELF

How many of the people you encounter in life are fine with attaching Jesus (or at least the portions of Him they like and approve) onto their package of belief systems? What are the big questions this tactic leaves unanswered as they try to live out their desires for a fulfilling life?

OFFENDING FALSE DISCIPLES

*But Jesus, conscious that His disciples grumbled at this, said to them,
"Does this cause you to stumble?"* —JOHN 6:61

Jesus knows the heart of every person, and here it was easy for Him to realize that the people were grumbling at His instructions. He used the Greek word translated "stumble," which can mean either "to take offense" (Matt. 13:57) or "to give up believing" (Matt. 24:10). Both meanings fit for these false disciples, who were offended by our Lord's teaching and consequently discarded their superficial faith in Him.

Because one of the Jews' key offenses was Jesus' claim to have come down from heaven, He asked them what they would think if they saw Him ascending back to heaven. Implicit in this question seems to be the Lord's wondering if such a sight would convince these doubters that He had indeed come from heaven. Some commentators see in this reference to the ascension an allusion to the crucifixion as well. In other words, Christ's point would be, If you false disciples are offended by My teaching, how much more will you be offended by My crucifixion (cf. 1 Cor. 1:23)?

Jesus knows that the only way anyone's offense toward Him will melt away is if he yields to "the Spirit who gives life," rather than his unprofitable flesh (John 6:63). Authentic spiritual life comes only when God's Spirit gives the Son's life to believers (Col. 3:3–4), never merely through "the will of the flesh" (John 1:13).

ASK YOURSELF

Why does belief in Jesus require the reaction of stumbling on our part? And what does this necessity take away from the human will and nature that we would much rather keep if we could? Why can there be no true salvation that doesn't cause us to fall on our knees?

FALSE DISCIPLES VERSUS THE WORD OF TRUTH

*Jesus knew from the beginning who they were who did not believe, and who it was
that would betray Him. And He was saying, "For this reason I have said to you,
that no one can come to Me unless it has been granted him from the Father."
As a result of this many of His disciples withdrew and were not walking with
Him anymore.* —JOHN 6:64–66

Believing or rejecting the divine Word is the crucial line of demarcation
between true and false disciples. True disciples will continue in God's
Word (John 8:31), which abides in them (15:7; cf. Col. 3:16; 1 John 2:14).
In stark contrast, false disciples will ultimately reject God's Word (John
8:37). Scripture is essential for bringing any sinner to salvation:

> Now the parable is this: the seed is the word of God. . . . The seed in
> the good soil, these are the ones who have heard the word in an hon-
> est and good heart, and hold it fast, and bear fruit with perseverance.
> (Luke 8:11, 15; cf. v. 21)

> For you have been born again not of seed which is perishable but im-
> perishable, that is, through the living and enduring word of God.
> (1 Peter 1:23; cf. James 1:18, 21)

Jesus held the false disciples personally responsible for their rejection of Him, not because they could not understand, but because they refused to believe. Their unbelief, however, was no surprise to Him
because He always knew who would and wouldn't have faith. These
teachings again underscore the tension between divine sovereignty and
human responsibility—God condemns unbelievers because of their unbelief, but they are also lost because He chooses not to draw them to saving faith. So, false disciples are always at odds with God's Word.

ASK YOURSELF

Do you find yourself resisting any clear teaching of Scripture? What are
the chief fears or factors at work that keep you from giving your
wholehearted best to obedience?

RIGHT REACTION OF THE TWELVE

Jesus said to the twelve, "You do not want to go away also, do you?" Simon Peter answered Him, "Lord, to whom shall we go? You have words of eternal life. We have believed and have come to know that You are the Holy One of God."
—JOHN 6:67–69

The false disciples' defection was an opportunity for Jesus to contrast that with the Twelve's faith. Peter here, as many other times, acted as their spokesman (cf. 13:36–37; Matt. 14:28; Mark 11:21; Luke 5:8). His faith declaration reminds us of his notable confession of Jesus as Messiah: "You are the Christ, the Son of the living God" (Matt. 16:16). Whereas the crowd wanted to accept Jesus only as some sort of second Moses who could supply the people's material needs, the apostles believed in the true Messiah and Savior from sin. Whom else could they turn to, because only He had (and has) the "words of eternal life" (cf. John 6:63)?

After Jesus dismissed Judas Iscariot the night of the Last Supper, He told the eleven of their being chosen for salvation: "You did not choose Me but I chose you, and appointed you that you would go and bear fruit, and that your fruit would remain, so that whatever you ask of the Father in My name He may give to you" (15:16). Christ's sovereign choice of the apostles—to salvation and apostleship—showed them that any pride they may have had was wrong.

Peter's wonderful affirmation in this passage contains two expressions of authentic disciples: saving faith ("we have believed") and faithfulness ("Lord, to whom shall we go?"). The initial faith of such disciples always results in ongoing commitment and loyalty to Jesus Christ.

ASK YOURSELF

Where else have you gone at times, hoping to find something more exciting and satisfying than you've found Christ to be? Why, after so many failed attempts to get our needs met, do we feel the need to keep searching? Only Jesus is sure to be enough for us.

JESUS THE COMPASSIONATE HEALER

When they had crossed over, they came to land at Gennesaret. And when the men of that place recognized Him, they sent word into all that surrounding district and brought to Him all who were sick; and they implored Him that they might just touch the fringe of His cloak; and as many as touched it were cured.
—MATT. 14:34–36

Jesus and the disciples probably intended to spend considerable time just by themselves in the beautiful, productive agricultural area of Gennesaret. But the people of that area sidetracked their plans by bringing many of the sick to Jesus. Obviously there were still many with afflictions in that vicinity, even though the Lord had healed thousands previously.

Confidence in Jesus' miracle powers was now so high that "they implored Him that they might just touch the fringe of His cloak." Because such a touch healed the woman with the bleeding (Matt. 9:20), people who heard about it assumed anyone could be healed exactly the same way. Whatever the case, the Lord had compassion on the crowds and honored the expressions of faith by healing everyone who touched His cloak.

As many people today who look to God only for their selfish needs and desires, most of the crowds wanted little to do with Jesus after the healings. It grieved Jesus that they sought nothing more from Him than physical blessings. But because they didn't want a full spiritual meal, He still gave them pieces of bread. Even though they cared nothing for spiritual help, Jesus nevertheless granted them physical healings. In the face of the people's ungrateful self-centeredness and carnal superficiality, the Lord yet graciously showed them the compassionate heart of God.

ASK YOURSELF

What are some of the common graces God showers on even those who want nothing of His salvation or simply ignore the fact that He is present around them? Why would God continue to extend life and blessing to those who reject or belittle His impact on their lives?

JUNE 13

CONFRONTATION OVER TRADITION

Then some Pharisees and scribes came to Jesus from Jerusalem and said,
"Why do Your disciples break the tradition of the elders? For they
*do not wash their hands when they eat bread." —*MATT. 15:1–2

The Jewish leaders who confronted Jesus did not conceal that they considered His offense to be against "the tradition of the elders" rather than God's law. For them such human tradition was actually superior to Scripture as a reliable guide to God's will and purpose. Similarly, Roman Catholics have long looked to church dogma to interpret Scripture, and many Protestants trust the traditional teachings of their denomination more than they do the Bible.

Sadly, the unconverted rabbis' ("elders") efforts to use traditions to protect the law actually undermined it. Instead of pointing the people to true worship from pure hearts, the rabbis led them to serve God by human means from unchanged hearts. Scripture became hidden behind a wall of tradition and thus was obscured and distorted rather than clarified and applied toward righteous ends.

Christ and the apostles did not adhere to the many man-made Jewish traditions, and the one here about washing was just representative of many that could have been cited. "Wash" had nothing to do with personal hygiene but referred to ceremonial rinsing. God had instituted such washings as part of the Mosaic covenant, but such ceremonies were never to be more than outward pictures of inward spiritual truths. God's Word never elevated them as having any merit or blessing in themselves. Instead, the Word itself always has primacy in teaching us the truths of salvation, practical holiness, and obedience to the Lord's commands.

ASK YOURSELF

What are our reasons for ever engaging in outward practices that have no effect on our hearts or lifestyle? How empty does it feel when Christian worship or service becomes little more than going through the motions? How does God desire to rescue us from that?

JESUS CONDEMNS UNBIBLICAL TRADITION

You hypocrites, rightly did Isaiah prophesy of you: "This people honors
Me with their lips, but their heart is far away from Me. But in vain do they wor-
ship Me, teaching as doctrines the precepts of men." —MATT. 15:7–9

Righteously indignant at the Jews' foolish adherence to traditions, Jesus compared those leaders to the hypocrites of Isaiah's day (see Isa. 29:13). And what identifies those hypocrites certainly applies to those of today.

Satan has no greater allies than hypocrites disguised as God's people. And such false disciples have no greater ally than human tradition, because they can follow it mindlessly, without real conviction, sincerity, or integrity. Traditions require no faith, trust, or dependence on God. Furthermore, they appeal to the pride and self-righteousness of the flesh.

Because of the nature of earthly religious traditions, people can easily substitute them for genuine worship and obedience. Therefore it becomes easy for people to give mere lip service to God while their rituals and ceremonies take them further from Him.

We can worship God in spirit and in truth (John 4:24) only if we have regenerate hearts, cleansed from sin and made righteous by Him. God has always offered such hearts to all who repent and trust Him: "I will give you a new heart and put a new spirit within you, and I will remove the heart of stone from your flesh and give you a heart of flesh. I will put My Spirit within you and cause you to walk in My statutes, and you will be careful to observe My ordinances" (Ezek. 36:26–27). Unless such transformation occurs for you, your righteousness will not exceed the superficial righteousness of the Jewish leaders, and you won't enter God's kingdom (Matt. 5:20).

ASK YOURSELF

Pray today that God would expose any hypocrisy that has been able to go undetected in your life, having become so ingrained and routine. Want nothing other than full, grateful, generous devotion to the Lord Jesus Christ, letting His righteousness flow from your submitted heart.

JUNE 15

THE PRINCIPLE OF SPIRITUAL DEFILEMENT, PART 1

*After Jesus called the crowd to Him, He said to them, "Hear and understand.
It is not what enters into the mouth that defiles the man, but what proceeds
out of the mouth, this defiles the man."* —MATT. 15:10–11

As elsewhere, Jesus based this illustration on His hearers' everyday experiences. Spiritual defilement concerns what's on the inside, not the outside. Thus Jesus told the people—and He tells us—that no spiritual defilement results from what a person eats. Hand washing before eating has nothing to do with making us morally undefiled. The crucial thing is the sinful heart, which eventually sends evil out of the mouth to defile the person.

Jesus' words should not have shocked His Jewish audience. Like the Sermon on the Mount, these were not new truths but simply reinforcements of what the Word always taught. Likely almost everyone in the crowd knew the story of God's choosing David to replace Saul as Israel's king. As Samuel considered Jesse's sons, the prophet thought Eliab surely would be the new king. "But the Lord said to Samuel, 'Do not look at his appearance or at the height of his stature, because I have rejected him; for God sees not as man sees, for man looks at the outward appearance, but the Lord looks at the heart'" (1 Sam. 16:7).

Jesus is concerned with what a person thinks and does, not merely what he or she says. He simply echoes here the principles God declared to Moses: "What does the Lord your God require from you, but to fear the Lord your God, to walk in all His ways and love Him, and to serve the Lord your God with all your heart and with all your soul. . . . So circumcise your heart" (Deut. 10:12, 16).

ASK YOURSELF

As you gauge the condition of your heart, what pleases you? We're often asked to be honest about our sin, to admit its presence and defilement. And we do. But what are the areas where Christ is indeed purifying you, gaining victory over long-held positions of sin and resistance?

THE PRINCIPLE OF SPIRITUAL DEFILEMENT, PART 2

After Jesus called the crowd to Him, He said to them, "Hear and understand. It is not what enters into the mouth that defiles the man, but what proceeds out of the mouth, this defiles the man." —MATT. 15:10–11

Adherence to ritual and tradition demands no repentance and fleeing from sin; rather, it permits people to flaunt religious symbols while clinging to their sins. Tradition involves style over substance, places works ahead of faith, and ends up being empty and hypocritical.

The Jews and their leaders not only failed to embrace the spiritual truths represented by ritual but added hundreds more rituals and traditions. The more such representations multiplied, the more people trusted in them and the less they trusted God. Thus when Jesus came among His countrymen, they were so entangled with their understandings of defilement and morality and so far from scriptural reality that they crucified Him.

Even Jewish believers in the early church had much difficulty in forsaking their former mind-set concerning traditions and what was clean and unclean. Peter needed a divine vision, repeated three times, and a special demonstration of the Spirit's power to convince him that all foods and peoples are accepted by God (Acts 10:1–33). Paul gives us a fitting summary:

> If you have died with Christ . . . why, as if you were living in the world, do you submit yourself to decrees, such as, "Do not handle, do not taste, do not touch!". . . in accordance with the commandments and teachings of men? These are matters which have, to be sure, the appearance of wisdom in self-made religion . . . but are of no value against fleshly indulgence. (Col. 2:20–23; cf. vv. 16–19)

ASK YOURSELF

What have you noticed about those who treat their religious practices with superstitious caution, as though these were good-luck charms meant to ward off any harm that might otherwise befall? What do they misunderstand most about God by exercising their faith in this way?

HYPOCRISY AND DEFILEMENT

*But He answered and said, "Every plant which My heavenly Father did not plant shall be uprooted. Let them alone; they are blind guides of the blind. And if a blind man guides a blind man, both will fall into a pit." —*MATT. 15:13–14

Our Lord's most frequent charge against the Jewish leaders concerned their hypocrisy, a sin that was so reprehensible and removed them so far from His kingdom that He told the disciples, "Let them alone." In other words Jesus said, "Stay away from and have nothing to do with them." That command echoed God's statement about the idolatrous Ephraim: "Let him alone" (Hos. 4:17)—words that connoted abandonment to divine judgment.

It is dangerous to hang around apostates or anyone resolutely opposed to the gospel. Even witnessing to them must occur with the utmost of caution, as it were "snatching them out of the fire" (Jude 23) and being careful not to become contaminated in the process. Christians should not even listen to "the opposing arguments of what is falsely called 'knowledge'" (1 Tim. 6:20; cf. 2 John 8–11).

Christ did not even waste His time debating the scribes and Pharisees. Whenever He responded to or confronted them, He simply corrected their doctrinal errors and condemned their spiritual and moral wickedness.

Believers must not engage or confront the severest of hypocrites as if to weed out of the church those who seem to be tares. Our discernment is imperfect and could uproot some good plants (believers) with the bad (hypocrites; cf. Matt. 13:29). We should not desire to take ultimate judgment into our own hands, because we are not qualified and the time is not yet come. God's truth will eventually expose hypocrites.

ASK YOURSELF

It may go against our compassionate sides to hear Jesus speaking in this way. But what is the wisdom behind taking this cautious approach toward those who hold such disdain for the gospel? Why is this a better way to show ultimate compassion toward the spiritually resistant?

THE DEFILEMENT PRINCIPLE DESCRIBED

For out of the heart come evil thoughts, murders, adulteries, fornications, thefts,
false witness, slanders. These are the things which defile the man; but
to eat with unwashed hands does not defile the man. —MATT. 15:19–20

Jesus here continues using the figure of eating to explicate the principle of defilement. In the Markan account, Jesus adds that food "does not go into [man's] heart" (7:19). Food and drink are only physical, therefore they can affect only the physical. They can't defile the inner person, represented by the heart, because the physical and spiritual are qualitatively different—of different realms. Outward ceremonial practices can't cleanse a person spiritually; neither can failure to observe them defile a person spiritually. All the ceremonial cleansings, prescribed sacrifices, and special observances in the Old Testament never did more than picture spiritual cleansing.

Christ rightly observes that the heart represents the inner person—his or her thoughts, attitudes, desires, loyalties, and motives. Therefore, what defiles is heart attitudes, like "evil thoughts, murders, adulteries, fornications, thefts, false witness, slanders." A person commits sin when he *wants* to, whether or not he ever actually carries it out in action—and therefore he is defiled in God's sight. Paul writes this: "To the pure, all things are pure; but to those who are defiled and unbelieving, nothing is pure, but both their mind and their conscience are defiled. They profess to know God, but by their deeds they deny Him" (Titus 1:15–16a).

The things that defile us come from an uncleansed heart, not from hands that might be unwashed. Therefore we always need the Lord and His Spirit to cleanse our hearts. When we have a pure heart—undefiled inside—we will see God (Matt. 5:8).

ASK YOURSELF

Part of what causes sin to keep coming out of us is that we allow our minds to dwell on things that foster it. What is God calling you to radically eliminate from your life in order to cut off much of sin's supply to your heart?

GREAT FAITH IS REPENTANT

A Canaanite woman from that region came out and began to cry out,
*saying, "Have mercy on me, Lord." —*MATT. 15:22a

This woman's faith was certainly great, not because it was stronger or better than the faith of those Jews who believed in Jesus, but because it derived from so little light. Her faith turned away from pagan idolatry and immorality and toward God, which is the essence of repentance. The woman's plea to Jesus, rather than being a demand, is further demonstration of her repentant attitude and acknowledgement that she was unworthy of His gracious mercy.

God declared Himself to the Israelites as "compassionate and gracious, slow to anger, and abounding in lovingkindness and truth; who keeps lovingkindness for thousands, who forgives iniquity, transgression and sin" (Ex. 34:6–7a; cf. Ps. 51:1).

Saving faith always involves repentance that derives from a deep and earnest sense of unworthiness and spiritual inability. Charles Spurgeon wrote:

> Repentance is the inseparable companion of faith. All the while that we walk by faith and not by sight, the tear of repentance glitters in the eye of faith. That is not true repentance which does not come of faith in Jesus, and that is not true faith in Jesus which is not tinctured with repentance. . . . Faith and repentance are but two spokes in the same wheel, two handles of the same plow. Repentance has been well described as a heart broken for sin and from sin, and it may equally well be spoken of as turning and returning.

ASK YOURSELF

How have you experienced the mercy of God, not only in salvation but also in the regular outworkings of life? Looking back, where would you be if not for His mercy reaching down to give you hope and a future? Worship Him today for this undeserved gift, still active and in force.

GREAT FAITH IS RIGHTLY DIRECTED

Son of David; my daughter is cruelly demon-possessed. —MATT. 15:22b

When poet John Greenleaf Whittier wrote, "The steps of faith fall on the seeming void and find the rock beneath," he proved himself a better poet than theologian. Whittier's kind of faith shows it does not understand that great faith—the genuine variety—must focus on the right object. Whittier's faith is basically faith in faith—in other words, no faith at all.

For faith to have real power, and thus be great faith, it must be like the Canaanite woman's and rest on a trustworthy object, namely the Lord, the Son of David. Even though a Gentile, she reverently addressed Jesus as her sovereign and all-powerful Lord. Her approach to Christ followed the same worshipful and trusting attitude of the leper who met Jesus after the Sermon on the Mount "and bowed down before Him, and said, 'Lord, if You are willing, You can make me clean'" (Matt. 8:2).

Compared to the irreverent treatment the Jewish leaders gave Jesus, He must have been encouraged by this Gentile woman's respect and submission. And she came with that attitude in spite of not fully grasping the significance of Jesus' lordship and messiahship.

The woman loved her daughter more than herself, and when the girl became demon-possessed, the woman came to the only source of help she believed to be adequate. By appealing to our Lord, she renounced her pagan religion, culture, and family and affirmed His superiority over those things. As the believers at Thessalonica did, she "turned to God from idols to serve a living and true God" (1 Thess. 1:9).

ASK YOURSELF

Do you know someone closely who makes his spiritual appeals in heaven's general direction, but not to the One who made heaven and earth? Make their condition a matter of specific prayer, and ask God for opportunities to encourage them in setting their faith aright.

GREAT FAITH IS PERSISTENT

He did not answer her a word. And His disciples came and implored Him, saying,
"Send her away, because she keeps shouting at us." But He answered and said,
*"I was sent only to the lost sheep of the house of Israel." —*MATT. 15:23–24

Great faith persists; it's not deterred by setbacks. Christ therefore tested the Canaanite woman's faith by placing barriers in her way. One of those was that He did not answer, which can be the most difficult response to accept. When the woman persisted in asking the Lord for help, the apostles came in frustration to Him and asked Him to do something about the nuisance. Finally, they simply demanded that He "send her away, because she keeps shouting at us."

That response was insensitive and prejudiced, and at first glance Jesus seemed to be equally insensitive to the woman—He did not even acknowledge her presence. But the Lord never did anything unloving or apart from His own wise and perfect purpose. Here He'd had enough of artificial and selfish faith that got what it wanted from Him and then departed. Thus He chose to test the woman's faith to bring it to fruition; so He put up barriers not to keep her away from Him but to draw her closer. At the same time, He taught the apostles the nature of genuine faith and the value of persisting in it.

Jesus' words to the disciples about the primacy of Israel in the plan of redemption may have reassured them, but they did not deter this Gentile woman. Her love for her daughter made her determined to free her from Satan. The woman's pagan gods did not care, and she knew her only hope was to turn to Christ. Her response reiterated Peter's sentiment, "Lord, to whom shall we go?" (John 6:68).

ASK YOURSELF

Have you experienced the silence of God during certain seasons of your life? How did you react to it? Why do you think He chose to delay His response to you? What have you learned from those occasions that can help your faith stay true when He forces you to wait?

GREAT FAITH IS HUMBLE

She came and began to bow down before Him, saying, "Lord, help me!"
And He answered and said, "It is not good to take the children's bread
and throw it to the dogs." But she said, "Yes, Lord; but even the dogs feed
*on the crumbs which fall from their masters' table." —*MATT. 15:25–27

The Gentile woman's bowing down might or might not have been an act of worship toward Jesus, but it was clearly an act of humility. She likely became prostrate at His feet and cried out even more desperately, "Lord, help me!"

But the Savior again put her off with symbolic words about children and dogs that at first hearing were far from complimentary. The woman would have known that *children* referred to the Jews, and *dogs* denoted the Gentiles—the Jews commonly used both figures. Jesus' answer no doubt sounded to her like the insults Jews frequently hurled at their Gentile neighbors.

The woman, however, was undaunted and showed incredible understanding of Jesus' words: "Yes, Lord; but even the dogs feed on the crumbs which fall from their masters' table." She conceded that she was sinful and less deserving than the Jews. This attitude showed a complete lack of the pride and self-reliance that often characterized the Jews. A small leftover portion of Jesus' power was enough to heal her daughter, and that was all she humbly asked.

The Lord's earthly ministry was primarily to the Jews, but crumbs of the gospel did fall from their table and feed humble Gentiles like this woman with the Bread of Life.

ASK YOURSELF

How has Christ tested your faith in days past, not to discourage or resist you, but rather to add new layers of muscle to your trust in Him? Why is it so easy to misunderstand this aspect of His lordship, and in what ways has it strengthened your faith and loyalty to Him?

JESUS' RESPONSE TO GREAT FAITH

Jesus said to her, "O woman, your faith is great; it shall be done for
you as you wish." And her daughter was healed at once. —MATT. 15:28

The Canaanite woman's seeking heart did not give up. Her faith remained great to the end of this encounter with Jesus—and undoubtedly
beyond. Her faith grew strong through God's testing, just as Abraham's
did (Rom. 4:20). Similar to Jacob wrestling with the Lord (Gen. 32:26),
the woman would not let go until the Lord blessed her. She witnessed the
promise of God fulfilled, which says, "'You will seek Me and find Me
when you search for Me with all your heart. I will be found by you,' declares the Lord, 'and I will restore your fortunes'" (Jer. 29:13–14a).

Sensing and hearing what He needed to know about the woman's
character, Jesus was greatly pleased with her response and declared, "O
woman, your faith is great." She did not even hear the Sermon on the
Mount, but came to the Lord with the kind of humble, mourning, meek,
and seeking heart God requires for entrance into His kingdom (Matt.
5:3–6). She displayed the earnest approach described in Luke 13:24 and
16:16 of straining every nerve and vigorously pressing forward to enter
the kingdom.

Because of her great faith so humbly and persistently displayed and
rightly directed toward Him, the Lord Jesus granted the woman's wish
that her daughter be delivered from a demon. As Spurgeon has observed,
"The Lord of glory surrendered to the faith of the woman." She truly
followed Christ's instruction of "Ask, and it will be given to you; seek,
and you will find; knock, and it will be opened to you" (Matt. 7:7).

ASK YOURSELF

God acts for His own good purposes. There's not a magic word or a
certain level of fervor on our part that finally attracts His attention. And
yet He thrills at the sight of "great" faith in His children. How could you
act in "great" faith in the face of your current circumstances?

FEEDING OF THE 4,000, PART 1

*He directed the people to sit down on the ground; and He took the seven loaves
and the fish; and giving thanks, He broke them and started giving them to the
disciples, and the disciples gave them to the people. And they all ate and were satisfied, and they picked up what was left over of the broken pieces, seven large baskets full. And those who ate were four thousand men, besides women and children.*
—MATT. 15:35–38

Jesus displayed compassion for people's spiritual needs and physical afflictions, but He also had compassion concerning their daily food. He
tells us to ask God to "give us this day our daily bread" (Matt. 6:11) because He cares about our practical needs. Here our Lord was determined
that the needy crowd not go home hungry and collapse on the way.

As with the 5,000, the apostles again wondered where they could get
enough food for so many people (15:33). They couldn't possibly have forgotten the miracle of a month earlier, but they were merely noting again
their lack of resources. This multitude was slightly smaller, but the Twelve
could no more provide enough food for them than they could for the 5,000.

This region of the Decapolis was likely even more desolate than the
area around Bethsaida Julius, where Christ fed the 5,000. If food was sparse
on that earlier occasion, it certainly would not be readily available here. But
surely the apostles did not doubt that their Lord could again miraculously
feed a large number of people; they remembered vividly the feeding of the
5,000. The apostles' words to Jesus simply emphasized their confidence
that He could satisfy such a multitude whereas they could not. Jesus had no
less power than before, and His disciples no more.

ASK YOURSELF

The size of our need does not determine the size of God's provision. He
meets needs completely, even when our lack is great. Yet even when our
needs are smaller by comparison, we must never think ourselves sufficient
to care for them. Are you depending on Him . . . for everything?

FEEDING OF THE 4,000, PART 2

He directed the people to sit down on the ground; and He took the seven loaves and the fish; and giving thanks, He broke them and started giving them to the disciples, and the disciples gave them to the people. And they all ate and were satisfied, and they picked up what was left over of the broken pieces, seven large baskets full. And those who ate were four thousand men, besides women and children.
—MATT. 15:35–38

Jesus could have miraculously distributed the food without the apostles as easily as He had miraculously multiplied it without human aid. After all, the Father had provided manna in the wilderness for the children of Israel—fresh every morning, distributed across the entire area of encampment, and available so the people needed only to gather what was needed outside their tents (Ex. 16:14). But here, in addition to simply feeding the crowd, Christ wanted to teach the apostles. He desired that they learn the practical as well as the theological reality of His compassion for people. Once again, our Lord wanted His men to participate firsthand in God's concern for people's daily needs. He wanted them to realize that divine compassion embraces every aspect of human need: eternal redemption, physical wellness, and the daily need of food and beverage.

Of the miraculous feedings, author Alfred Edersheim observes:

The Lord ended each phase of His ministry with a feeding. He ended the ministry in Galilee with the feeding of the five thousand. He ended the ministry in the Gentile area with the feeding of the four thousand. And He ended the Judean ministry before His death on the cross with the feeding of His own in the upper room.

ASK YOURSELF

How concerned are you for the hunger of those around you? You cannot do everything for everyone, but you can do something for someone. Ask God to keep your eyes open to human need, and to give you direction on how you can truly minister to them in His name.

THE LESSONS OF MINISTRY, PART 1

Sending away the crowds, Jesus got into the boat and
came to the region of Magadan. —MATT. 15:39

We can learn a number of lessons from Jesus' ministry to Gentiles in the Decapolis area. First, He displayed unrivaled divine power because only God could multiply the loaves and fish many thousandfold to feed people. Just as He replaced diseased tissues with healthy ones, deformed and missing limbs with complete ones, and blind eyes with seeing ones (cf. Rom. 4:17), he multiplied inadequate food into superabundance. Our Lord did all this in His own name and power because He was and is the source of that power.

Second, Jesus not only cured diseases and restored physical faculties, He restored the maimed and deformed, thus setting Himself totally apart from so-called healers of contemporary times. Their "healings" are at best psychosomatic and extremely minor compared to the many miraculous ones the Son of God did during His earthly ministry.

God can still sovereignly heal the most hopeless sick person or restore the most gravely injured adult or child, even creating new limbs as He wills. But the church era has had only one genuine age of healing, and that to authenticate Christ and His Word through the apostles' ministries. Once those purposes were accomplished, the need for miracles or the gift of miracles ceased.

ASK YOURSELF

Rather than reading about Jesus' miraculous ministry with well-worn familiarity, stop to consider in absolute astonishment what He did for the sick and hurting of His earthly time. How do you respond to such power when its reality rushes over you again? We serve a mighty God!

THE LESSONS OF MINISTRY, PART 2

*Sending away the crowds, Jesus got into the boat
and came to the region of Magadan.* —MATT. 15:39

As we continue evaluating the lessons of Christ's ministry to the Gentiles, we see, third, that the true goal of ministry is worship. Although the vast majority of those who witnessed Jesus in Decapolis were Gentiles, when they saw His overwhelming and superlative power, they were astounded and "glorified the God of Israel" (Matt. 15:31). The perfection of what He said and did demanded reverential worship, and many of the Gentiles offered it as best they could. But Christ was infinitely more concerned to save their souls from eternal damnation and make them citizens of His kingdom. The final goal of evangelism and Christian living is always to "worship the Father in spirit and truth; for such people the Father seeks to be His worshipers" (John 4:23).

The primacy of worship is an especially vital lesson for today when our evangelism likes to make the way of salvation wide, even though Jesus defines it as narrow (Matt. 7:14). We also like to present the Christian life as an easy one, whereas the Lord says believers must take up their crosses (Matt. 10:38–39).

A fourth lesson is that we must depend on God's resources. Like the apostles, we are most usable for the kingdom when we admit the lack of our own resources and turn to the Lord. Jesus did not command the disciples to be His "witnesses both in Jerusalem, and in all Judea and Samaria, and even to the remotest part of the earth" until He first promised empowering from the Holy Spirit (Acts 1:8).

ASK YOURSELF

Let this be a day when you deliberately seek to worship, not only through song and prayer, but in giving excellence to your many tasks and serving those around you in His name and for His glory. How many ways can you think of to worship with what's ahead of you?

THE LESSONS OF MINISTRY, PART 3

Sending away the crowds, Jesus got into the boat
and came to the region of Magadan. —MATT. 15:39

Our continued look at the important lessons from Jesus' ministry at this juncture reveals three more for today. Fifth, Matthew's narrative says God's resources are never diminished or exhausted. Jesus did not need bread and fish to feed the crowd, because He could have made food from nothing, just as He created the world from nothing. The loaves and fish taught the apostles and now us to give what we have into His care (cf. Luke 6:38).

The sixth lesson is that of the servant's usefulness. Although Christ can do His work without us, He graciously chooses to accomplish it through us. In an instant He could have distributed the bread and fish for the 4,000, whereas it took the apostles several hours for that. God today chooses to use human agents to proclaim the gospel and minister to the world's needs. In obediently serving others in the Lord's name and power, we also serve Him, which prepares us for serving Him through all eternity.

Today's third lesson—and the seventh overall—is that God gives liberally, in "good measure—pressed down, shaken together, and running over" (Luke 6:38). Everyone on the mountainside ate to his or her satisfaction. By analogy, God always provides for all our physical and spiritual needs—and sometimes far beyond (cf. Eph. 3:20–21).

ASK YOURSELF

How do you sense God wanting to use you in greater ways for His kingdom's sake? Do you receive this as the honor it is—the God of heaven allowing you to participate in His eternal work? Follow up on what He is leading you to do, considering it a privilege to be in His service.

THE LESSONS OF MINISTRY, PART 4

*Sending away the crowds, Jesus got into the boat
and came to the region of Magadan.* —MATT. 15:39

Two more important lessons from Jesus' ministry await our consideration today. Eighth in our ongoing list is the lesson of spiritual investment. When the apostles gave the Lord all they had so He could use it to feed the 4,000, they ended up with seven basketsful for themselves. "He who sows sparingly will also reap sparingly, and he who sows bountifully will also reap bountifully" (2 Cor. 9:6).

The ninth and final lesson is Christ's limitless compassion for all our needs—daily, lifetime, and eternal. His compassion extends to all nationalities, and on the merely hungry as well as the severely afflicted. Thus believers should follow their Lord's example and "do good to all people, and especially to those who are of the household of the faith" (Gal. 6:10). The attitude and generosity of our giving measures our compassion, not superficial sentiments.

John Wanamaker, founder of the Philadelphia department store bearing his name, was a dedicated Christian. While observing missionary work in China, he entered a village where believers lacked money to complete a church building. In a nearby field he saw a boy yoked with an ox as the two pulled a plow guided by the boy's father. Wanamaker's guide explained that the boy had promised his father he'd help plow if his father would sell one ox to raise money for the church. The businessman reportedly fell to his knees and prayed, "Lord, let me be hitched to a plow that I may know the joy of sacrificial giving."

ASK YOURSELF

What keeps you from being as available to the Lord as He wants you to be? What intereferes with your recognition of areas where you could serve and be useful to others for the glory of God? Deal radically and deeply with anything that prevents your full surrender to His lordship.

CURSING THE LIGHT, PART 1

The Pharisees and Sadducees came up, and testing Jesus, they asked Him to show them a sign from heaven. But He replied to them, "When it is evening, you say, 'It will be fair weather, for the sky is red.' And in the morning, 'There will be a storm today, for the sky is red and threatening.' Do you know how to discern the appearance of the sky, but cannot discern the signs of the times?" —MATT. 16:1–3

The Jewish elite did not want to find truth from Jesus but only wanted to discover His "falsehood." They demanded a sign (miracle) they believed was beyond Jesus, seeking to prove that He was not from God. Thus they could publicly discredit Him and vindicate themselves.

In their blindness the Jews could not recognize that Christ Himself was "a sign from heaven." This refusal to accept God's ultimate Sign meant they already had rejected Jesus' lesser signs, even in the face of irrefutable evidence of their validity. As Abraham warned about the brothers in Jesus' story of the rich man and Lazarus, "If they do not listen to Moses and the Prophets, they will not be persuaded even if someone rises from the dead" (Luke 16:31). Like Pharaoh, the more the Jews witnessed divine power, the more they hardened their hearts against it (Ex. 7–11). God will display more heavenly signs in the future (Matt. 24:29–30; Luke 21:11; Rev. 15:1), but they will indicate the end of the age.

The famous French philosopher and atheist Voltaire once declared, "Even if a miracle should be wrought in the open marketplace before a thousand sober witnesses, I would rather mistrust my senses than admit a miracle." Unbelief always finds a way to reject God's truth, even if it must deny the undeniable. How much better a heart that is open to the truth, receives it, and rejoices to obey it.

ASK YOURSELF

Rather than getting frustrated with the lack of spiritual soundness around you, make this a day when you begin asking God often to reveal Himself to those who are resisting Him. How could you make yourself ready to answer others' questions with His sure Word of truth?

CURSING THE LIGHT, PART 2

Do you know how to discern the appearance of the sky,
but cannot discern the signs of the times? —MATT. 16:3b

People today curse the light just as the Jewish leaders did. Unbelieving scholars prefer the speculations of human learning to the wise truths of Scripture. Agnostics and atheists don't refuse to believe because it is impossible to know God but because they will not know Him. They embrace the "evidence" from rationalism, evolutionary naturalism, and skepticism to explain life—not because there is no evidence for the truth of Christ, but because they despise that truth.

For expiation of sin and guilt, such people often turn to man-made religion with its acts of penance, self-affliction, confessionals, and other resources. But they fail to deal with the root of their problem—their sinful hearts—because they don't want to change.

Knowing that the Jewish leaders' true intent was to discredit Him, Jesus pointed to the incongruity of their trust in folk meteorology while completely distrusting Him. In spite of their religious heritage and training, their primitive insights on the weather superseded their knowledge of Messiah. Many postmodern people also have great insight into worldly matters but no comprehension of the things of God. They predict all sorts of earthly trends, but they know nothing of God's plan for this world and that it's still the "last time," a time calling for repentance and faith.

All the signs that mark the end times (see Matt. 24:3, 6–7, 11–12) are indicative of contemporary society. Believers' concern should thus be for what Scripture says and what God is doing, not for what human experts are saying and what they're doing to disprove God.

ASK YOURSELF

How do you square the simplicity of faith with the pursuit of knowledge? Should Christians be viewed as downplaying the importance of staying current and valuing complex thought? Where do you strike the balance between heart and mind?

FALLING DEEPER INTO SIN

"An evil and adulterous generation seeks after a sign; and a sign will not be given it, except the sign of Jonah." And He left them and went away. —MATT. 16:4

The spiritually blind, such as the Pharisees, will never see the light because they sink further and further into sin. They think that seeking additional signs will make them pleasing to God, but such experiences and observations merely drive them further away. Jesus refused to grant such sinners any miracles that would feed their wicked, hypocritical desires.

Jesus' final sign to the world was "the sign of Jonah," the great indicator of His victory over Satan's kingdom through His resurrection. On an earlier occasion Christ declared to some scribes and Pharisees,

> An evil and adulterous generation craves for a sign; and yet no sign will be given to it but the sign of Jonah the prophet; for just as Jonah was three days and three nights in the belly of the sea monster, so will the Son of Man be three days and three nights in the heart of the earth. The men of Nineveh will stand up with this generation at the judgment, and will condemn it because they repented at the preaching of Jonah; and behold, something greater than Jonah is here. (Matt. 12:39–41)

Of course, the Jewish elite would reject this final sign as well as earlier ones. God ultimately abandons those who persist in their sin and rejection of His light (cf. Rom. 1:24, 26, 28). Stubborn, satanic blindness becomes God's sovereign blindness—He chooses to leave them behind and focus His blessings on those whose spiritual eyes are open to salvation.

ASK YOURSELF

How do you keep yourself from becoming closed off to the vibrancy and freshness of life with Christ? What are some of the signals that indicate you're letting yourself grow stale and inflexible, operating out of sheer habit rather than from an eager desire to let the Word truly live?

SEEKING THE LIGHT

The disciples came to the other side of the sea. —MATT. 16:5

Unlike the scribes and Pharisees, the Twelve followed Jesus to the other side of the Sea of Galilee. They knew He was the true light of redemption and followed Jeremiah's promise: "You will seek Me and find Me when you search for Me with all your heart. I will be found by you" (Jer. 29:13–14*a*).

One day as Jesus taught in the temple, He proclaimed, "I am the Light of the world; he who follows Me will not walk in the darkness, but will have the Light of life" (John 8:12). The apostles believed this truth and knew Christ was not merely to be seen but obediently followed. All who truly believe realize they cannot have spiritual sight apart from God's gracious work on their behalf through His Son. Long before this time, the psalmist wrote: "Open my eyes, that I may behold wonderful things from Your law. . . . Teach me, O Lord, the way of Your statutes, . . . Incline my heart to Your testimonies. . . . Your hands made me and fashioned me; give me understanding, that I may learn Your commandments (Ps. 119:18, 33, 36, 73).

The apostles had a spiritual hunger that diligently sought God's light and truth, and they were eager learners as they followed Jesus. They were as naturally blind as the religious leaders, but unlike the unbelieving Jews, the apostles recognized their blindness and came to the Messiah for the light of salvation and sanctification.

ASK YOURSELF

What are some of the discoveries and insights God has brought into the light in recent days as you've spent steadfast time in the Word, in prayer, in worship, and in church fellowship? How do these rays of illumination keep you encouraged and prepared for greater service?

RECEIVING GREATER LIGHT, PART 1

"How is it that you do not understand that I did not speak to you concerning bread? But beware the leaven of the Pharisees and Sadducees." Then they understood that He did not say to beware of the leaven of bread, but of the teaching of the Pharisees and Sadducees. —MATT. 16:11–12

Even though hearing and seeing Christ's teaching at the highest levels—God's words, a perfect example, and irrefutable miracles—the apostles still tended to operate on the physical level. After rowing to the other side of the lake and being hungry, they did not think of Jesus' provision but their own lack thereof. And typically, the Lord used this as an opportunity to instruct them.

This is a wonderful example of how believers should be discipled—one comes alongside and helps another interpret life's difficulties, problems, and opportunities in light of God's truth and His resources. Christians gain maturity by learning to live one day at a time and trusting in the Lord's provisions.

Jesus at this time knew His death would occur in just a few months, and He had much more for the apostles to learn. One day without bread—they had forgotten to bring some along—should have been of no consequence for the disciples. But like saints in every era, the apostles were preoccupied with the temporal and its concern for physical supplies. They needed, as do all who trust Christ, to have their spiritual vision extended and their spiritual attention span enlarged.

ASK YOURSELF

How has your preoccupation with the daily, routine matters of life blinded you to the greater activity of God happening around you? How can you work to keep your perspectives large and eternal, with so many responsibilities to perform, with so many people depending on you?

RECEIVING GREATER LIGHT, PART 2

Then they understood that He did not say to beware of the leaven of bread,
but of the teaching of the Pharisees and Sadducees. —MATT. 16:12

The Twelve were confused about Jesus' definition of bread because
their dominant earthly perspective clouded their spiritual vision. Their
misplaced response to Him prompted an expression He had used numerous times before, "You men of little faith" (v. 8; cf. 6:30; 8:26; 14:31).
Their confusion and misunderstanding was not because of limited information or intellect, but because of limited faith.

When Christians walk obediently by the Spirit, God will make provision for all their temporal needs. That's why in the Sermon on the
Mount, Jesus admonished His listeners,

> Do not worry then, saying, "What will we eat?" or "What will we
> drink?" or "What will we wear for clothing?" For the Gentiles ea-
> gerly seek all these things; for your heavenly Father knows that you
> need all these things. But seek first His kingdom and His righteous-
> ness, and all these things will be added to you. (Matt. 6:31–33; cf.
> 2 Cor. 9:10)

Christ was grieved with the apostles because, after hearing much
sound teaching and witnessing many convincing miracles, they were still
walking by sight rather than faith. The believer needs regular exposure
to God's Word and the constant illumination the Holy Spirit provides.
Only by these means can he rise above the concerns, burdens, perplexi-
ties, and anxieties that are inevitable in this life, especially when viewed
and lived strictly from a human standpoint.

ASK YOURSELF

How often could the words "you of little faith" be appropriately applied
to your actions, behaviors, and beliefs? What would it take for you to
begin exercising great faith amid the challenges you face and the
opportunities that could potentially be coming up in your life?

RECEIVING GREATER LIGHT, PART 3

"How is it that you do not understand that I did not speak to you concerning bread? But beware the leaven of the Pharisees and Sadducees." Then they understood that He did not say to beware of the leaven of bread, but of the teaching of the Pharisees and Sadducees. —MATT. 16:11–12

Jesus' use of the term "leaven" here represents the tainted spiritual influence of the Pharisees and Sadducees. Such teachings and lifestyles have no part in His kingdom of righteousness. For the Pharisees it was hypocrisy (Luke 12:1)—religiosity marked by external purity that sought to cover up internal unrighteousness. For the Sadducees it was religious liberalism, whose system was focused primarily on temporal ends.

Later in Matthew, Jesus denounces the Pharisees' legalism and ritualism: "Woe to you, scribes and Pharisees, hypocrites! For you are like whitewashed tombs which on the outside appear beautiful, but inside they are full of dead men's bones and all uncleanness" (Matt. 23:27). For the Sadducees the problem was their human-centered, antisupernatural approach (Acts 23:8) that was thoroughly materialistic. Both phony religions adversely permeated and influenced Israel's religious scene.

Neither kinds of leaven are friends of the gospel (cf. Gal. 3:2–3; Col. 2:8). Both varieties corrupt God's truth and His people. We must never trifle with false doctrine or minimize its potential adverse effects. In fact Jude tells us how carefully we must act when trying to deliver another person from a false system: "And have mercy on some, who are doubting; save others, snatching them out of the fire; and on some have mercy with fear, hating even the garment polluted by the flesh" (Jude 22–23). We must shun error and heresy and, if need be, oppose them wherever and however we encounter them.

ASK YOURSELF

Do you sometimes grow weary with so many false religions and incorrect belief systems floating around, taking scores of people captive, corrupting their minds and distorting their take on truth? How can you keep discouragement from weakening your prayerfulness?

THE DISCIPLES ARE TAUGHT BY CHRIST, PART 1

*Then they understood that He did not say to beware of the leaven of bread,
but of the teaching of the Pharisees and Sadducees.* —MATT. 16:12

Jesus' brief teaching session with the apostles concluded positively, and they understood the difference between physical leaven and the evil spiritual leaven of the religious leaders. During His earthly ministry our Lord always wanted to bring to greater maturity those who believed, especially the Twelve. Even after His resurrection He taught them for another forty days until His ascension (Acts 1:3). And He provided for continued teaching after that: "The Helper, the Holy Spirit, whom the Father will send in My name, He will teach you all things, and bring to your remembrance all that I said to you" (John 14:26; cf. 16:12–15).

Believers today primarily receive God's teachings through His Word, whether they study it or hear it proclaimed; and the indwelling Spirit is the agent to make Scripture clear and understandable. After this, He graciously applies the Word to the hearts, minds, and lives of all who believe. The apostle John enlarges on this:

> You have an anointing from the Holy One, and you all know. . . . As for you, the anointing which you received from Him abides in you, and you have no need for anyone to teach you; but as His anointing teaches you about all things, and is true and is not a lie, and just as it has taught you, you abide in Him. (1 John 2:20, 27)

Similarly, Paul knew his message came not "in word only, but also in power and in the Holy Spirit and with full conviction" (1 Thess. 1:5; cf. 1 Cor. 2:4–5).

ASK YOURSELF

What would be different about your Bible reading experience if not for the influence of the Holy Spirit? What are some of the clear ways He has drawn your attention to certain Scriptures, or how He has brought them to mind at the most uncanny, appropriate times?

THE DISCIPLES ARE TAUGHT BY CHRIST, PART 2

*Then they understood that He did not say to beware of the leaven of bread,
but of the teaching of the Pharisees and Sadducees.* —MATT. 16:12

Most people who heard Jesus' teachings had no desire for the kingdom
of God (cf. Matt. 13:11b). The truths He declared that made so much
sense to the apostles were lost on the crowds, as He noted:

> While seeing they do not see, and while hearing they do not hear,
> nor do they understand . . . for the heart of this people has become
> dull, with their ears they scarcely hear, and they have closed their
> eyes, otherwise they would see with their eyes, hear with their ears,
> and understand with their heart and return, and I would heal them.
> (Matt. 13:13, 15; cf. Isa. 6:9–10; 64:4; 65:17; 1 Cor. 2:9–10)

But Christ assured the disciples, "Blessed are your eyes, because they
see; and your ears, because they hear" (v. 16). What made the difference
is that the apostles were willing to learn from Jesus, which had nothing to
do with their innate ability or intelligence. Just like the unbelieving
masses, they were originally spiritually blind, but through faith, by the
Spirit, our Lord enabled them to see and become disciples.

As Christians study the Bible and allow the Holy Spirit to interpret it
and apply it to their lives, the Father enables them to understand the most
profound things of His kingdom. As with the two Emmaus disciples,
their hearts should burn with wonder and glory as Jesus Christ makes
His truth come alive to them (Luke 24:32).

ASK YOURSELF

How do you keep your heart willing to learn from God's Word? During
those seasons of time when this is harder than others, what have you
discovered from persevering in Bible study, pushing past your desires for
other pursuits to keep your devotion for Scripture alive?

EXAMINING JESUS' IDENTITY, PART 1

He was asking His disciples, "Who do people say that the Son of Man is?" And they
said, "Some say John the Baptist; and others, Elijah; but still others, Jeremiah, or
one of the prophets." He said to them, "But who do you say that I am?"
—MATT. 16:13*b*–15

"Son of Man" was Jesus' favorite designation of Himself, and it's used
approximately eighty times in the New Testament. The Jews recognized
it as a title for Messiah, but because it emphasized His humanity, many
preferred not to use it. Likely that is why Jesus did use this title often—
He wanted to focus people's attention on the humiliation of His incarnation and His redemptive work.

To reveal Himself to the world—to teach and demonstrate that He
was God's Son—He asked the apostles, "Who do people [the Jews] say
that the Son of Man is?" By asking that question, Jesus was not showing
unawareness of what the crowds said about Him, but He was directing
the apostles to think carefully about the swirl of popular perceptions concerning Him. Christ was not so concerned about the unbelieving opinions of the Jews, but He did want to mold the thoughts of those who
received Him favorably and realized, although sometimes uncertainly,
that He was more than an ordinary religious teacher.

So, after witnessing many miracles and hearing much teaching, what
was the peoples' conclusion about the Son of Man, according to the apostles? Some thought He was John the Baptist returned from the dead to
continue his forerunner ministry. Others offered the possibility of Elijah,
perhaps the supreme Old Testament prophet. And others believed Jesus
was Jeremiah, one of the so-called major prophets. Each of these opinions, however, falls far short of Jesus' true identity as Son of God.

ASK YOURSELF

What kinds of answers do you think you would get to the question,
"Who do you think Jesus is?" if you used it as a conversation starter?
Would you be surprised by the opinions you'd get? How could you use
the possible responses to defend the Bible's teachings about Him?

EXAMINING JESUS' IDENTITY, PART 2

He was asking His disciples, "Who do people say that the Son of Man is?" And they said, "Some say John the Baptist; and others, Elijah; but still others, Jeremiah, or one of the prophets." He said to them, "But who do you say that I am?"
—MATT. 16:13*b*–15

W hy did the people want to fasten inaccurate identities to Jesus? Some saw in Him the character and message of John the Baptist. Others perceived He had the fire and intensity of Elijah. Still others thought He displayed the lament and grief of Jeremiah. But whomever the Jews thought Jesus to be, they considered Him only Messiah's forerunner who possessed God-given powers.

Others in the crowds did not speculate about Christ's specific identity but merely considered His uniqueness and thought perhaps He was "one of the prophets" who was "risen again" (Luke 9:19).

None of the people who had opinions about Jesus could deny His supernatural powers—however, they refused to believe in Him as the true Messiah. Likewise, since that time, many prominent people have spoken highly of the Lord, yet without embracing His lordship or deity. Pontius Pilate said, "I find no guilt in this man" (Luke 23:4). Napoleon observed, "I knew men, and Jesus was no mere man." David Friedrich Strauss, the German philosopher, called Him "the highest model of religion." More contemporary observers have called Him "Jesus Christ Superstar." However, all of those labels are not remotely close to accurately identifying Christ as the Son of God and Redeemer. The apostles knew this, and therefore Jesus prompted them for a genuine identification of Him.

ASK YOURSELF

How would it make life easier if you didn't feel the need to take Christ so seriously? But what would you miss as a result? Try to describe to yourself the greatest losses that weigh on a person who tolerates Jesus but doesn't let Him outrank their other gods in importance?

EXAMINING JESUS' IDENTITY, PART 3

Simon Peter answered, "You are the Christ, the Son of the living God."
—MATT. 16:16

Here Simon Peter was again the spokesman, "the director of the apostolic choir," as church father Chrysostom called him. In a concise and emphatic manner, with no hesitation, Peter declared Jesus to be the Messiah.

Peter's fellow disciples had paved the way for his decisive identification of our Lord. Andrew had enthusiastically proclaimed Him to be the Messiah, and Nathaniel had called Him "the Son of God . . . the King of Israel" (John 1:49). The apostles also knew that John the Baptist testified to Jesus' being the Son of God (1:34), and the more time they spent with Him, the more they were convinced of His divine nature, power, and authority.

However, the apostles, like their fellow Jews, had long expected a conquering and reigning Messiah who would defeat Israel's enemies and establish His righteous, eternal kingdom on earth. And when Jesus' humility, meekness, and subservience failed to match up with that preconceived picture, it tended to delay the Twelve's confident conclusion concerning His real identity and role. That Messiah would experience so much opposition and suffering, not to mention eventual execution, was inconceivable to them (cf. John 14:5). But now they were all (though of course not Judas Iscariot, ultimately) ready to stand firmly on the truth of Peter's ringing confession of faith.

ASK YOURSELF

Does your confidence ever waver concerning who Christ is? If so, what are the most common conditions that bring about such doubts? If you were to start with the unshakable belief that Jesus is truly the Son of God, how would that change your reaction to these doubt-inducers?

CONFESSING JESUS

Simon Peter answered, "You are the Christ, the Son of the living God." And Jesus said to him, "Blessed are you, Simon Barjona." —MATT. 16:16–17a

Finally, the apostles accepted the truth of Jesus' sonship and messiahship beyond question. They would still experience times of failing and bewilderment (cf. Matt. 8:26; 14:31) regarding what He said and did, but they would have no further doubt about who said the words or performed the deeds. The Holy Spirit had confirmed the truth of Jesus' identity in their hearts and minds. Without question, the apostles now knew Christ was the fulfiller of their hopes, the source of their salvation, and the desire of all nations.

Some of the things the disciples later said and did demonstrated that they did not at this time fully comprehend the Trinity or the full nature and work of Christ. But they knew He was truly the Messiah and truly the Son of God. "Son" here reflects the concept of oneness in essence— a son is one in nature with his father. Therefore Christ was and is one in nature with the Father (cf. John 5:17–18).

People who confess that Jesus is God, which means to genuinely agree that He is Lord and Savior (1 John 4:14–15), the Father will eternally bless them (Eph. 1:3–5). God pours out all His powerful, all-sufficient resources on those who come to Him through saving faith in His Son, because through the Son they become the Father's own children.

ASK YOURSELF

Try to enumerate the blessings that have been poured into your life since you acknowledged Jesus as Lord, remembering that blessings are not only things that make you feel happy and energized, but rather the positive, eternally beneficial aspects of God's mercy and favor.

THE SOURCE OF TRUTH ABOUT JESUS, PART 1

Flesh and blood did not reveal this to you, but My Father who is in heaven.
—MATT. 16:17*b*

The teachings and miracles of Jesus, amazing as they were, were not enough by themselves to convince the apostles of their Lord's rightful identity. In this respect the Twelve were hardly any better, humanly speaking, than the thrill-seeking multitudes who heard the same messages and saw the same signs. Human capabilities, represented here by Christ's expression "flesh and blood," can't give us a comprehension of divine, spiritual truths (cf. 1 Cor. 2:14). God, through the Holy Spirit, must reveal them to us and allow us to understand His Son.

From the gospel narratives we can infer that the Father disclosed His Son primarily through the Son Himself. Nothing suggests that the apostles ever received divine revelation from anyone other than the Lord Jesus. Christ made many astonishing claims about Himself, such as that He came to fulfill the law and the prophets (Matt. 5:17) and that in the last days many would call Him Lord (7:22). He also asserted, "I am the living bread that came down out of heaven; if anyone eats of this bread, he will live forever" (John 6:51), and, "I am the door; if anyone enters through Me, he will be saved" (10:9; cf. 14:6). And along with such teachings Jesus did numerous amazing miracles (e.g., Matt. 4:24; 8:26; John 2:6–11; 11:38–44).

God's Spirit, through His written Word, still reveals Jesus Christ as Lord and Savior to sinners and allows them to confess this to the world and to grow in knowledge of Him (see Rom. 8:29; 10:17; 1 Cor. 15:49).

ASK YOURSELF

Why is it so important that God reveals Himself to us, rather than merely leaving us clues that we can piece together on our own? What would be the result of a Christian faith that depended on our ability to figure it out? How can we avoid concluding that we do figure everything out?

THE SOURCE OF TRUTH ABOUT JESUS, PART 2

Flesh and blood did not reveal this to you, but My Father who is in heaven.
—MATT. 16:17*b*

Perhaps the greatest source of truth as to Jesus' identity was His claim to be Lord of the Sabbath (Matt. 12:8). Not only the Jews' week but their entire calendar rested on the concept of sabbath, which means rest or cessation. The seventh day of the week (Ex. 20:11) and every other sabbath observance was a time of rest and worship (see Leviticus 23 and 25).

All nine sabbath-based events picture the eternal rest of the saints of God, when Messiah comes to earth, frees His people, and establishes His kingdom. Thus for Jesus to claim fulfillment of Isaiah 61:1–2, as He did in the Nazareth synagogue (Luke 4:18–21), was clearly to assert messiahship. To present Himself the source of rest (Matt. 11:28) meant He was the source of holiness, and to claim lordship of the Sabbath meant He was Lord over everything.

The order to keep the Sabbath day is the only one of the Ten Commandments not binding on Christians today (cf. Col. 2:16–17; Heb. 4:3, 9–10). The Lord graciously gives every believer a jubilee liberation, which entails a perfect, final, and eternal rest.

Jesus well summarizes His perfect lordship over all things, including those who know Him and ultimately enjoy His Sabbath rest forever: "All things have been handed over to Me by My Father; and no one knows the Son except the Father; nor does anyone know the Father except the Son, and anyone to whom the Son wills to reveal Him" (Matt. 11:27).

ASK YOURSELF

How do you experience God's eternal rest already in your relationship with Him? In what areas are you inviting turmoil, stress, and chaos even though His rest is available to you? How could you better demonstrate through your lifestyle the rest that God offers His people?

THE FOUNDATION OF THE CHURCH, PART 1

I also say to you that you are Peter, and upon this rock I will build My church.
—MATT. 16:18*a*

Here Jesus addresses Peter as representative of the apostles, which explains two different Greek forms for "rock": *petros* for Peter the man and *petra* for Peter as group spokesman. The foundation of Christ's church is the apostles as His uniquely appointed teachers of the gospel. Because it is God's Word that the disciples, and subsequently the true church, always taught, Christ is the cornerstone of its foundation (cf. John 5:39). Paul declares, "For no man can lay a foundation other than the one which is laid, which is Jesus Christ" (1 Cor. 3:11; cf. Eph. 2:20).

The early church gave highest priority, not to the prestige of the apostles as persons or title holders but rather to their doctrine—"continually devoting themselves to the apostles' teaching" (Acts 2:42*a*). Peter himself warned the crowd not to credit him only with the healing of the crippled man: "Why are you amazed at this, or why do you gaze at us, as if by our own power or piety we had made him walk?" (3:12). He did command the man to walk (v. 6), but he spoke on God's behalf and his fellow apostles', as well as his own.

Because they joined the apostles in proclaiming the gospel, the prophetic teachers of the young church were also part of the church's foundation. Martin Luther noted that "All who agree with the confession of Peter are Peters themselves setting a sure foundation." That process continues through believers today, "as living stones . . . built up as a spiritual house for a holy priesthood" (1 Peter 2:5).

ASK YOURSELF

Are you ever guilty of taking too much credit for what God accomplishes through you, enjoying the insufficient, temporary fruits of pride, forgetting that you are merely a vessel of His goodness and glory? How do you counteract this, and why is it so terribly important to do so?

THE FOUNDATION OF THE CHURCH, PART 2

I also say to you that you are Peter, and upon this rock I will build My church.
—MATT. 16:18*a*

Christ did not make the foundation for the church Peter or his papal successors. That is clear from what happened shortly after the teaching here. When the apostles asked Him who is the greatest in the kingdom, He placed a small child before them and said, "Whoever then humbles himself as this child, he is the greatest in the kingdom of heaven" (Matt. 18:4; see also vv. 1–3). Had the church's foundation been the greatness of Peter alone, the apostles would not have asked who is the greatest. Or if the Twelve had forgotten a previous teaching about Peter as the special rock of the church, Jesus would have reminded them and likely rebuked them for not remembering (cf. Matt. 14:31; John 14:9).

Not long after this, James and John's mother asked that her sons have the main places of honor in Christ's future kingdom (Matt. 20:20–21). Such a request would not have been made had these disciples understood that Peter already was Jesus' most favored apostle as head of His church on earth. Our Lord also did not use this instance of misunderstanding to correct the brothers about the nature of Peter's supremacy.

Peter himself never claimed a superior rank in the church but simply called himself a "fellow elder" (1 Peter 5:1) and "a bond-servant" (2 Peter 1:1) and warned fellow elders not to lord it over the sheep (1 Peter 5:3). Like all saints, Peter looked for the glory that is yet "to be revealed . . . when the Chief Shepherd appears" (vv. 1, 4).

ASK YOURSELF

Why is Jesus' servanthood model such a difficult one for us to grasp, much less to live? If this truth were to really take root in you, what changes could you begin making this week, this month, to orient your life toward greater service and sacrifice . . . toward God's style of greatness?

THE CERTAINTY OF THE CHURCH

I will build My church. —MATT. 16:18a

With this brief statement, Jesus points up the certainty of His church. It is the divine promise of the divine Savior, therefore it will be built. Only the Father through His Son can produce the godly results that equal the church.

When believers study and obey the Word, walk in the Holy Spirit, and produce the fruit of the Spirit, they can be certain they are where Christ is building His church. They are not the ones who ultimately build the church, but Christ ministers through them to build His church. The true church is always "under construction," even if Christians in certain local assemblies become complacent or disobedient.

The New Testament clearly asserts the certainty of Christ building His church. He told the people, "All that the Father gives Me will come to Me" (John 6:37). Peter told the crowds at Pentecost that the Lord adds to His church "as many as the Lord our God will call to Himself" (Acts 2:39b; cf. v. 47; 11:24). When the Gentiles of Pisidian Antioch heard Paul and Barnabas, "they began rejoicing and glorifying the word of the Lord; and as many as had been appointed to eternal life believed. And the word of the Lord was being spread through the whole region" (Acts 13:48–49). God's sovereign choice of those who believed ensured the building of Christ's church.

ASK YOURSELF

How can you attest to the fact that Christ is building the church where you worship and serve on a weekly basis—that it's not the work of man but the work of God? What have you seen Him do that couldn't be attributed merely to good planning, hard work, and follow-through?

THE INTIMACY OF BELIEVERS' FELLOWSHIP

I will build My church. —MATT. 16:18*a*

In describing the church, Jesus also alludes to the intimacy of the fellowship of believers: it is "My church." He is the Architect and Lord of His own church. Thus He guarantees that believers are His personal possession, eternally under His love and care. Believers constitute Christ's Body, "purchased with His own blood" (Acts 20:28). As such, they are also one with Him in an intimate, holy fellowship: "The one who joins himself to the Lord is one spirit with Him" (1 Cor. 6:17). In that fellowship there is a mutual respect and love, whereby Jesus is not ashamed to call His followers "brethren" (Heb. 2:11), and "God is not ashamed to be called their God; for He has prepared a city for them" (11:16).

Such close fellowship explains why when people attack the church, they actually attack God Himself. For instance, when the risen and ascended Christ confronted Saul of Tarsus (soon to be Paul) on the Damascus road, He asked, "Saul, Saul, why are you persecuting Me?" (Acts 9:4). By persecuting the saints, Saul had been persecuting Christ as well.

Whether it is the church or His chosen people Israel, God has always closely identified Himself with His own and jealously guarded their well-being. "He who touches you, touches the apple of His eye" (Zech. 2:8). The front part of the eye, the cornea (or "apple"), is the most sensitive of all the exposed parts of the human body. Harm done to God's people is like sticking a finger into His eye. That's why we must nourish the fellowship of the church.

ASK YOURSELF

What are some of the things that threaten the intimacy shared between members of the church, between members of God's family? Seeing how seriously God takes this, what could you do to join Him in restoring the unity and fellowship that's broken when brothers collide?

THE IDENTITY OF BELIEVERS

I will build My church. —MATT. 16:18*a*

J esus' short statement here also emphasizes the identity of His people, "My church." This is the first New Testament usage of the Greek *ekklesia* for "church," and with no qualifying explanation. Thus the Twelve would have understood it only in its most commonplace sense as meaning "called out ones"—or as one of its synonyms, such as "assembly," "community," or "congregation." The fact that Christ likely spoke in Aramaic does not change the basic understanding the apostles would have had, namely "an invited gathering," a term regularly used of synagogue meetings.

After the Day of Pentecost, *ekklesia* took on a new and technical significance in the epistles (which contain instructions for its proper functioning and leadership), denoting God's redeemed community established on Jesus Christ by the Spirit's coming.

The author of Hebrews mentions "the general assembly and church of the firstborn who are enrolled in heaven" (Heb. 12:23), speaking of the redeemed throughout the ages. Jesus undoubtedly uses the term "church" here in this same way, as a synonym for citizens of His eternal kingdom (see Matt. 16:19). Therefore believers today can take great comfort and confidence that Jesus never builds His kingdom apart from His church or His church apart from His kingdom.

ASK YOURSELF

How well do you think you understand the central mission and purpose of the church? Would you say your church is built around those core, biblical objectives? How are you living them out as a body, and how could you reposition certain things to do it better?

THE INVINCIBILITY OF THE CHURCH

And the gates of Hades will not overpower it. —MATT. 16:18*b*

With this memorable phrase Jesus clearly declares His church's invincibility: not even the power of death ("Hades") can by its "gates" hold God's redeemed people captive. The formidable doors at the entrance of death are not nearly strong enough to keep God's church imprisoned. Her Lord and Savior has conquered sin and death on her behalf (Rom. 8:2). "Because I live, you will live also," Christ promised the disciples (John 14:19). Our Lord's ultimate victory over Satan is so certain that the book of Hebrews speaks of it in the past tense: "Therefore, since the children [believers] share in flesh and blood, He Himself likewise also partook of the same, that through death He might render powerless him who had the power of death, that is, the devil" (2:14; cf. Acts 2:24; Rev. 1:18).

The apostle Paul upheld the same truth for the Corinthian believers who wavered in their belief in the resurrection:

> "Death is swallowed up in victory. O death, where is your victory? O death, where is your sting?" The sting of death is sin, and the power of sin is the law; but thanks be to God, who gives us the victory through our Lord Jesus Christ. (1 Cor. 15:54*c*–57)

In view of what Jesus was about to teach the apostles regarding His own death and resurrection and their willingness for self-denial (Matt. 16:21–24), He assures all who would ever believe—the church—that the dreaded shackles of death could never permanently capture them and hold them captive.

ASK YOURSELF

How does it change your view of the day ahead to know that nothing—not even death or hell itself—can thwart God's plans for your life and the lives of His people? How could you exercise this freedom and confidence in practical, specific ways? What fears could it erase?

THE AUTHORITY OF THE CHURCH

*I will give you the keys of the kingdom of heaven; and whatever you
bind on earth shall have been bound in heaven, and whatever you
loose on earth shall have been loosed in heaven.* —MATT. 16:19

Here Jesus tells Peter and his colleagues, and by extension the entire
church, that they had (and have) authority to declare what is divinely
forbidden or permitted on earth. Later on, in His instruction on church
discipline to all His followers, our Lord would teach that a sinning member, unrepentant after several stages of counseling, must be treated as an
unbeliever (Matt. 18:15–18; cf. John 20:23). Therefore, a properly constituted body of believers has a duty to tell an unrepentant member that he
or she is disobeying God's Word and must not have fellowship in the
church.

The source of such authority resides not in church members themselves, any more than did the apostles' authority reside only in their exalted position. With authority believers can declare what is acceptable to
God or forbidden by Him because they possess His Word. They don't
have to determine what is right or wrong, but based on Scripture they
simply recognize and teach what God has already determined. Because
they have God's Word on "everything pertaining to life and godliness,
through the true knowledge of Him who called us by His own glory and
excellence" (2 Peter 1:3), Christians can be sure their assessment of important spiritual matters corresponds with that of heaven. With this kind
of authority on their side, they can even discern a person's spiritual condition by comparing that life to the Word of God.

ASK YOURSELF

Certainly we know of ways people (and churches) can abuse our high-
ground claims of biblical authority, but in truth we are much more likely
to fear exercising its demands, not calling ourselves and others to live
under its protective truths. How have you seen this happen?

THE CHURCH IS A SPIRITUAL REALITY

Then He warned the disciples that they should tell no one that He was the Christ.
—MATT. 16:20

At first glance it seems strange to conclude from this sentence that the church is a spiritual reality. But this warning, taken with the context of the preceding verses and the political-religious mind-set of the times, reminds the apostles that Christ's church is a spiritual entity, not a political force. Like most Jews, the Twelve had expected Messiah to enter the scene as a political and military leader who would free them from Rome. They looked for a conquering king, not a savior who would redeem them from sin. The Jews' expectations were so skewed and self-centered that to tell them at this time that Jesus was the Messiah would be to throw pearls before swine (cf. Matt. 7:6).

Jesus later told Pilate, "My kingdom is not of this world. If My kingdom were of this world, then My servants would be fighting so that I would not be handed over to the Jews; but as it is, My kingdom is not of this realm" (John 18:36). Even though God has ordained human government (Rom. 13:1–7; Titus 3:1; 1 Peter 2:13), the state should not be an instrument of the church any more than the church should be an instrument of the state.

Like the kingdom of God, the church is temporarily concerned with this world, but its ultimate nature and priorities are spiritual and eternal. True members of the church are "righteousness and peace and joy in the Holy Spirit. For he who in this way serves Christ is acceptable to God and approved by men" (Rom. 14:17b–18).

ASK YOURSELF

It takes work to stay reminded that this earth is temporary, merely serving God's purposes for a time. How do you maintain this perspective amid the problems, issues, and pressures upon you? How do you keep worldly concerns from clouding eternity in your mind and heart?

THE PLAN OF GOD: FOUR NECESSITIES

From that time Jesus began to show His disciples that He must go to Jerusalem,
and suffer many things from the elders and chief priests and scribes, and be
killed, and be raised up on the third day. —MATT. 16:21

Jesus now "began to show His disciples" deeper and more challenging truths about His divine plan and earthly work. He had alluded to these truths before, but now He would present them more clearly and in greater detail. Previously, our Lord had mentioned His death with words like this: "The Son of Man [would] be three days and three nights in the heart of the earth" (Matt. 12:40). He told the Jewish leaders in Jerusalem, "Destroy this temple, and in three days I will raise it up" (John 2:19). After that time Jesus would continue to teach about His burial (12:7) and predict that He would rise from the grave after suffering at His enemies' hands (e.g., 17:9, 12, 22–23).

The Father's plan for the Son was not one of human devotion to a great cause, but a divine imperative and absolute necessity. It rang forth from eternity as an essential, unalterable arrangement God set in motion before the foundation of the world.

Four things necessitated this plan. First was human sin, for which Christ had to give His life to pay the penalty for sinners, as "a ransom for many" (Matt. 20:28). Second was God's requirement that "without shedding of blood there is no forgiveness" (Heb. 9:22). Third was God's decree of His sovereign foreknowledge (Rom. 8:29; Eph. 1:4–5). Finally, there was the prophetic promise that Messiah must die (Pss. 16; 22; Isa. 53). People can believe this redemptive plan or they can reject it—but they can never alter it.

ASK YOURSELF

Be careful not to let the familiarity of God's plan grow old on your ears, sounding a hollow tone that diminishes its magnificence. Whenever you have that kind of reaction, what does it reveal about where your heart is? What seems more glorious and exciting to you right now?

THE PLAN OF GOD: PHASE 1

He must go to Jerusalem. —MATT. 16:21*a*

After a stay in Caesarea Philippi, Jesus and the apostles headed toward Jerusalem. His men feared that death by stoning at the Jews' hands awaited both Jesus and them in the city (John 11:16). The legalistic, unbiblical Judaism that flourished there hated Jesus because He exposed its sinfulness and rejected its man-centered traditions (see Matt. 15:3–9). But the Jews would not have to seek out His arrest because Christ would willingly present Himself to them. "I lay down My life so that I may take it again. No one has taken it away from Me, but I lay it down on My own initiative. I have authority to lay it down, and I have authority to take it up again" (John 10:17–18; cf. 19:11).

The Jews alternately lost and recaptured Jerusalem, but they always identified it as the city of God (cf. Ps. 137:5–6). But by Jesus' day it was hardly living up to that title. During the first Passover of His ministry, He had to drive the money changers and merchants out of the temple (John 2:13–16). At the second Passover, the Jewish leaders tried to kill Him for violating Sabbath traditions (5:16–18). Jesus deliberately stayed away from the third Passover; and later at the Feast of Booths the Jews again attempted to apprehend Him (7:1–19, 44–45).

Had Jesus not finally gone to Jerusalem, He could not have redeemed His own from sin, no matter what else happened. Christ had to become the Passover Lamb, offering Himself "once for all" (Heb. 7:27; cf. Luke 13:33).

ASK YOURSELF

Imagine the courage required of Christ not to go into hiding but rather to walk headlong into the boiling heat of danger, knowing full well what awaited Him. What is He calling you to boldly wade into at this time in your life—or else you will miss His plan for you for this hour?

THE PLAN OF GOD: PHASES 2–4

. . . and suffer many things from the elders and chief priests and scribes,
and be killed, and be raised up on the third day. —MATT. 16:21*b*

The remaining three phases of God's redemptive plan were all clear,
distinct, and essential. The second was that His Son, Jesus Christ, would
"suffer many things from the elders and chief priests and scribes." Those
religious leaders constituted the Sanhedrin, the Jewish ruling council.
Their political power, joined to their rejection of Jesus, would cause Him
much pain at their hands.

The third phase in God's plan was that Jesus "be killed." In this context the Greek word translated "killed" denotes murder; thus what happened to Jesus goes beyond a legal execution. He was not even legally
found guilty of wrongdoing but rather sentenced to death on false and
vindictive charges from the Jewish leaders. But this was all according to
the Father's sovereign plan (Acts 2:22–23).

The fourth and climactic phase was that Jesus would be "raised up
on the third day." It is likely, however, that because of their distress regarding the first three phases, the apostles didn't really hear this final one
at all. But this was the great truth of victory over sin and death that made
the other phases bearable and conquered those seeming defeats (cf.
1 Cor. 15:13–14, 20–22, 26, 50–57). This was the final phase of triumph
and glory that all believers should constantly remember and rejoice in.

ASK YOURSELF

What was Jesus trying to communicate to His disciples by letting them
in on the culmination of the Father's plan, the reality of resurrection?
How deeply are you encouraged by knowing that this final hope and joy
is attached to every problem and difficulty you face?

PETER'S PRESUMPTION

Peter took Him aside and began to rebuke Him, saying, "God forbid it, Lord!
This shall never happen to You." —MATT. 16:22

We can be quick to rebuke Peter for such arrogant presumption against the Lord. But we should be candid to recognize that we have contradicted Christ numerous times, as when we complain about our sufferings and trials. It's easy to accept God's blessings, but not His testings; the prosperity and health He brings, but not the hardship and sickness. Like Peter, we easily rejoice at God's pleasant news, but we often second-guess God's wisdom in the difficult news.

Peter's presumptuous words may have derived from a self-important attitude and awareness that he was the leader of the apostles. Jesus had just commended him for his great confession and imparted key words about the church. This apparently gave Peter the brashness to speak out now, typical of his self-confident personality. Surely his love for and dependence on the Savior made any prospect of Jesus' death a fearful thing for Peter. Whatever the case, the apostle's sinful pride placed his human understanding above God's.

In this context, the expression translated "God forbid it" is in that colloquialism's most negative connotation. Thus, when Peter used it with "Lord" the words resonate with hypocrisy because the apostle was placing himself above his Master. To further compound the sinfulness of his statements, Peter totally contradicted what Christ had just declared as being necessary when he said, "This shall never happen to You." Because the elements of God's plan of redemption were humanly unthinkable to him, Peter outspokenly rejected them. Sometimes the best of human "wisdom" is sadly antagonistic to God's.

ASK YOURSELF

What have you been saying "never" to as you look down the road? What are you refusing to do, refusing to accept, refusing to forgive, refusing to endure patiently? What is the source of your "nevers," and what have you learned from the ones you've spoken in the past?

CHRIST PROTESTS TO PETER, PART 1

He turned and said to Peter, "Get behind Me, Satan!
*You are a stumbling block to Me." —*MATT. 16:23*a*

Jesus' words here undoubtedly were a stinging, devastating reply that shook Peter to the core. Before he could declare any further objections to God's plan, his Lord abruptly cut off Peter's words and accused him of being Satan's mouthpiece. This would have shaken Peter because superficially his statement meant well—he could not bear the idea of his Friend and Master suffering and dying. In addition, he and the other apostles had become completely dependent on Jesus for everything—instruction, food, even tax money.

Christ had spoken similar words to the devil himself after the wilderness temptations (Matt. 4:10). Even though Satan departed at that time, Luke says it was "until an opportune time" (Luke 4:13). Thus Satan sought other opportunities to tempt Jesus and now placed into Peter's mind the same ideas he had tempted the Lord with: the plan of redemption is too hard; support me and realize my way is superior to God's.

The same disciple who had just acknowledged Jesus to be the Christ and God's Son now contradicted Him. God had revealed the greatest of all confessions to Peter, but now Satan was the one "inspiring" him. If Peter could engage in such a drastic turnaround, so can anyone who believes. When we as Christians follow our own wisdom instead of the Holy Spirit's, we can find ourselves unwittingly siding with the devil rather than remaining firmly at our Lord's side.

ASK YOURSELF

Have you ever experienced a time when you were sincerely seeking the Lord one minute, then chasing an impure desire or indulgence the next? What does your potential for this kind of about-face reveal about where your righteousness comes from? It's all God, isn't it?

CHRIST PROTESTS TO PETER, PART 2

*He turned and said to Peter, "Get behind Me, Satan!
You are a stumbling block to Me." —*MATT. 16:23a

With Peter here taking the side of Satan in opposition to God's plan of salvation, the apostle at that moment became "a stumbling block" to the Lord Jesus. "Stumbling block" is from the Greek *skandalon* (which yields the English *scandal*), originally denoting an animal trap and its bait. The word later came to refer to the luring of a person into captivity or destruction. Peter had become Satan's instrument to trap Jesus on His way to the cross.

The temptation to avoid crucifixion was a real one to Jesus, because He knew how agonizing it would be to bear all the consequences of sin and be for a time separated from the Father. That's why He prayed, "Father, if You are willing, remove this cup from Me" (Luke 22:42).

The enemy knew the way to the crucifixion was the way to his defeat. He therefore opposed the cross with all his strength. Because they are the spiritual children of Satan (John 8:44), unbelievers consider the cross of Christ to be foolish and a stumbling block (1 Cor. 1:18, 23). The devil knows that Calvary is the place of sinners' deliverance from his dominion, the only path from his kingdom of darkness to God's kingdom of light. After Jesus' death, Satan wanted Him to stay in the grave; but death could not hold Him (cf. Ps. 16:10). Similarly, death and Satan will ultimately have no power over Christ's church (Matt. 16:18), which is the redeemed fellowship of all who put their trust in Him.

ASK YOURSELF

Is there anything in your lifestyle, your opinions, your advice, or your counsel that causes others to throttle back their own spiritual enthusiasm? How could you become a more effective encourager, serving as an inspiring example of someone who's serious about conforming to Christ?

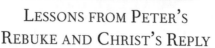

LESSONS FROM PETER'S
REBUKE AND CHRIST'S REPLY

You are not setting your mind on God's interests, but man's. —MATT. 16:23*b*

With this statement Jesus gives the reason Peter became an agent of Satan: he was reasoning from his sinful, finite mind, trusting in his own perspective rather than God's. When believers focus solely on themselves and their worries, they become easy victims for Satan's traps and can also ensnare others. Thus James writes,

> Consider it all joy, my brethren, when you encounter various trials, knowing that the testing of your faith produces endurance. And let endurance have its perfect result, so that you may be perfect and complete, lacking in nothing. (James 1:2–4; cf. v. 12)

From Peter's rebuke and the Lord's reply, we can learn two vital lessons. First, God's plan of redemption doesn't correspond to humanity's. People insist on their own kind of Messiah and on coming to God on their own terms. But mankind's fallen propensities never lead to saving faith. To reject the cross is to reject Christ, no matter how much people might profess Him and praise Him.

Second, there is pain in the divine refining process. Christ calls His disciples to share His suffering and cross. He exhorts them to deny themselves and take up their crosses as they follow Him (Matt. 16:24). To produce spiritual gold from believers, God must first burn off their sinful dross. Through the prophet He declares, "I will . . . refine them as silver is refined, and test them as gold is tested. They will call on My name, and I will answer them" (Zech. 13:9*a*).

ASK YOURSELF

Where in your own life do you have the hardest time determining the difference between God's interests and your own? When you're really not sure whether you're thinking clearly about a matter, how do you go about determining the truth of a situation, decision, or action?

THE PRINCIPLE OF SELF-DENIAL, PART 1

Jesus said to His disciples, "If anyone wishes to come after Me, he must deny himself, and take up his cross and follow Me." —MATT. 16:24

To the apostles, Jesus' words "come after Me" reminded them of when they had left all to travel with Him. To unbelievers who heard Him, the words referred to initially coming to Him for salvation. And to believers, including the apostles, the reminder was for a life of daily obedience to Christ.

Any person not willing to "deny himself" cannot be Jesus' disciple. "Deny" means to completely disown or utterly separate yourself from someone. Christians must have that kind of denial toward themselves. They must utterly disown and refuse to acknowledge their old, sinful selves and refuse any companionship with the former self.

Jesus is not referring to the believer's identity as a distinct individual and unique child of God (cf. Luke 10:20). Rather, here He refers to the natural, sinful, rebellious, unredeemed self that characterizes every sinner and can temporarily even reassert control over a believer. It has often been called the flesh, "the old self, which is being corrupted in accordance with the lusts of deceit" (Eph. 4:22). To exercise self-denial here is to confess with Paul, "I know that nothing good dwells in me, that is, in my flesh" (Rom. 7:18). Such a confession results in a genuine belief that you have nothing in your humanness (flesh) to commend you to God, no merit to offer apart from trust in the saving work of Christ.

ASK YOURSELF

How convinced have you become that "nothing good" comes out of following your basic desires, that if there is to be any holiness issuing forth from your life, it will be only by the grace and empowerment of the Lord Jesus? What has happened lately to remind you of this reality?

The Principle of Self-denial, Part 2

Jesus said to His disciples, "If anyone wishes to come after Me, he must deny himself, and take up his cross and follow Me." —MATT. 16:24

God makes sinners acceptable before Him when they trust in Christ and stand clothed in "the new self, which in the likeness of God has been created in righteousness and holiness of the truth" (Eph. 4:24). But even after salvation a believer has no more goodness in himself (his or her flesh, or humanness) than before salvation. To deny self is to "make no provision for the flesh" (Rom. 13:14; cf. Phil. 3:3). Such an attitude and action, if genuine, will subject you to Christ's lordship and absolutely reject self-centeredness.

According to Jesus, the first requirement for membership in God's kingdom is to be "poor in spirit" (Matt. 5:3). Only when someone realizes how spiritually poor he naturally is will he ever realize how rich he can be in Christ. Only when one sees his hopelessness will he appreciate how precious God's forgiveness is (Pss. 34:18; 51:17). The penitent and humble rather than the arrogant and self-righteous will be saved. It was not the proud, self-satisfied Pharisee but the contrite, broken-hearted tax collector—the one who asked God for mercy—who "went to his house justified" (Luke 18:14).

The truly redeemed sinner will have denied himself or herself so as to "consider the members of [their] earthly body as dead to immorality, impurity, passion, evil desire, and greed, which amounts to idolatry" (Col. 3:5). Self-denial is to "lay aside the old self, which is being corrupted in accordance with the lusts of deceit, and . . . be renewed in the spirit of your mind" (Eph. 4:22–23).

ASK YOURSELF

If you have been battling particularly hard lately to keep yourself pure and submitted to Christ—perhaps losing more than you've been winning—what kind of voice would you give in prayer today to ask for God's help and deliverance? Have you gotten desperate enough for Him yet?

Taking Up the Cross, Part 1

Jesus said to His disciples, "If anyone wishes to come after Me, let him deny himself, and take up his cross, and follow Me." —Matt. 16:24

A true disciple will not only deny himself, but also take up his cross. To take up your cross does not refer to gaining some mystical, elite level of spiritual life. Nor does it refer to experiencing trials and hardships common to all people. To take up your cross is simply to be willing to pay any price for Christ's sake, even if that means enduring shame, reproach, persecution, or martyrdom.

In Jesus' day the cross was the instrument of execution reserved for Rome's worst enemies. It symbolized the torture and death that awaited those who dared raise a hand against Roman authority.

So when the disciples and the crowd heard Jesus speak of taking up the cross, they pictured a poor, condemned soul walking along the road carrying the instrument of his execution on his back. A man who took up his cross began his death march.

To be a disciple of Jesus Christ is to be willing to start on a death march in His service—to be willing to suffer the indignities, pain, and even death of a condemned criminal.

And why would you do that? It is your opportunity to share in the sufferings of the One who suffered the most to save you.

ASK YOURSELF

What needs to be offered up to death in your heart today? What has been taking far too much of your time, focus, and attention, distracting you from pure and wholehearted devotion to Christ? How far must it drag you down before you realize it can do nothing else?

Taking Up the Cross, Part 2

Jesus said to His disciples, "If anyone wishes to come after Me, let him deny himself, and take up his cross, and follow Me." —MATT. 16:24

What does it mean to become a disciple of Jesus Christ? It means you want to come to the end of yourself and your sin so much that you long for Christ and His righteousness, making absolutely any sacrifice for Him. The extent to which sacrifice results in suffering and persecution varies from believer to believer, from time to time, and from place to place. Not all the apostles were martyred, but all of them were willing to be martyred. Not every disciple is called on to be martyred, but every disciple is commanded to be willing to be martyred.

The cross represents the suffering that is ours because of our relationship to Christ. As Jesus moved unwaveringly toward Jerusalem, His place of execution, He had already taken up His cross and was beginning to bear on His back the sins of all who would believe. And in His train, millions of disciples, each with their own cross, have since borne reproach with Him.

Christ does not call you to Himself to make your life easy and prosperous, but to make you holy and productive. Willingness to take up your cross is what marks you as a true disciple.

ASK YOURSELF

How has Christ called you to bear reproach for His name? What has your allegiance to Him cost you, whether in relationships, in hardship, in reputation, or in some other area of sacrifice? How can you become more steadfast and sure in honoring Him at any price?

THE DISCIPLE'S LOYAL OBEDIENCE

*Jesus said to His disciples, "If anyone wishes to come after Me, let him deny himself, and take up his cross, and follow Me." —*MATT. 16:24

Only after a person denies himself and takes up his cross, Jesus said, is he prepared to "follow Me." True discipleship is submission to the lordship of Christ. The apostle John wrote, "The one who says he abides in Him ought himself to walk in the same manner as He walked" (1 John 2:6).

Paul calls salvation the "obedience of faith" (Rom. 1:5; 16:26). Peter describes God's sovereign saving work in a life as "the sanctifying work of the Spirit, to obey Jesus Christ and be sprinkled with His blood" (1 Peter 1:2). Obviously, obedience is an integral feature in salvation and is as characteristic of a believer as is the sanctifying work of the Holy Spirit and the sacrificial saving work of the Son. The Holy Spirit is given only to those who obey God (Acts 5:32), and since every believer has the Holy Spirit (Rom. 8:9), every believer is also characterized by obedience to God as a pattern of life.

As Jesus said, "If anyone serves Me, he must follow Me; and where I am, there My servant will be also; if anyone serves Me, the Father will honor him" (John 12:26).

ASK YOURSELF

Why would someone try to divorce personal holiness from personal faith, insisting that an individual's consistency (or inconsistency) in godliness cannot be used as a gauge of their Christian testimony? What else can it say when a person rebels against His lordship?

THE PARADOX OF DISCIPLESHIP, PART 1

Whoever wishes to save his own life will lose it; but whoever loses his life for My sake will find it. For what will it profit a man if he gains the whole world and forfeits his soul? Or what will a man give in exchange for his soul? —MATT. 16:25–26

This is a simple truth: whoever lives only to save his earthly, physical life will lose his opportunity for eternal life. But whoever is willing to give it up to suffer and die, if necessary, for Christ's sake will find eternal life.

The true disciple is willing to pay whatever price faithfulness to the Lord requires. He will be willing to abandon his safety, personal resources, health, friends, job, and even his life for Christ.

Jesus reinforced the paradox by adding, "For what will it profit a man if he gains the whole world and forfeits his soul? Or what will a man give in exchange for his soul?" Jesus was saying, "Of what lasting benefit would it be to somehow possess the whole world if in gaining it you forfeited your soul?"

"Or," Jesus continued, "what could possibly be worth having during this lifetime, if to gain it you would have to exchange your soul?" To gain every possession possible in this world and yet be without Christ is to be bankrupt forever. But to abandon everything for the sake of Christ is to be rich forever.

ASK YOURSELF

What do those who lose themselves to sin and self-serving behaviors really hope to gain from their so-called freedom? What do they expect to receive and enjoy in return? What have you learned (and lost) from directing your own energies toward fleshly habits?

THE PARADOX OF DISCIPLESHIP, PART 2

Whoever wishes to save his own life will lose it;
but whoever loses his life for My sake will find it. —MATT. 16:25

The story is told of a plantation slave in the old South who was always happy and singing. No matter what happened to him, his joy was always great. One day his master asked him, "What makes you so happy?" The slave replied, "I love the Lord Jesus Christ. He has forgiven my sin and put a song in my heart."

"Well, how do I get what you have?" his master asked him.

"Go and put on your Sunday suit, then come down here and work in the mud with us and you can have it," came the reply.

"I would never do that," the owner retorted indignantly as he rode off in a huff.

Some weeks later, the master asked the same question and was given the same answer. A few weeks later, he came back a third time and said, "Now be straight with me. What do I have to do to have what you have?"

"Just what I've told you the other times," answered the slave. In desperation, the owner said, "All right, I'll do it."

"You don't have to do it now," the slave said. "You only had to be willing."

A disciple doesn't have to be a martyr, but he must be willing to be a martyr if faithfulness to Christ demands it.

ASK YOURSELF

What are you willing to do and to be for the sake of your Lord? Is there anything you simply are not ready to part with or give up in order to walk in unfettered faithfulness with Him? Why is Jesus so insistent on having your full allegiance? Why is this not asking too much of you?

THE PAROUSIA

The Son of Man is going to come in the glory of His Father with His angels, and will then repay every man according to his deeds. —MATT. 16:27

Parousia is a noun form of the Greek verb behind "to come" and is often used to refer to Christ's second coming. A day of judgment is coming, Jesus reminded the disciples and the multitude, when He will return with His angels and "repay every man according to his deeds." He will raise "those who did the good deeds to a resurrection of life" and "those who committed the evil deeds to a resurrection of judgment" (John 5:29).

This general truth had been proclaimed long before by the psalmist, "You recompense a man according to his work" (Ps. 62:12). It was also echoed by Paul in his letter to the church at Rome: "Each one of us will give an account of himself to God" (Rom. 14:12).

Those whose works are pleasing to the Lord are those who, by God's sovereign grace and power, have trusted in Christ as saving Lord, while denying self, taking up their crosses, and following Him. They will receive everlasting life and the blessings of heaven. Those whose works are rejected by the Lord are those who put their hope and trust in the ephemeral things of this life. They will receive eternal damnation and all the torments of hell.

ASK YOURSELF

When was the last time that, coming to the end of a day, you felt really good about the way you'd honored Christ, submitted to His leadership, and availed yourself of His victory over sin? What are the main obstacles that keep you from feeling that way more often?

THE PROMISE OF JESUS' RETURN, PART 1

The Son of Man is going to come in the glory of His Father with His angels.
—MATT. 16:27*a*

One of the highlights of Jesus' ministry on earth is found in Matthew 16:27–17:6. It looks ahead to His return to earth in exaltation and glory, when all His enemies will be placed under His feet and He will establish the long-hoped-for eternal kingdom.

At the time Jesus spoke to the disciples about His return, they were in desperate need of encouragement. Recently they had heard much of pain but little of gain, much of suffering but little of glory, and much of the cross but little of the crown. Jesus therefore assured them that He was indeed the Son of Man who would "come in the glory of His Father with His" thousands upon thousands and myriads upon myriads of holy angels to receive the kingdom and execute judgment.

Here was Jesus' first specific revelation to His disciples of His second coming. After just telling them that He was God in human flesh, that He was the promised Messiah, that He would build a kingdom that nothing could hinder or destroy—but that He first had to be rejected, killed, and raised from the dead—He now informed them that He will one day return in great glory and righteous judgment to establish His throne.

ASK YOURSELF

"The glory of [the] Father with His angels" may not be a sight with which you can do justice in your imagination. But spend a few moments trying to sense the majesty and drama of this coming event. How could meditating on this reality help you do real justice to this day?

THE PROMISE OF JESUS' RETURN, PART 2

The Son of Man is going to come in the glory of His Father with His angels.
—MATT. 16:27a

In Scripture, the word for "glory" is often used to represent the totality of God's nature, character, and attributes. When He came to earth as a man, Jesus' deity was veiled (cf. Phil. 2:6–8), and there was nothing in His human appearance to mark Him as being different from other men (cf. Isa. 53:2). That very fact made it difficult for many Jews to acknowledge Him as the Messiah, whose divine power and glory they thought would be immediately manifest. But that was not God's plan.

When Moses asked God, "I pray You, show me Your glory!" the Lord replied, "I Myself will make all My goodness pass before you, and will proclaim the name of the Lord before you; and I will be gracious to whom I will be gracious, and will show compassion on whom I will show compassion" (Ex. 33:18–19). To witness God's attributes is to have a glimpse of His glory, all that the fullness of His name implies.

The message that the Messiah would come in glory was not new. It was perhaps the messianic truth with which the Jews of that day were most familiar. Jesus now affirmed and gave a more complete perspective to that truth.

ASK YOURSELF

Why do we have a desire to experience "glory"? Even those who won't turn their hearts to receive God's mercy and grace, who don't value or believe in the glory of God, seek transcendence in other ways. What does that tell us about the true need of mankind?

The Promise of Jesus' Return, Part 3

The Son of Man is going to come in the glory of His Father with His angels.
—Matt. 16:27*a*

For those of us who know and love the Lord Jesus Christ, His return in glory is a comforting and thrilling promise that fills us with great hope and anticipation. Like the saints under the heavenly altar (Rev. 6:9–10), we wonder how long the Lord will allow the world to go its sinful way before intervening in sovereign power and bringing righteousness, equity, and justice to the world. We wonder with the psalmist, "How long, O God, will the adversary revile, and the enemy spurn Your name forever?" (Ps. 74:10).

At this point in Jesus' ministry the disciples especially needed a word of hope from their Lord. He had just told them of His impending suffering and death and of the demanding conditions of true discipleship, of taking up one's cross, and of giving up one's own life in order to save it (Matt. 16:21–25). Perhaps for the first time it was becoming clear to them that the way of Christ is the way of self-denial, sacrifice, rejection, persecution, and quite possibly martyrdom. It was beginning to dawn on them that the way of Christ is the way of willing obedience at any price. They were learning that a disciple says no to ease, comfort, money, and pleasure and says yes to pain, struggle, persecution, and spiritual warfare for His sake.

ASK YOURSELF

Identify those things that you are more than ready to give up to the sweeping eraser of Christ's coming, as well as those things that keep you more attached to this world than you should be. Ask Him to help you maintain a healthy, holy desire for His return.

Warning about His Return, Part 1

[He] will then repay every man according to his deeds. —Matt. 16:27*b*

At His glorious coming Jesus also "will then repay every man according to his deeds." The believer looks forward to the second coming in the hope of sharing His Lord's glory, but the unbeliever can look forward to it only in fear of being condemned under the Lord's judgment.

In speaking here of repaying "every man according to his deeds," Jesus was pointing out that it will be a time of glory and reward for those who belong to Him and a time of judgment and punishment for those who do not. On that day every man will be judged on the basis of his deeds. It is not that deeds are the means of salvation, which is by grace through faith alone. But a person's outward deeds are the surest evidence of his inward spiritual condition. People are best known by their fruits, Jesus said (Matt. 7:16). James declared that "faith, if it has no works, is dead" (James 2:17).

The Lord's return is bittersweet for believers who are sensitive and loving. Like John as he tasted the little book he took from the angel's hand (Rev. 10:10), they think of the second coming as "sweet as honey" regarding their own destiny but "bitter" regarding the destiny of the many lost souls who reject Christ. His coming ultimately will resolve the destiny of every person (cf. John 5:25–29).

ASK YOURSELF

How motivated are you by the reward of being honored at judgment for the ways you've let God's righteousness, love, and mercy flow through you—the many evidences of fruit borne in you by His Holy Spirit? Forsake all that would cost you His greatest blessings.

Warning about His Return, Part 2

[He] will then repay every man according to his deeds. —Matt. 16:27*b*

Among the last words of Scripture is Jesus' declaration, "Behold, I am coming quickly, and My reward is with Me, to render to every man according to what he has done" (Rev. 22:12).

Unbelievers are unable to produce genuinely righteous works because they don't have the indwelling Holy Spirit to produce them nor a godly new nature through which the holiness of the Spirit can be expressed. Conversely, believers are characterized by righteous works because they have God's life and Spirit within them as the source and power for those works. A person who has no evidence of righteous behavior in his life has no basis for assurance of salvation, no matter how long and vocally he may have professed being a Christian.

Yet the honest believer knows that no matter how faithfully he studies and obeys God's Word and has fellowship with Him in prayer, he still falls short of the Lord's perfect righteousness. But he also knows, "If we confess our sins, He is faithful and righteous to forgive us our sins and to cleanse us from all unrighteousness" (1 John 1:9). When a believer has given his life to Jesus Christ, His own Spirit produces in him works that are worthy of God's reward. For the believer, therefore, the truth that the Lord "will then repay every man according to his deeds" is a wonderful promise.

ASK YOURSELF

If anything assures us that grace is much more than a one-time event, it is our daily experience of realizing how much we need Him to do anything that is lasting, truly meaningful, and worthwhile. How have you learned again how dependent you are on His grace?

Warning about His Return, Part 3

[He] will then repay every man according to his deeds. —Matt. 16:27b

For unbelievers this truth is a dire warning, because at Christ's judgment they will have no acceptable deeds to present to the Lord as evidence of salvation. Many professing Christians will say on that day, "'Lord, Lord, did we not prophesy in Your name, and in Your name cast out demons, and in Your name perform many miracles.' And then I will declare to them, 'I never knew you; depart from Me, you who practice lawlessness'" (Matt. 7:22–23).

For unbelievers, this will be a day of unending fear as they finally realize the good works they relied on to make them right with God were nothing more than filthy garments (cf. Isa. 64:6) that leave them totally unfit to stand before the righteous King and Judge. At Jesus' second coming, Paul warns, He will deal out "retribution to those who do not know God and to those who do not obey the gospel of our Lord Jesus" (2 Thess. 1:8).

There will be a day of reckoning for all people. For the cross-bearing, obedient Christian it will be a day of great rejoicing and glory, because he will have evidence that the life of God is within him by faith in Jesus Christ. But for the unrepentant, Christ-rejecting sinner, it will be a day of great terror and torment, because he will have no evidence of divine life.

ASK YOURSELF

When you think of those whose carefully built defenses will be exposed before God's holy fire at judgment, how seriously does this make you want to take your responsibility for personal evangelism? What keeps you from being more deliberate in sharing what you know?

PROMISE OF HIS RETURN RESTATED, PART 1

Truly I say to you, there are some of those who are standing here who will not taste death until they see the Son of Man coming in His kingdom.
—MATT. 16:28

In light of Jesus' growing opposition by the Jewish leaders and His predictions of impending death, it was surely with some skepticism that the disciples heard their Lord's promise of one day returning in glory. Understanding the disciples' bewilderment and weak faith, Jesus repeated the promise, adding that "some of those who are standing here . . . will not taste death until they see the Son of Man coming in His kingdom."

"Taste death" was a common Jewish expression that referred to drinking the cup of death, or in other words, to dying. Jesus assured the Twelve that some of them would see Him "coming in His kingdom" before they died.

To understand correctly what Jesus meant, it is first of all helpful to know that the Greek word *basileia* (kingdom) was often used as a metonym to mean "royal majesty" or "regal splendor"—in much the same way that *scepter* has been used figuratively to represent royal power and authority. Used in that way, *basileia* would refer to a manifestation of Jesus' kingliness rather than His literal earthly reign. His promise could therefore be translated, "until they see the Son of Man coming in His kingly splendor." That's exactly what Peter, James, and John saw six days later at His transfiguration (Matt. 17:1–8).

ASK YOURSELF

What do you do with selected statements of Scripture that seem obviously contradictory to each other or to your own experience? In light of this one, which seems on its face to be untrue, what do you gain by beginning with confidence in the truthfulness of His Word?

PROMISE OF HIS RETURN RESTATED, PART 2

Truly I say to you, there are some of those who are standing here who
will not taste death until they see the Son of Man coming in His kingdom.
—MATT. 16:28

It was not uncommon for Old Testament prophecies to combine a prediction of a far distant event with a prediction of one in the near future, with the earlier one even prefiguring the latter. Such prophecies would thereby have near, soon-to-come fulfillments as well as distant ones. The fulfillment of the near prophecy served to verify the reliability of the distant one. It seems reasonable to assume that Jesus verified the reliability of His second coming prophecy by giving a glimpse of His second coming glory to some of the disciples before they would "taste death."

In light of that interpretation—and because in all three Synoptic Gospel accounts the promise of seeing His glory is given immediately preceding the account of the transfiguration (see Mark 9:1–8; Luke 9:27–36) and *basileia* can be translated "royal splendor"—it seems Jesus must have been referring specifically to His transfiguration before Peter, James, and John only six days later (see Matt. 17:1). Those three disciples were the "some" among the Twelve who would not die until, in a most miraculous preview, they would "see the Son of Man coming in His kingdom."

ASK YOURSELF

Seeing the layers upon layers of meaning that make up His Word, what does this tell you about the knowledge and wisdom of God, as well as the vastness of His plan for us, for the world, and for time itself? Lose yourself in wonderment at your Lord's immensity.

Eyewitnesses of the Transfiguration

Six days later Jesus took with Him Peter and James and John his brother,
and led them up on a high mountain by themselves. —MATT. 17:1

Peter, James, and John were the most intimate disciples of Jesus, so it isn't surprising that it was these three Jesus took with Him. Four reasons seem likely for Jesus' taking only these three men to witness His transfiguration. First, they would be reliable witnesses of His manifested glory, able to confirm the event to the other disciples and to the rest of the church. The Lord's promised display of His kingdom glory (Matt. 16:27–28) would be confirmed by the testimony of these three trustworthy witnesses.

Second, these three men were probably chosen because of their intimacy with Jesus. They were with Him the most and understood Him the best, and they frequently accompanied Him when He went away for times of intense fellowship with His heavenly Father (Mark 5:37; 14:33).

Third, as the acknowledged spokesmen among the Twelve, the ones whose word was most respected, these three men could most reliably and convincingly articulate what they witnessed on the mountain.

The fourth possible reason is negative. If all twelve disciples plus the crowds were to have seen Jesus transfigured, the entire region likely would have been in turmoil, with Jesus feeling more pressure to become the political and military deliverer the people expected the Messiah to be (see John 6:15; 12:12–19). That was a situation best avoided.

ASK YOURSELF

We often focus merely on the facts of these accounts from Scripture, as well as in the ongoing, personal situations we face in life. Seeing that Jesus had specific purposes for doing what He did, what purposes of His could you see for some of your current circumstances?

CHRIST'S TRANSFORMATION

He was transfigured before them; and His face shone like the sun,
and His garments became as white as light. —MATT. 17:2

During this brief display of divine glory, Jesus "was transfigured."
That is the translation of the Greek word *metamorphoo*, from which get
metamorphosis. It basically means "change into another form." From
within Himself Jesus' divine glory was manifested before Peter, James,
and John.

Here Jesus revealed Himself as He truly is, the Son of God. As the
divine glory radiated from His face, it illumined even His garments,
which became "white as light" in supernatural testimony to His spiritual
splendor.

The "light" portrayed Jesus' glory and majesty, as Peter testified
years later in his second epistle: "For when He received honor and glory
from God the Father, such an utterance as this was made to Him by the
Majestic Glory, 'This is My beloved Son with whom I am well-pleased'"
(2 Peter 1:17). John later testified that "we saw His glory, glory as of the
only begotten from the Father, full of grace and truth" (John 1:14).

In His human form Jesus Christ was veiled, but when He comes
again to earth, He will come in His full divine majesty and glory, a
glimpse of which Peter, James, and John witnessed on the mountain.
From now on there could be no doubt He was God incarnate, and there
should have been no doubt He would come some day in the fullness of
His glory.

ASK YOURSELF

How encouraging of Christ to use this event to provide a context for the
hard realities He had just told to His followers, as well as to confirm the
glorious realities still to come. How has Jesus encouraged your heart in
recent days, and how have you responded?

OLD TESTAMENT GREATS TESTIFY OF JESUS

Behold, Moses and Elijah appeared to them, talking with Him. —MATT. 17:3

Out of the many godly Old Testament believers God could have chosen to appear with Jesus, why did He choose Moses and Elijah? As no others, Moses and Elijah represented the Old Testament, the law and the prophets. And they could give testimony to Christ's divine majesty and glory. By their presence together, they affirmed, in effect, "This is the One of whom we testified, the One in whose power we ministered, and the One in whom everything we said and did has meaning. Everything we spoke, accomplished, and hoped for is fulfilled in Him."

Luke says that these two great saints were talking with Jesus "of His departure which He was about to accomplish at Jerusalem" (Luke 9:31). They were not simply there to reflect on the Lord's glory, but they were talking with Him as friend to Friend about His departure, His imminent sacrifice, which was the supreme objective and work of His earthly ministry.

It was significant that the discussion was about Christ's saving work through His death, because it was this truth the disciples found most difficult to accept. Moses and Elijah gave confirmation not only of Jesus' divine glory, but also of His divine plan. Their supernatural testimony no doubt later gave the apostles added conviction and courage as they proclaimed that Jesus was "delivered over by the predetermined plan and foreknowledge of God" (Acts 2:23).

ASK YOURSELF

If even the revered leaders and prophets of ancient Israel are in awe of Christ, recognizing Him as their Lord, how much more readily should we bow before His presence, honoring Him for His majesty, thanking Him for His loving sacrifice on our behalf?

PETER TESTIFIES OF JESUS

Peter said to Jesus, "Lord, it is good for us to be here; if You wish, I will make three tabernacles here, one for You, and one for Moses, and one for Elijah."
—MATT. 17:4

Luke gives us the additional information that Peter spoke "not realizing what he was saying" (Luke 9:33). Peter completely failed to comprehend the significance of Jesus' glory or of Moses' and Elijah's testimony. In his combined bewilderment and fear, Peter could think of nothing but making three tabernacles with his own hands in which Jesus and the two Old Testament saints could dwell.

We can only guess at Peter's motive for making the suggestion. He had no interest in Jesus' going to Jerusalem or in His coming again. He wanted the Lord to stay, not leave and return. He especially did not want Him to leave by way of death (Matt. 16:2). As usual, he was caught up in his own plans and his own will rather than the Lord's.

Peter's idea was not so much wrong as foolish. He was foolish in perhaps thinking that Jesus might not have to die after all, that there was now opportunity to fulfill His mission by avoiding the cross and therefore avoiding the need of later returning. Peter was also foolish in placing Moses and Elijah, great as they were, on the same level as Christ by wanting to build tabernacles for all three of them. Only Christ is supreme.

ASK YOURSELF

If you were to take a brash, reactionary approach to the issues in your life right now that seem too big to handle, what would you probably do? And looking back from a point in the near or distant future, how do you think that action would appear? Always better to wait and worship.

THE FATHER'S TESTIMONY OF THE SON, PART 1

While he was still speaking, a bright cloud overshadowed them,
and behold, a voice out of the cloud said, "This is My beloved Son,
*with whom I am well-pleased; listen to Him!" —*MATT. 17:5

Another confirmation of Jesus' deity was the terror caused by the intervention of the Father while Peter was still speaking. Through the form of a bright cloud God overshadowed the three disciples and spoke to them in "a voice out of the cloud." The Father spoke identical words at Jesus' baptism (Matt. 3:17), and during Jesus' last week in Jerusalem—only a few days before His betrayal, arrest, and crucifixion—the Father again publically and directly declared His approval of the Son (John 12:28).

In calling Jesus His Son, the Father declared Him to be of identical nature and essence with Himself (cf. John 5:17–20). Jesus is the essence of divine nature as the apostles repeatedly emphasize (see Rom. 1:1–4; Col. 1:3).

In calling Jesus His "beloved Son," the Father declared not only a relationship of divine nature but also a relationship of divine love. They had a relationship of mutual love, commitment, and identification in every way.

In saying, "with whom I am well-pleased," the Father declared His approval with everything the Son was, said, and did. Everything about Jesus was in perfect accord with the Father's will and plan.

ASK YOURSELF

Would you say you are "well-pleased" with your Lord and Savior today? Or do you perhaps take issue with Him about some of the things He has said, done, or allowed into your life? Begin or end this day by getting your trust and love for Him settled again in your heart.

THE FATHER'S TESTIMONY OF THE SON, PART 2

A voice out of the cloud said, "This is My beloved Son, with whom
I am well-pleased; listen to Him!" When the disciples heard this,
they fell face down to the ground and were terrified. —MATT. 17:5–6

Directly addressing the three disciples—perhaps Peter in particular—
God said, "Listen to Him!" He was saying, in effect, "If My Son tells you
He must go to Jerusalem to suffer and die, believe Him. If He tells you
He will be raised up on the third day, believe Him. If He tells you to take
up your own cross and follow Him, then do it. If He says He will come
again in glory, then believe Him and live accordingly."

Peter and his two companions now knew they stood in the awesome
presence of Almighty God. As would be expected, all three fell to the
ground in fear.

The combined awareness of the Lord's grace and His majesty, His
love and His justice, His friendship and His lordship should cause a kind
of spiritual tension in every believer. On the one hand you rejoice in your
loving fellowship with the Lord because of His gracious kindness, and on
the other hand you have reverential fear as you contemplate His awesome holiness and righteousness. As you walk in obedience, you'll experience the comfort of His presence. But if you are disobedient, you ought
to feel the terror of His presence as well.

ASK YOURSELF

When was the last time you fell facedown in awe before the Lord, or
even in desperation because of your sins or other problems that caused
you to pour out your heart before the only One able to help? Why is this
not our natural tendency, and how can we change that?

AFTERMATH OF THE TRANSFIGURATION

Jesus came to them and touched them and said, "Get up, and do not be afraid."
And lifting up their eyes, they saw no one except Jesus Himself alone. As they
were coming down from the mountain, Jesus commanded them saying, "Tell the
vision to no one until the Son of Man has risen from the dead." —MATT. 17:7–9

Jesus' first actions and words after His mighty display of splendor were those of gentle and loving care. Knowing the great fear of His three beloved companions, Jesus "came to them and touched them and said, 'Get up, and do not be afraid.'" As they hesitatingly looked up, it must have been a great relief to see "no one except Jesus Himself alone."

The disciples realized they had witnessed a preview of the Lord's second coming glory. And once they regained their composure, they must have had a strong and understandable desire to run down and report their astounding experience to the other disciples and to anyone else who would listen. But then the Lord said, "Tell the vision to no one until the Son of Man has risen from the dead." How extremely difficult it must have been to keep the vision to themselves.

But the wait would be worth it for the people. For when they would hear the story after Jesus had risen from the dead, it would be clear that He had not come to conquer the Romans but to conquer death.

ASK YOURSELF

From terrifying glory to gentle compassion—that is the blessed comprehensiveness of our dear Lord's nature. And He knows just when to reveal either or all of them to us, depending on our need, depending on His purposes. Worship Him today for His absolute completeness.

MISUNDERSTANDING ABOUT ELIJAH

His disciples asked Him, "Why then do the scribes
say that Elijah must come first?" —MATT. 17:10

Having just seen Elijah in the mountain, a natural question for Jesus' disciples was, "Why then do the scribes say that Elijah must come first?" That particular teaching of the scribes was not based simply on rabbinical tradition but on scriptural teaching. Through Malachi the Lord declared, "Behold, I am going to send you Elijah the prophet before the coming of the great and terrible day of the Lord. He will restore the hearts of the fathers to their children and the hearts of the children to their fathers, so that I will not come and smite the land with a curse" (Mal. 4:5–6).

The prediction that the actual Old Testament person of Elijah would be the forerunner of the Messiah and His judgment was well-known to Jews of Jesus' day. Therefore, Peter, James, and John could not have helped wondering how the appearance of Elijah they had just witnessed fit in with Malachi's prophecy. They wanted to know why Elijah did not appear before Jesus began His ministry.

Unfortunately, the scribes had made many embellishments to Malachi's prophecy. They taught that Elijah would come again as a mighty miracle-working reformer who would bring order out of chaos and holiness out of unholiness. But that is not an accurate picture of Jesus' forerunner, whose description He would immediately clear up. Check out tomorrow's entry for Jesus' explanation.

ASK YOURSELF

How do some of our cultural traditions and "givens" cause us to misread certain aspects of the Bible, including the words and teachings of Christ? What are some of the most common misunderstandings that you hear people make, and how can you respond to them?

True Link to John the Baptist

He answered and said, "Elijah is coming and will restore all things; but I say to
you that Elijah already came, and they did not recognize him, but did to him
whatever they wished. So also the Son of Man is going to suffer at their hands."
Then the disciples understood that He had spoken to them about John the Baptist.
—Matt. 17:11–13

Jesus responded by first acknowledging that there is an Elijah who is yet
to come, and when he arrives he "will restore all things" just as Malachi
prophesied. But the Elijah prophesied by Malachi was not to be a reincar-
nation of the ancient prophet. Rather, as the angel of the Lord told
Zacharias regarding his son, John the Baptist, the prophesied forerunner
would come "in the spirit and power of Elijah" (Luke 1:17). John would
minister in much the same style and power as had Elijah.

Why then, some wonder, did John himself disclaim being Elijah
(John 1:21)? He denied being Elijah because like Jesus, he realized the
question was about a literal, reincarnated Elijah. He also understood that
the questioning of the Jewish leaders originated from unbelief, which
they manifested when they imprisoned him and then beheaded him.

The full wickedness of the Jewish leaders became clear when they
rejected and persecuted the Son of Man Himself. But in the last days, the
Lord will send another like Elijah, and the Messiah Himself will return,
this time to establish His eternal kingdom in power, righteousness, and
glory.

ASK YOURSELF

These wide-eyed students of Christ's would go on to become the pillars
of the early church. It's interesting to see them here—so young, so
green, so needy of Jesus' teaching. Is there a younger someone in your
life who needs the direction and counsel you could give?

A FATHER PLEADS FOR HIS SON

When they came to the crowd, a man came up to Jesus, falling on his knees before Him and saying, "Lord, have mercy on my son, for he is a lunatic and is very ill; for he often falls into the fire and often into the water." —MATT. 17:14–15

From somewhere within the crowd of people, which included the other nine disciples, this man approached Jesus with humility and reverence. He fully believed that Jesus could bring sanity and wholeness to his son, his "only boy" (Luke 9:38), who had had this terrible affliction since childhood (Mark 9:21).

Like the Greek term it translates, "lunatic" literally refers to something related to the moon (*lunar*). The Greek word was used to describe what we now understand to be various nervous disorders, including epilepsy, that cause convulsions.

The father sensed what Jesus verified, that the boy's affliction was not simply physiological or mental but demonic. When he brought him to Jesus, he described his son as being "possessed with a spirit which makes him mute" (Mark 9:17). Whenever the "spirit seizes him . . . he suddenly screams, and it throws him into a convulsion with foaming at the mouth; and only with difficulty does it leave him, mauling him as it leaves" (Luke 9:39).

You can well understand the father's deep anguish and why he pleaded with Jesus to have compassion on his son and restore him to health. He came to the only One who could help.

ASK YOURSELF

When you feel overwhelmed or outmatched by the various challenges of life—be they job-related, or family crises, or health issues—how quick are you to run to Jesus as your source of help? In what ways could you testify to His ability to meet your deepest needs?

THE POWERLESSNESS OF THE DISCIPLES

I brought him to Your disciples, and they could not cure him. —MATT. 17:16

While Jesus had been on the mountain with Peter, James, and John, the man had brought his demon-possessed boy to the other disciples for healing. But they couldn't heal him. It seems strange that the disciples now failed where once they had succeeded. When Jesus had sent them out the previous year (Matt. 10:6–8), the disciples were highly successful in "casting out many demons and were anointing with oil many sick people and healing them" (Mark 6:13).

What had gone wrong or changed? They still had Jesus' promise and His power, yet "they could not cure" the boy. The explanation for their failure is therefore obvious. They failed to appropriate the power available to them.

With increasing frustration and anguish, the father understandably despaired of help from the disciples and turned to Jesus Himself.

Throughout the history of the church, the faithlessness, weakness, and indifference of Christians has caused many seeking unbelievers to despair of help from God's people. Sometimes, like the father in this story, they turn to the Lord Himself. And He is always the best One to turn to.

ASK YOURSELF

What have you sometimes sought help in, only to find the resulting aid to be unsuccessful or (at best) incomplete? What have you learned from putting more trust in others than in Jesus, from allowing your faith to be dependent on even the most faithful people in your life?

A PERVERSE FAITHLESSNESS

Jesus answered and said, "You unbelieving and perverted generation, how long shall I be with you? How long shall I put up with you? Bring him here to Me."
—MATT. 17:17

Here Jesus gives us a rare glimpse into the depths of His divine heart and soul. Having been accustomed to having angels instantly do His bidding, He was grieved at the blindness and faithlessness of God's people Israel, especially His disciples, whom He had personally chosen, taught, and endowed with unique power and authority.

The entire generation of Jews was faithless, represented on this occasion by the crowd, the disciples, and the self-righteous scribes who were there to entrap and discredit the Lord if they could.

The people were not only unbelieving but perverted as well. Although many of His listeners doubtlessly were also morally perverted, Jesus was here speaking primarily of the spiritual perversion that is inevitable in those who are unbelieving. Any person who does not genuinely trust God cannot escape having a distorted view of Him and His will.

But Jesus would not vary from His divine mission nor succumb to Satan's temptation to despair over the faithlessness of the people. He was on earth to do His Father's business, from which nothing would deter Him. So He said to the boy's father, "Bring him here to Me."

ASK YOURSELF

What do you make of Jesus' frustration? Do you sometimes sense His frustration with you? Do you not know that even though His every action toward you is love, true love can sometimes be demanding— because true love is intent on taking you where you really need to be?

A DEMON EXPELLED

*Jesus rebuked him, and the demon came out of him,
and the boy was cured at once. —*MATT. 17:18

When Jesus rebuked him, the demon had no choice but to come out of the boy. But before he departed, the evil spirit made a last attempt to destroy the boy: "Crying out and throwing him into terrible convulsions, it came out; and the boy became so much like a corpse that most of them said, 'He is dead!'" (Mark 9:26).

As soon as the demon was gone, "the boy was cured at once." While the child was still in the deathlike stupor in which the demon left him, "Jesus took him by the hand and raised him; and he got up" (Mark 9:27). He could now play like other boys, with no fear of suddenly being thrown into a fire to be burned or into water to be drowned. He would have no more seizures, no more foaming at the mouth or grinding of teeth.

Although Jesus already had successfully cast out countless demons from people, Luke reports that on this occasion the crowds "were all amazed at the greatness of God" (Luke 9:43). "Greatness" is from a word that refers to great splendor or magnificence. Peter used it to describe the divine majesty that he, James, and John witnessed at the transfiguration. It was perhaps with that glory in mind that Luke here used that term to describe the crowd's amazement.

ASK YOURSELF

What does it take for you to be vividly aware of the "greatness" of God? Must it always be something loud or amazing or obviously miraculous? Or would you say you've sensed His greatness in quiet places, with little fanfare, on very ordinary days? If not, why not?

AUGUST 28

THE POWER OF FAITH, PART 1

The disciples came to Jesus privately and said,
"Why could we not drive it out?" And He said to them,
*"Because of the littleness of your faith." —*MATT. 17:19–20a

Little faith is the kind of faith that believes in God when you have something in your hand, when His provision is already made. When things were going well with the disciples and everything seemed under control, they found it easy to trust their Lord. But as soon as circumstances became uncertain or threatening, their faith withered. Their faith was like the faith of most believers in all ages. When we are healthy and have the necessities of life, our faith is great and strong, but when we are in need, our faith is small and gives way to doubt.

Great faith trusts God when there is nothing in the cupboard to eat and no money to buy food. Great faith trusts in God when health is gone, work is gone, reputation is gone, or family is gone. Great faith trusts God while the windstorm is still howling and persecution continues.

It is encouraging to realize that even the apostles always had to rely on Jesus to minister effectively. To strengthen their faith and their sense of dependence, the Lord sometimes made them wait—just as He does with believers today. And as He does so, we will grow stronger in faith by ever-increasing challenges that expose our own weakness and drive us to the Lord.

ASK YOURSELF

What is the Lord causing you to wait for today? If you could step back and look at it objectively, not being as spun up by the fears and emotions involved, what would you say you've learned in your waiting times? What have they helped you see in yourself?

THE POWER OF FAITH, PART 2

*Truly I say to you, if you have faith the size of a mustard seed,
you will say to this mountain, "Move from here to there," and it
will move; and nothing will be impossible to you.* —MATT. 17:20*b*

Jesus seems to contradict Himself, first rebuking the disciples for having
small faith and then telling them that even the smallest faith can move
mountains. But as He made clear in the parable of the mustard seed, the
seed does not represent littleness as such, but rather littleness that grows
into greatness. "When it is full grown," He explained, "it is larger than
the garden plants and becomes a tree" (Matt. 13:32). Small faith can accomplish great things only if, like a mustard seed, it grows into something greater than it was. Only when small faith grows into great faith
can it move a mountain.

Mustard-seed faith is persistent faith. It continues to grow and become productive because it never gives up. It's the sort of faith exercised
by the importunate man who kept knocking on his neighbor's door late at
night until he got a response (Luke 11:8).

Jesus also illustrated mustard-seed faith in the parable of the oppressed widow (Luke 18:1–8), a parable He gave specifically "to show
that at all times they ought to pray and not to lose heart" (Luke 18:1).

When we are tempted to become discouraged, that's when we need
to be persistent in prayer.

ASK YOURSELF

How have you seen your faith grow throughout the years? And what
have been some of its greatest catalysts? Knowing that seasons of ease
and plenty are rarely fertile ground for an increase of faith, how does
this affect your reaction to the troubles you're facing now?

THE POWER OF FAITH, PART 3

Truly I say to you, if you have faith the size of a mustard seed,
you will say to this mountain, "Move from here to there," and it
will move; and nothing will be impossible to you. —MATT. 17:20*b*

W hat is Jesus referring to here? Is He talking about moving a literal mountain? The expression "able to move mountains" was a common figure of speech in that day, which represented the ability to surmount great obstacles. So Jesus was talking about mountain-size difficulties, such as the nine disciples had just experienced in not being able to cure the demonized boy.

The promise "nothing will be impossible to you" is conditional, valid only within the framework of God's will. Mountain-moving faith is faith in God. Jesus' point was "nothing will be impossible to you when you prayerfully and persistently trust in Me." The disciples could not heal the demonized boy because they did not persist in dependent prayer.

Nineteenth-century Christian leader George Mueller provides a good example of persistent prayer. Early in his ministry, he began praying for five friends. Five years later one of them came to Christ. After five more years, two more became Christians, and after twenty-five years the fourth man was saved. He prayed for the fifth friend until the time of his death, a few months after which the last friend came to salvation. For that friend, George Mueller had prayed more than fifty years!

ASK YOURSELF

How have you seen this "nothing will be impossible" promise misinterpreted to mean something much different, much more self-serving than Jesus' assurance of His own unlimited power in the submitted, believing heart? What makes us want to turn this into a magic lamp?

JESUS' DEATH WAS WITHIN GOD'S PURPOSE

While they were gathering together in Galilee, Jesus said to them, "The Son of Man is going to be delivered into the hands of men; and they will kill Him, and He will be raised on the third day." And they were deeply grieved.
—MATT. 17:22–23

Jesus was neither helpless nor passive in going to the cross. He willingly accepted the cross so that "all things which are written through the prophets about the Son of Man will be accomplished" (Luke 18:31). He willingly laid down His life (John 10:15, 17), which no one could have taken from Him without His consent.

In His willingness to give His life a ransom for many, Jesus submitted Himself to the evil plans of men and to the righteous plan of His heavenly Father (see Acts 2:22–23). Because of His willing submission to wicked men, He was "going to be delivered" by the treachery of Judas "into the hands of men." Also because of His willing submission to wicked men, the Jewish and Roman leaders would "kill Him." But because of His willing submission to His righteous heavenly Father, He would "be raised on the third day."

The disciples needed this reminder that Jesus' suffering and death were in God's plan, that these events would not destroy the Messiah's work. The crucifixion did not catch Jesus or His heavenly Father by surprise; it was the reason the Father sent Him to earth and that He willingly came.

ASK YOURSELF

Jesus' obedience even to death is our gold standard, the most complete example in history of perfect faithfulness to the Father's will, no matter the cost. How does His pattern inspire you? Where is God calling you in particular right now to follow Him entirely, without wavering?

PETER AND THE TAX PAYMENT

*When they came to Capernaum, those who collected the two-drachma tax
came to Peter and said, "Does your teacher not pay the two-drachma tax?"
He said, "Yes." —*MATT. 17:24–25a

Rome allowed the Jews to collect the two-drachma tax so the Jews
could fund the operation of their temple. "Two-drachma" commonly denoted the Jewish temple tax and equaled the half shekel, the amount required to cover the tax.

When the Israelites first built the tabernacle, God made an annual
assessment of half a shekel on every male twenty and older for the tabernacle's maintenance and operation. The money was used "for the service
of the tent of meeting, that it may be a memorial for the sons of Israel before the Lord" (Ex. 30:16). Because the temple tax was due by Passover,
collectors went throughout the region ahead of time. It was collectors
such as these who asked Peter, "Does your teacher not pay the two-
drachma tax?"

The way the tax collectors asked the question suggests the Jewish
leaders had instructed them to challenge Jesus on the subject of paying
taxes. They likely might have reasoned that, because He claimed to be
Messiah, He would have considered Himself exempt from taxation. If
that were so, the leaders would have had another accusation to make
against Jesus.

Peter didn't have to ask Jesus for the answer, because he already knew
He had always paid His taxes, whether to Rome or the Jews. He therefore
simply answered "Yes," implying that Christ had a God-oriented view of
the believer's relationship to earthly governmental authorities.

ASK YOURSELF

Christians are sometimes accused of being too other-worldly, not
placing enough value on current events, human need, or the earth itself.
Jesus obviously was aware of His real-time obligations. What have you
found to be the best ways to honor both, to maintain a balance?

PETER INSTRUCTED ON TAXES

Jesus spoke to [Peter] first, saying, "What do you think, Simon? From whom do the kings of the earth collect customs or poll-tax, from their sons or from strangers?" When Peter said, "From strangers," Jesus said to him, "Then the sons are exempt. However, so that we do not offend them . . ."
—MATT. 17:25b–27a

Jesus' tax question was rhetorical, and the answer obvious. It would be nonsense for a father to collect revenue from his sons who were dependent on him. Such an action would amount to self-taxation. Here the term "strangers" is a general word identifying people outside the king's family, namely his subjects.

Peter's answer—"From strangers"—prompted Jesus to give the corollary truth on taxation, "Then the sons are exempt." In those days, rulers' families, represented by the sons, were excused from paying taxes. Had the Lord ended the instruction with this, believers could easily argue that, as children of God, they too should be exempt from earthly taxation. But there is more to Jesus' teaching.

As Lord of all the earth, including the temple that was built to honor His Father (cf. Luke 2:49) and whose sacrifices and offerings were directed to Him, Christ could have exempted Himself from any temple tax obligation. After all, He had declared Himself as greater than the temple (Matt. 12:6). But when He set aside His divine glory (Phil. 2:7), He also relinquished the prerogatives to it. Thus to avoid offense to the authorities, Jesus told Peter to pay the tax.

If God's Son claimed no tax exemption, but said it should be paid willingly, how much less can His followers claim an exemption?

ASK YOURSELF

Have you sometimes done things, not because you were forced to, but simply because complying served the purpose of setting a good example, going above and beyond? Where have you been the most tempted lately to do only the bare minimum, just enough to get by?

A Lesson on Government and Taxes, Part 1

Go to the sea and throw in a hook, and take the first fish that comes up;
and when you open its mouth, you will find a shekel. Take that
and give it to them for you and Me. —Matt. 17:27b

This was the only time we know of that Jesus supplied tax money miraculously. He told Peter "to go to the sea," apparently to any place along the Sea of Galilee that he chose. There the Lord would provide a fish with the necessary coin in its mouth.

Usually two Jewish men paid the temple tax together since there was no two-drachma coin. They would use a shekel, equal to a pair of two-drachmas, to pay the tax for each man. The coin in the fish's mouth was that exact amount which Peter and Jesus needed to meet the tax obligation.

Although the tax was primarily for support of the temple, the Jews no doubt misappropriated a large portion of the total for other purposes. Some of the money Jesus and Peter paid also went to support Rome, its army, rulers, and pagan religions.

Even with the negative aspects involved, we can derive a positive principle from this account. Jesus wants us to be good citizens of this world. Even though all human governments are to varying extents corrupt and believers are ultimately citizens of heaven, we must obey the governing authorities while we are in this life. The only exception we can claim is when a government edict would cause us to directly disobey God and His Word.

ASK YOURSELF

Have you ever come up against an issue where strict obedience to an order challenged your conscience, forcing you to choose between God's directives and the present authority? How did you handle this situation? What might have happened if you'd handled it differently?

A Lesson on Government and Taxes, Part 2

*Go to the sea and throw in a hook, and take the first fish that comes up;
and when you open its mouth, you will find a shekel. Take that
and give it to them for you and Me.* —MATT. 17:27b

God has chosen Christians to be citizens of His kingdom, His priests specially called to minister to the unsaved world around them (1 Peter 2:9). Before we believed, we were outside of the divine mercy, but now we receive it in abundance (v. 10). Therefore Peter exhorts us:

> Beloved, I urge you as aliens and strangers to abstain from fleshly lusts which wage war against the soul. Keep your behavior excellent among the Gentiles, so that in the thing in which they slander you as evildoers, they may because of your good deeds, as they observe them, glorify God in the day of visitation. (vv. 11–12)

Concerning the matter of the Christian and government, and despite the godlessness of Rome, Paul wrote:

> Every person is to be in subjection to the governing authorities. For there is no authority except from God, and those which exist are established by God. . . . For because of this you also pay taxes, for rulers are servants of God, devoting themselves to this very thing. Render to all what is due them: tax to whom tax is due; custom to whom custom; fear to whom fear; honor to whom honor. (Rom. 13:1, 6–7; cf. 1 Peter 2:13–14)

Most human laws are not godly or just, but God has ordained government for social and civil order, thus His people must respect and obey its laws, even though they're imperfect.

ASK YOURSELF

What are some of the matters that concern you the most in today's legislative and judicial debates? What are believers to do in regard to those issues that contradict the clear teaching of Scripture?

A LESSON ON GOVERNMENT AND TAXES, PART 3

Go to the sea and throw in a hook, and take the first fish that comes up;
and when you open its mouth, you will find a shekel. Take that
and give it to them for you and Me. —MATT. 17:27*b*

Christians must exercise civil obedience willingly, "not only because of wrath, but also for conscience' sake" (Rom. 13:5). The early church experienced increased persecution and oppression from the Roman Empire, yet the New Testament letters commanded believers to be loyal, law-abiding, helpful citizens. They could easily have mounted an organized opposition to corruption or slavery, but the Spirit made slavery related terms (*slave, bond-slave, bondage, servant*) into symbols of Christian dedication and submission.

God also providentially used the Empire to spread the Greek language so His New Testament could be understood far and wide, as well as building an extensive, quality network of roads over which His messengers could carry the gospel. Rome's relative peace also allowed the apostles to travel safely. These factors all sovereignly converged to set the ideal stage for Christ's earthly ministry.

There are obvious limits to a Christian's obedience to authority. When the Jews forbade John and Peter from preaching the gospel, the apostles refused and said, "Whether it is right in the sight of God to give heed to you rather than to God, you be the judge; for we cannot stop speaking about what we have seen and heard" (Acts 4:19–20; cf. 5:29).

The believer's first duty is always to obey God (cf. Matt. 22:35–38). When human directives oppose God's law, His law must prevail.

ASK YOURSELF

Even when things seem the most out-of-control and beyond hope, the sovereign Lord of the ages is working all things in accordance with His eternal purposes, turning them to His desired ends. What kind of peace and contentment can this give you in troubling times?

A Lesson on Government and Taxes, Part 4

Go to the sea and throw in a hook, and take the first fish that comes up;
and when you open its mouth, you will find a shekel. Take that
*and give it to them for you and Me. —*Matt. 17:27b

Christians do have the right to help change unjust laws or governments as opportunities arise. But especially in democracies, major wrongs never derive primarily from bad laws or governments, but from sinful people who disrespect both human and divine law. It's useless to strive for the reform of evil laws or the removal of corrupt leaders without first seeking to transform the wicked hearts of people in the society.

Like the submissive wife who wants to see her unsaved husband come to Christ (2 Peter 3:1–2), effective witnessing starts with submission. The best example of godly submission is Jesus Himself, who

> also suffered for you, leaving you an example for you to follow in His steps, who committed no sin, nor was any deceit found in His mouth; and while being reviled, He did not revile in return; while suffering, He uttered no threats, but kept entrusting Himself to Him who judges righteously. (1 Peter 2:21–23)

Jesus committed no sin, in thought or deed, yet He submitted to ungodly religious and political authorities. He accepted unjust abuse so He might better win sinners to Himself—Christ is the role model for everyone who calls Him Lord.

If you are a citizen of God's kingdom, that does not exempt you from responsibility to human kingdoms, including their tax requirements. By being a good citizen, you demonstrate that you love God as well as your country and fellow citizens. Such testimony compels the watching world to consider the supreme power that makes such love possible.

ASK YOURSELF

What are some of the most effective ways to deal with the wicked hearts and corrupted minds of our generation? How can we be praying? Where can we be working? What can we be boldly doing?

WHO IS THE GREATEST?—PART 1

At that time the disciples came to Jesus and said, "Who then is greatest
in the kingdom of heaven?" And He called a child to Himself and set him
before them, and said, "Truly I say to you, unless you are converted and become
like children, you will not enter the kingdom of heaven." —MATT. 18:1–3

A selfish question betraying the apostles' sinful ambitions prompted
our Lord's teaching on greatness and His kingdom. The question here
stemmed from an argument they'd had among themselves "as to which
of them might be the greatest" (Luke 9:46). When Jesus asked them what
they were discussing, the disciples were so ashamed that "they kept
silent" (Mark 9:33–34). That silence shows they knew they had been acting inconsistently with Jesus' teaching on humility and that they were as
proud and ambitious as ever.

Even as they had not really accepted what Jesus taught about humility, the apostles had not genuinely embraced what He taught about the
kingdom. Much like Isaiah's audience (Isa. 6:9), the Twelve listened but
did not perceive and looked but did not understand. They still anticipated
a soon establishment of Christ's earthly kingdom (cf. Acts 1:6), with each
of them having a high ranking and one of them being the highest.

Although the apostles did not fully understand what Jesus told them
about His upcoming suffering and death (Matt. 17:22–23), they should
have sensed its gravity. But they were so caught up in their own desires
for personal prestige and glory that they were unreceptive to most of
what the Lord said about His suffering, crucifixion, and resurrection.
The apostles thereby showed no concept of humility or compassion, and
certainly no willingness to take up their own crosses and follow Him to
death as He had taught them (10:38–39; 16:24–26).

ASK YOURSELF

Why the need among ourselves to outrank and outperform, to be
thought of more highly than others? What freedom would you be able
to possess and enjoy if you were relieved of needing to appear more
important, more together, more impressive, or more valuable?

WHO IS THE GREATEST?—PART 2

At that time the disciples came to Jesus and said, "Who then is greatest in the kingdom of heaven?" And He called a child to Himself and set him before them, and said, "Truly I say to you, unless you are converted and become like children, you will not enter the kingdom of heaven." —MATT. 18:1–3

Several months after this lesson, at the probable instigation of James and John, their mother kept ambition alive when she told Jesus, "Command that in Your kingdom these two sons of mine may sit one on Your right and one on Your left" (Matt. 20:21). To the Lord it must have been especially painful that this request came right after He had predicted His suffering and death (v. 19). Similarly, on the night before His death, at the Last Supper, the apostles were still arguing about their own greatness (Luke 22:24). On neither occasion was there any indication of sympathy or grief concerning what Christ would soon endure on their behalf and on behalf of all who believe.

Concerning rank and greatness, the other apostles might at times have been jealous of Peter, since he was most intimate with Jesus and their leading spokesman. Peter was privileged, along with James and John, to see the transfiguration, and only Peter had walked on water and had his temple tax miraculously provided. But Jesus commanded only him to "Get behind Me, Satan!" (Matt. 16:23). The other disciples may have thus thought that the position of greatest among them was not yet finalized.

What the church today desperately needs to draw from the apostles' displays of selfish ambition is a realization that personal greatness is not the issue for the Lord. Rather believers must accept their obligation to selflessly serve fellow believers.

ASK YOURSELF

Have you ever experienced someone being oblivious to your suffering, perhaps entering into flippant, meaningless conversation while you were dealing with something heavy and severe? How can you keep from being the one who is insensitive to the needs of those around you?

THE KINGDOM OF HEAVEN

Truly I say to you, unless you are converted and become like
children, you will not enter the kingdom of heaven. —MATT. 18:3

Jesus here uses the phrase "kingdom of heaven" as a synonym for kingdom of God. The Jews had adopted, out of reverence for God's name,
the word *heaven* instead of *Yahweh* (the covenant name for God). Therefore this usage made "heaven" simply another way of saying "God." The
phrases "kingdom of heaven" and "kingdom of God" both indicate the
rule of God, with the first emphasizing the sphere and character of His
rule and the second pointing to the ruler Himself. The Father rules His
kingdom with heavenly principles and blessings and in heavenly power
and majesty. Any person in that kingdom willingly comes under the sovereign rule of God.

When Jesus speaks here of entering the kingdom of heaven, He
means one must come in by saving faith. He uses it two other times in the
gospel of Matthew (7:21; 19:23–24), and in each instance it denotes personal salvation (cf. 18:8; 25:21). God wants people to enter His kingdom
and does not wish "for any to perish but for all to come to repentance"
(2 Peter 3:9). The purpose of Jesus' earthly ministry and those of John
the Baptist and the apostles was to call people into the divine, heavenly
kingdom. And that is still the overarching task for today's church.

ASK YOURSELF

What kinds of causes or issues have become more important to you and
to your church than the ingathering of lost souls into the kingdom? Why
do you suppose we are so susceptible to being lured off-message,
distracted with other "good" but less eternal undertakings?

ENTERING THE KINGDOM, PART 1

Truly I say to you, unless you are converted and become like
children, you will not enter the kingdom of heaven. —MATT. 18:3

The gospel of Matthew spends much of its focus on persons entering
the divine kingdom through faith in Jesus Christ. The first component
for entering is repentance. John the Baptist declared, "Repent, for the
kingdom of heaven is at hand" (Matt. 3:2). This is the very same message
with which Jesus began His own ministry (4:17). Repentance calls for
people to recognize their sin and have a genuine desire to turn from it.
This essential component of salvation is not a human work but a gift that
only God can grant (2 Tim. 2:25).

The second component necessary for kingdom entrance is the recognition of spiritual bankruptcy. This too is a divine work, beyond human
capability because the Holy Spirit must convict a person of sin (John
16:8–11). The Beatitudes point us in that direction with Jesus' call to humility, expressed there as poverty of spirit (Matt. 5:3). Someone with
poverty of spirit sees himself as utterly unworthy and undeserving of
kingdom membership and brings a sense of guilt and frustration over his
inability to remove sin. The Greek term from which we get "poor in
spirit" denotes a beggar who has absolutely no personal merit to boast of.
Because the repentant and bankrupt person recognizes his or her sin, they
mourn over it (v. 4); because they know they don't have their own righteousness, they hunger and thirst for God's (v. 6); and because they can't
cleanse their own sin, they long for the purity of heart (v. 8) that God
must provide for kingdom entrance.

ASK YOURSELF

Are you as convinced as you'd like to be that your sinful flesh has no
ability at all to generate good deeds and pure motives? Why is this so
important to admit and honestly believe? And what always remains
missing from the believer's life until he is sure of it?

ENTERING THE KINGDOM, PART 2

Truly I say to you, unless you are converted and become like children, you will not enter the kingdom of heaven. —MATT. 18:3

Another faith component that permits entrance into God's kingdom is meekness. The meek neither claim nor demand any glory for themselves, but are committed to fighting for God's causes. They will also have a desire for obedience. This goes far beyond a simple wish to be in the kingdom or a mere awareness that Jesus is its Lord (cf. Matt. 7:21). God will produce in the souls of those entering His kingdom a personal submission to Christ as Lord and a new heart that longs to obey Him.

Entering the kingdom means following Jesus' call to salvation (cf. Matt. 19:21). And such people are willing to make a public confession of their desire to obey Him. Our Lord says,

> Therefore everyone who confesses Me before men, I will confess him before My Father who is in heaven. But whoever denies Me before men, I will also deny him before My Father who is in heaven. (10:32–33)

Another component necessary for entering the kingdom of heaven is persistence. For example, the woman with the demon-possessed daughter did not quit when Jesus initially ignored her, when the apostles wanted to send her away, or when Jesus reminded her she was a Gentile. She persisted even with spiritual leftovers until Christ met her need. In response to such childlike persistence, the Lord said, "O woman, your faith is great; it shall be done for you as you wish" (15:28).

ASK YOURSELF

Meekness is not often a highly valued or highly desired character trait. But what are some of the blessings God provides to those who choose to let God determine their worth rather than demanding their way, insisting that others recognize their value and importance?

THE LESSON OF CHILDLIKE HUMILITY

Whoever then humbles himself as this child,
he is the greatest in the kingdom of heaven. —MATT. 18:4

Like all believers, the apostles needed repeated reminders of the need for humility. Here Jesus uses a child to illustrate His lesson. The Greek word for "child" indicates a very young child, perhaps an infant or toddler. This particular child (see also v. 2) may have belonged to Peter's family and already been known to Jesus. The child likely cooperated readily with Jesus' illustration and happily went to His arms. Jesus and children got along well with one another, and this setting was a wonderful opportunity for Him to teach childlike humility for His followers.

It's impossible to miss that Jesus' teaching on humility was directed at His apostles—and by extension to us—because they so much needed to grasp its significance. From their arguments about who was the greatest, they undoubtedly were not living by their Lord's standard of humility. Instead they allowed themselves to be caught up in pride and self-interest. Perhaps some who heard this teaching were not even saved yet (certainly that would include Judas Iscariot, who was ultimately lost). Others had already entered the heavenly kingdom but had allowed their fallen flesh rather than their new natures to dictate their attitudes. This ought to remind any of us who are Christians of how often we still fall victim to the power of sin that still seeks to influence us.

Jesus' lesson on childlike humility illustrates a crucial and far-reaching requirement for membership in the kingdom. Entrance into it demands humble, childlike faith. There is simply no other way to receive God's saving grace.

ASK YOURSELF

Jesus was a master at using simple, memorable object lessons to teach deep truths of His kingdom. What are some of the most profound insights and concepts you've learned, not from long, laborious study, but simply from everyday occurrences God used to catch your eye?

THE HUMILITY OF CONVERSION, PART 1

Unless you are converted and become like children,
you will not enter the kingdom of heaven. —MATT. 18:3

Jesus' phrase "are converted" translates a form of the Greek word that elsewhere in the New Testament is always rendered with the meaning of "turning" or "turning around." The idea is that a person must make an about-face and head in the opposite direction. Peter used a form of the same word twice in his sermon shortly after Pentecost as he urged his audience to "repent and return, so that your sins may be wiped away" and said of Christ that "God raised up His Servant and sent Him to bless you by turning every one of you from your wicked ways" (Acts 3:19, 26; cf. 11:21; 26:18, 20). Paul used this word in describing what the Thessalonian believers did—they had "turned to God from idols to serve a living and true God" (1 Thess. 1:9).

Conversion complements repentance. Repentance entails being sorry for sin and turning away from it. Conversion is the humble expression of the will that completely turns from sin to God. The psalmist alludes to these two sides of the salvation coin when he asserts, "sinners will be converted to You" (Ps. 51:13). That Jesus used our key word here in the passive voice proves that the apostles or anyone else could not experience conversion on their own efforts. In order to flee from sin to righteousness, a person needs someone else to turn him or her around. Certainly in this process we must exert our will, but ultimately it is God through the Holy Spirit who has the power to accomplish conversion.

ASK YOURSELF

It would be much easier and more convenient if this turnabout negated the need to continue turning away from sin on a daily, routine basis. But what does God accomplish in us by keeping us trusting Him, not yet experiencing (as we one day will) ultimate freedom from sin?

THE HUMILITY OF CONVERSION, PART 2

*Unless you are converted and become like children,
you will not enter the kingdom of heaven.* —MATT. 18:3

Genuine conversion, according to our Lord, requires people to "become like children." Little children often exhibit the sort of traits—simplicity, dependency, helplessness, unpretentiousness—that God demands of adults who desire true spiritual conversion. Children are not naturally unaffected by sin, displaying the effects of the Fall from the earliest age. However they are generally naïve and unassuming, humbly trusting others, with no ambition for personal greatness.

The sinner who "humbles himself as this child," Jesus proclaimed (Matt. 18:4), is like the one who realizes the humility of conversion and finds greatness in the kingdom. The verb translated "humbles" literally means to make low. From the Lord's perspective, any man or woman who lowers themselves is the one whom God elevates. Jesus told the Pharisees, "Whoever exalts himself shall be humbled; and whoever humbles himself shall be exalted" (23:12). Anyone not willing to humble himself as Jesus did (Phil. 2:8) will have no place in His kingdom.

Jesus instructed that believers will rise higher in His kingdom as their pride decreases and they sink lower in their sense of self-importance. The New Testament commentator R. C. H. Lenski observed, "He who thinks of making no claims shall have all that others claim and by claiming cannot obtain. . . . Only an empty vessel can God fill with his gifts. And the emptier we are of anything that is due to ourselves, the more can God pour into these vessels his eternal riches, honors, and glories."

ASK YOURSELF

What are your greatest challenges to practicing humility in your life? When you think about the most humble people you know, how do you believe they deal with the very situations and attitudes that cause you to trip over your pride and your sense of self-importance?

THE HUMILITY OF CONVERSION, PART 3

Unless you are converted and become like children,
you will not enter the kingdom of heaven. —MATT. 18:3

We can't stress enough that young children make no claims of worthiness or greatness. They merely submit to the care of their parents and others who love them. Average youngsters recognize they have no resources to stay alive or put toward their needs. This is the kind of humble submissiveness that can and must lead someone to the humility of conversion.

And this is the childlike faith-response that produces greatness in God's sight and His kingdom. Such people are ones who are humble, not greedy or ambitious, genuinely sincere, selfless, receptive to all the Father offers, and earnest to obey whatever their Lord commands.

What a contrast to the contemporary "gospel" that propagates self-fulfillment and promises personal success and wealth. Such understandings are the antithesis of Christ's gospel and make a mockery of the New Testament teaching on Christian living. The Lord Jesus taught unequivocally that anyone who, on his or her own terms, "has found his life will lose it" (Matt. 10:39). Those who arrogantly glorify themselves not only will not be great in the kingdom, but will never enter it.

James restates the imperative of humble conversion:

"God is opposed to the proud, but gives grace to the humble." Submit therefore to God. Resist the devil and he will flee from you. Draw near to God and He will draw near to you. Cleanse your hands, you sinners; and purify your hearts, you double-minded. . . . Humble yourselves in the presence of the Lord, and He will exalt you. (James 4:6–8, 10)

ASK YOURSELF

God is always present with us, of course, but there is hard work involved in drawing near to Him when sinful temptations are pushing us away. What have you always done without by keeping your distance, and what does He always provide when you do come close?

CHILDREN OF GOD, PART 1

Whoever receives one such child in My name receives Me. —MATT. 18:5

It is impossible to separate Jesus Christ from His people. Therefore, whatever affects believers affects Him.

The context of this verse makes it clear that Jesus was not speaking of the particular toddler on His lap but was using the child to symbolize and describe the spiritual children of God. No matter how weak and unimpressive a believer may be, we must treat him as a precious child of God because there is a solidarity between God and saints and among all who share His life by the indwelling Spirit.

Jesus affirmed this truth to His apostles with these profound words, "The one who listens to you listens to Me, and the one who rejects you rejects Me; and he who rejects Me rejects the One who sent Me" (Luke 10:16). When Saul of Tarsus (soon to be the apostle Paul) was persecuting Christians, Christ stopped him on the way to Damascus by asking, "Saul, Saul, why are you persecuting Me?" (Acts 9:4). Later Paul rebuked the Corinthian believers for their sexual immorality with prostitutes: "Do you not know that your bodies are members of Christ? Shall I then take away the members of Christ and make them members of a prostitute? May it never be!" (1 Cor. 6:15). Jesus is not personally contaminated by believers' sins any more than sunlight is contaminated by shining on a garbage dump. But His name is stained and His work hindered when His children sin, just as He is blessed when they are received.

ASK YOURSELF

How often do you find yourself getting annoyed with or at cross purposes to other believers? Though you may have valid grounds for being upset, how can you turn a potential clash into a potential site for unity and reconciliation? Why is it so important to avoid disharmony in the body?

CHILDREN OF GOD, PART 2

Whoever receives one such child in My name receives Me. —MATT. 18:5

"Receives" translates a Greek word that means purposefully taking something or someone to yourself. People often used the term to denote the meeting of a guest's needs with special attention and kindness. Our Lord's point here is that the way anyone treats God's children is the way he treats Christ. When someone welcomes with an open heart a Christian as an honored guest, that person does the same to Jesus. When a person treats any believer with tenderness and kindness, he does the same to Christ.

When the Lord portrayed the judgment of the nations, He reaffirmed this principle of unity. After placing the sheep, believers, on His right and the goats, unbelievers, on his left,

> The King will say to those on His right, "Come, you who are blessed of My Father, inherit the kingdom prepared for you from the foundation of the world. For I was hungry, and you gave Me something to eat; I was thirsty, and you gave Me something to drink; I was a stranger, and you invited Me in; naked, and you clothed Me; I was sick, and you visited Me; I was in prison, and you came to Me." Then the righteous will answer Him, "Lord, when did we [do those things]? . . . The King will answer and say to them, "Truly I say to you, to the extent that you did it to one of these brothers of Mine, even the least of them, you did it to Me." (Matt. 25:34–40)

We are to care for one another like precious children.

ASK YOURSELF

How could you do a better job of expressing love and camaraderie with your fellow believers? What are some of the sweetest blessings received from seeking their good and welfare, as well as having it returned to you in a full-circle celebration of what God has done for us?

Do Not Cause a Brother to Sin, Part 1

Whoever causes one of these little ones who believe in Me to stumble, it would be better for him to have a heavy millstone hung around his neck, and to be drowned in the depth of the sea. Woe to the world because of its stumbling blocks! For it is inevitable that stumbling blocks come; but woe to that man through whom the stumbling block comes! —MATT. 18:6–7

The truth that whatever affects believers also affects Christ also has a negative side. Therefore whenever someone mistreats a believer, he mistreats Christ. Whether the person is the most reprobate unbeliever who harms a Christian, or a careless, sinning believer who harms a fellow believer, the effect is the same: Jesus is harmed and dishonored. Thus it is crucial that Christians take extra care not to sin against other Christians.

The verb "to stumble" literally means "to cause to fall" and refers to moral and spiritual stumbling, namely sinning. Jesus thus told the disciples of trapping or influencing a believer so that he sins or finds it easier to sin than otherwise.

With graphic and sobering language, Jesus declares that one who causes one of God's children to sin would be better off dying a terrible death such as drowning in the sea. The millstone was used to grind grain and often weighed hundreds of pounds. The Romans would tie the stone around a criminal's neck and drop him overboard into deep water. Such a pagan form of execution was reprehensible to the Jews, maybe even more so than crucifixion. Yet Jesus did not back away from saying that suffering such a terrifying death would be preferable than causing even one child of God to sin.

ASK YOURSELF

Sometimes we fail to remember how patient God continues to be with us as He does His work of sanctification in our hearts. What makes us think we are at liberty to demonstrate a lack of patience toward others of His children—our spiritual brothers and sisters?

Do Not Cause a Brother to Sin, Part 2

Whoever causes one of these little ones who believe in Me to stumble, it would be better for him to have a heavy millstone hung around his neck, and to be drowned in the depth of the sea. Woe to the world because of its stumbling blocks! For it is inevitable that stumbling blocks come; but woe to that man through whom the stumbling block comes! —MATT. 18:6–7

In the wake of the apostles' heated argument over who was the greatest in the kingdom of heaven, this illustration must have been especially sobering to them. The disagreement no doubt caused each man's resentment to rise as each one asserted, likely more than once, why he was due the label of greatest. They not only sinned with their pride and boasting, but they incited one another to envy and anger.

As children of God, each Christian needs protection, care, and understanding. For one saint to sin against another and retard his or her spiritual growth is heinous to God, because it equals sinning against Christ.

The prophet Zechariah states that whoever harms God's people (Israel) "touches the apple of His eye" (Zech. 2:8). The expression "apple of the eye" is an ancient metaphor for the cornea, the most delicate external part of the human body. The illustration is that anyone who harms believers jams his finger, as it were, into God's eye, seriously grieving our heavenly Father.

Anyone in the church who lives an ungodly life and pulls others into sin is effectively sticking a finger into God's eye and would be better off dead. Therefore, how we treat fellow believers in God's church is a matter of immense importance.

ASK YOURSELF

Your example touches more people than you probably know—whether for good or for ill. In what ways are you often forgetful of this fact? Think of the people in your own life whose diligent faithfulness (or perhaps frequent faithlessness) has a telling influence on you.

WAYS TO CAUSE SIN, PART 1

Woe to the world because of its stumbling blocks! For it is inevitable that stumbling blocks come; but woe to that man through whom the stumbling block comes!
—MATT. 18:7

Eve is the original example of a person who directly tempted another to sin. After falling to Satan's temptation, Eve lured Adam into joining her disobedience. Moses' brother Aaron caused Israel to sin by condoning production of the golden calf for worship while his brother received God's commandments on Sinai. Jeroboam was the supremely sinful king in Israel, the one to whom other kings were compared as "walking in the sins of Jeroboam" (cf. 1 Kings 16:31; 2 Kings 3:3).

Jesus indicted the hypocritical Jewish leaders with causing others to sin. Although not always guilty of physical adultery themselves, the Jews enabled others to commit it through the human tradition of allowing a husband to divorce his wife without proper cause (Matt. 5:32). Our Lord rebuked the churches at Pergamum and Thyatira because members in both places tolerated false teaching and sinful standards of living (Rev. 2:14, 20).

Today, a husband might tell his wife, "Let's claim this deduction on our tax return. Maybe it doesn't really qualify, but we need to save as much tax as possible, and no one will know." In doing this the man commits the double sin of cheating on his taxes and inducing his wife to go along with the fraud.

Those examples qualify as ways of leading another, especially a child of God, to sin. It's amazing how reluctant we are of exposing our physical children to harm. Yet it's sad how we often are not nearly as eager to protect those in our spiritual family from evil.

ASK YOURSELF

Could you identify some pockets of compromise in your life where you have allowed dishonesty, or bitterness, or impatience, or revenge to interrupt not only the free flow of relationship with God, but also the integrity of your relationship with others? How could you correct this?

WAYS TO CAUSE SIN, PART 2

Woe to the world because of its stumbling blocks! For it is inevitable that stumbling blocks come; but woe to that man through whom the stumbling block comes!
—MATT. 18:7

The apostle Paul warns parents against indirectly causing their children to stumble: "Do not provoke your children to anger" (Eph. 6:4). Such things as partiality, unrealistic demands, and being too critical can drive children to sinful reactions. Being detached and indifferent to your children's concerns can also provoke sin. Neglecting children (even because of church commitments) and showing little interest in their opinions can also prompt sinful responses. Your children's resentment and anger can spill over to affect friends, relatives, and fellow church members and cause them to stumble.

Another way people can cause God's children to stumble is through sinful example. Believers can tumble into sinful attitudes and practices merely by following the bad example of others. This is another area in which parents must be on guard, realizing they continually provide examples, good and bad, for their children to emulate.

An alcoholic father left his house one night and headed for his favorite tavern. He soon heard a crunching noise in the snow behind him and looked back to see his young son close behind him. When asked what he was doing there, the son said, "I'm trying to follow in your footsteps, Dad." The father reportedly never took another drink.

Paul admonished Timothy that "in speech, conduct, love, faith and purity" he was to be "an example to those who believe" (1 Tim. 4:12). Church leaders, no matter in what capacity, can't escape being examples, for better or worse, to those believers given into their care.

ASK YOURSELF

What could you do to rectify any errors of yours that have sent your children an inaccurate, unintended message about who God is and how He works? What might be the consequence of refusing to humble yourself in regard to these sins, not owning up to them for others' sake?

WAYS TO CAUSE SIN, PART 3

Woe to the world because of its stumbling blocks! For it is inevitable that stumbling blocks come; but woe to that man through whom the stumbling block comes!
—MATT. 18:7

When a strong believer carelessly flaunts his liberty on a matter that is not itself sinful, he could be causing the weak to sin. If the immature believer follows the mature one's example, while still convinced that the particular practice is sinful, the immature Christian is sinning. Thus stronger brethren can lead weaker ones to sin because the weaker person ends up violating his or her conscience.

Paul instructed both sides of this issue in Corinth (1 Cor. 8; cf. Rom. 14) that the important thing was not the eating of or abstaining from certain foods nor the observing or disregarding of certain holy days. The important concern was the mutual respect of believers' consciences. Strong believers who do not share a certain inhibition should respect those who still have it. The strong must not flaunt their liberty but even refrain from the practice if that will help the weak not to sin. Paul summarizes:

> All things indeed are clean, but they are evil for the man who eats and gives offense. It is good not to eat meat or to drink wine, or to do anything by which your brother stumbles. The faith which you have, have as your own conviction before God. Happy is he who does not condemn himself in what he approves. (Rom. 14:20–22)

Jesus doesn't want us to be insensitive about our liberties in Him, causing our brethren offense. To lead them into any conscience-violating action or inaction can mean we've caused them to sin. And "woe to that man through whom the stumbling block comes!"

ASK YOURSELF

What are some of the more common areas where young believers can become confused by other Christians' behaviors? How have you experienced some of these yourself, either by observing the example of another, or by your own example being held to account?

LEADING OTHERS TO RIGHTEOUSNESS

It is inevitable that stumbling blocks come. —MATT. 18:7*b*

The most common way that believers contribute to other believers' sins may be the failure to lead others into righteousness. To keep God's truth and all its rich resources strictly to ourselves is to withhold from others insights and experiences that can help them grow spiritually.

By contrast, the New Testament repeatedly urges saints to encourage one another in righteousness. Hebrews admonishes us to "consider how to stimulate one another to love and good deeds" (Heb. 10:24). In the Lord's Prayer, Jesus tells His children to petition their heavenly Father, "Do not lead us into temptation." We know, however, that He would never tempt us, because it is His desire to "deliver us from evil" (Matt. 6:13). James further assures us that "God cannot be tempted by evil," and that He sets the standard in that "He Himself does not tempt anyone" (James 1:13). Like the Father, the mature Christian never causes others to sin but shields them from it and leads them into righteousness.

The story is told of a very distraught old man on his deathbed. When asked why he was so upset, he said, "When we were boys at play, one day at a crossroads we reversed a signpost, and I've never ceased to wonder how many people were sent in the wrong direction by what we did." How many times does that sort of bad communication occur in the church when believers send other believers wrong signals that lead them down the road to sin?

ASK YOURSELF

Who have been some of the most winsome examples of Christlikeness you've been around in your life—those whose words, reactions, and expressions always draw out of you a fresh desire to follow Christ more completely? How badly do you want to become that for others?

THE EVIL OF THE STUMBLING BLOCK

It is inevitable that stumbling blocks come; but woe to that
man through whom the stumbling block comes! —MATT. 18:7*b-c*

The world today is under God's curse (the word "woe" is a term of cursing and condemnation) because of its sinfulness, but also because of the stumbling blocks it constantly places across believers' paths. The mass media, especially the ever-expanding numbers of Internet sites and blogs, are relentless at sending forth false and corrupt messages and images that seek to pull God's children into sin. In fact, the world seems to delight in victimizing those who follow the Lord.

It is inevitable that such ungodly influences will come and continue until Christ returns. But Jesus further emphasizes that, unless they repent, it will be horrifying for those who place stumbling blocks before others. He had already declared the gravity of such offenses by saying it was better for the guilty person to drown. Better off dead if someone has caused Christ's precious believers to sin. But now He asserts that being a stumbling block can bring on divine judgment.

Many years ago one of the handicapped young men at our church remorsefully told me he had gotten drunk recently. I ascertained that, as a prank, his brother and others had forced alcohol down his throat until he was intoxicated. The worst thing for him was not the intoxication but the guilt it produced afterwards. He felt ashamed and responsible, wondering if Jesus would forgive him. I assured him that our Lord had forgiven him and that the guilt really belonged to his abusers. They were the ones who needed to repent and escape God's judgment.

ASK YOURSELF

Think of the many ways the young and impressionable are being deceived on any number of fronts in our culture today. How can you be a barrier of protection for them, helping them see truth in the midst of such destructive lies, helping them avoid the trap of being drawn in deeper?

PREVENTION OF STUMBLING

If your hand or your foot causes you to stumble, cut it off and throw it from you;
it is better for you to enter life crippled or lame, than to have two hands or
two feet and be cast into the eternal fire. If your eye causes you to stumble,
pluck it out and throw it from you. It is better for you to enter life with one
eye, than to have two eyes and be cast into the fiery hell. —MATT. 18:8–9

J esus obviously is giving us a figurative statement here because no bodily part per se causes us to sin—and He would never advocate mutilation because that will not cleanse our hearts or prevent us from sinning. But Jesus is pointing the way, with graphic hyperbole, to deliverance from heart sin (cf. Matt. 5:29–30). Plucking out an eye or severing a foot or hand would be useless. The remaining bodily member could simply carry on with the sinful action the discarded one had engaged in.

Our Lord's point is that we should be willing, no matter how painful or extreme, to keep from sinning and to keep others from sinning. He implies that there is plenty of divinely provided grace available to overcome any temptation or sin. If any habit, situation, or relationship leads you to stumble, you should forsake it permanently. Even if the sacrifice causes "maiming" or "blinding"—socially, financially, professionally—that's infinitely preferable to entering the fire of hell forever.

Christ here gives believers a vivid exhortation to drastic action against sin. Only unbelievers are in danger of hell, but believers can't miss the seriousness of this statement. To keep others from sin, we must protect ourselves from its ravages. Paul affirmed, "I discipline my body and make it my slave, so that, after I have preached to others, I myself will not be disqualified" (1 Cor. 9:27). If a believer is truly concerned that he not sin, he will also be prepared and eager to help others not stumble.

ASK YOURSELF

The call to discipleship is indeed a radical one, and the path to victory cannot be considered a part-time job. What in your life needs a drastic shock to the system, a complete refusal to comply any longer?

DESPISING OTHER BELIEVERS

See that you do not despise one of these little ones. —MATT. 18:10*a*

J esus' negative command here is a stern warning (the grammar in the Greek intensifies the prohibition) strongly implying God's displeasure with disobedience of it. Our Lord had already established the seriousness of harming any of God's children—it would be better for such a violator "to have a heavy millstone hung around his neck, and to be drowned in the depth of the sea" (Matt. 18:6).

To despise literally means "to think down on," or to look down on another person as inferior or not worthy of consideration or care, and to treat him or her with contempt. Thus Jesus warns us not to treat a fellow believer—one of the Father's precious children—with disdain and contempt.

In the context of what had just happened with Jesus and the apostles, He was instructing them that their arguing over who was the greatest was a form of despising God's little ones—in this case each other. As each one exalted himself, he was pushing his fellow apostles down. Instead of proudly elevating himself, each should have been showing concern for the others and building them up. As Paul exhorted the Philippians:

> Do nothing from selfishness or empty conceit, but with humility of mind regard one another as more important than yourselves; do not merely look out for your own personal interests, but also for the interests of others. Have this attitude in yourselves which was also in Christ Jesus, who . . . humbled Himself by becoming obedient to the point of death, even death on a cross. (Phil. 2:3–6*a*, 8)

ASK YOURSELF

The habit of making comparisons has a way of turning personal temperaments and preferences into points of extreme judgment and disapproval of others. Have you let this become a favorite sport or pastime in your life? What does it usually leave you feeling like when you're done?

HOW CAN WE DESPISE ONE ANOTHER?—PART 1

See that you do not despise one of these little ones. —MATT. 18:10a

Believers can despise one another in various ways. First, they can despise other brethren when they flaunt their Christian liberty before weaker Christians, causing them to violate their consciences or fall into legalism. "The one who eats is not to regard with contempt the one who does not eat, and the one who does not eat is not to judge the one who eats, for God has accepted him" (Rom. 14:3). Such behavior uses liberty "as a covering for evil" (1 Peter 2:16) rather than in service to God.

Believers also despise each other when they demonstrate partiality. James commands us never to hold "faith in our glorious Lord Jesus Christ with an attitude of personal favoritism" (James 2:1). God loves His children equally and "is not one to show partiality, but in every nation the man who fears Him and does what is right is welcome to Him" (Acts 10:34–35). The mature Christian never looks down on other "lesser" believers or shows favoritism to some:

> If . . . you pay special attention to the one who is wearing the fine clothes, and say, "You sit here in a good place," and you say to the poor man, "You stand over there, or sit down by my footstool," have you not made distinctions among yourselves, and become judges with evil motives? . . . did not God choose the poor of this world to be rich in faith and heirs of the kingdom which He promised to those who love Him? But you have dishonored the poor man. Is it not the rich who oppress you and personally drag you into court? Do they not blaspheme the fair name by which you have been called? If, however, you are fulfilling the royal law according to the Scripture, "You shall love your neighbor as yourself," you are doing well. (James 2:2–8)

ASK YOURSELF

Do you see any of these behaviors operating in your church or among your Christian friends? What makes us want to ingratiate ourselves to those who are perceived as more impressive and important?

How Can We Despise One Another?—Part 2

*See that you do not despise one of these little ones. —*Matt. 18:10*a*

Another way Christians despise other Christians is by withholding help from ones who are needy. Paul rebuked such a problem at Corinth:

> When you meet together, it is not to eat the Lord's Supper, for in your eating each one takes his own supper first; and one is hungry and another is drunk. What! Do you not have houses in which to eat and drink? Or do you despise the church of God and shame those who have nothing? What shall I say to you? Shall I praise you? In this I will not praise you. (1 Cor. 11:20–22)

It would be as if a church today had a potluck before a Communion service and the well-to-do brought all the food and shared none with poorer members (cf. James 2:15–16; 1 John 3:17–18).

Further, saints can despise other saints by ridiculing their appearances. Some of the arrogant, carnal members of the Corinthian church derided Paul: "His letters are weighty and strong, but his personal presence is unimpressive and his speech contemptible" (2 Cor. 10:10). Conversely, Paul commended the Galatian believers for not depreciating his "bodily condition," possibly a serious eye infection, when he first preached to them (Gal. 4:14). There is simply no room for such demeaning ridicule within God's family—it is contemptible in His sight and the sight of fellow men and women, believers and unbelievers.

ASK YOURSELF

Whenever you interact with those who suffer from handicaps or other unfortunate conditions, what are some of the healthy ways to make them feel at ease and welcomed in your presence—as brothers and sisters in the Lord—not treated differently because of their differences?

HOW CAN WE DESPISE ONE ANOTHER?—PART 3

See that you do not despise one of these little ones. —MATT. 18:10a

Our brief study of how believers despise other believers concludes with three more ways. We despise others when we are indifferent to or judgmental of one who stumbles. When one of our brethren sins, we can be prone to dismissing them with this thought: "They knew better and made a bad choice—let them live with the consequences. Until they change, I'll stay at arm's length." But Paul admonished the Galatians: "Brethren, even if anyone is caught in any trespass, you who are spiritual, restore such a one in a spirit of gentleness; each one looking to yourself, so that you too will not be tempted. Bear one another's burdens, and thereby fulfill the law of Christ" (Gal. 6:1–2). Jesus wants us to humbly help a sinning brother or sister, realizing that we also could fall into an equally bad or worse sin, and knowing that only by God's grace we don't.

Another way we despise fellow saints is when we resent one who confronts our sinfulness. Instead of being grateful and repenting of the sin, our old self often charges the other person with being judgmental, legalistic, and hypocritical. Even if a church carries out discipline in careful conformity to Scripture (Matt. 18:15–18) and with grace and love, the one confronted often resents his brethren.

Finally, believers can despise other believers by taking advantage of them for personal gain. Although referring to sexual immorality, Paul's warning applies here—a believer should not "defraud his brother" in any way, "because the Lord is the avenger in all these things" (1 Thess. 4:6).

ASK YOURSELF

Have you ever been confronted by another who was genuinely concerned with the direction you were taking in life, someone who cared enough to lovingly warn you about the way sin was blinding you to important priorities? How did you receive that? How would you now?

CHRISTIANS' RELATION TO ANGELS

Their angels in heaven continually see the face of My Father who is in heaven.
—MATT. 18:10*b*

J esus' mention of believers' relationship to angels is the first reason Christians should never despise other Christians. God had commanded the angels to care for His people. The book of Hebrews states that angels are "all ministering spirits, sent out to render service for the sake of those who will inherit salvation" (1:14). Holy angels live in the presence of God, where they attentively await His commands to serve and care for His people. Jesus implies here that the angels never look away from the Father so as not to miss any instructions from Him about serving His children.

These truths, however, do not teach the concept of individual guardian angels for each Christian. Such a concept merely followed Jewish tradition. Upon seeing that Peter was released from prison and at the door of Mary's house, the servant girl Rhoda was so overjoyed she forgot to open the gate. When Rhoda told the believers gathered inside praying for Peter's release that he was outside, it was likely this superstitious concept of guardian angels that prompted their insistence she had only seen "his angel" (Acts 12:12–15). The Acts passage simply reflected the people's understanding—neither it nor any other passage teaches the notion as true.

The angels Jesus refers to care for, protect, and serve all who believe in Him. Because the Father is so concerned about His children that He has hosts of angels ready to aid them shows how valuable believers ("little ones") are and how sinful it is to even contemplate despising or harming ones God so highly prizes.

ASK YOURSELF

It may be hard to imagine that angels are this involved in our lives, serving the Lord by ministering His care and protection to us. But what does this tell you about His concern for our welfare and safety? Wonder how many ways we've been spared from harm without knowing it?

BELIEVERS' RELATION TO CHRIST: SHEEP AND SHEPHERD, PART 1

What do you think? If any man has a hundred sheep, and one of them has gone astray, does he not leave the ninety-nine on the mountains and go and search for the one that is straying? If it turns out that he finds it, truly I say to you, he rejoices over it more than over the ninety-nine which have not gone astray.
—MATT. 18:12–13

Jesus here tells the parable of the lost sheep that further illustrates why believers must not despise one another—because of their intimate relationship to Him. To consider any other Christian useless or worthless is to despise Jesus Himself (Luke 10:16).

Jesus' hearers were familiar with sheep and their keepers. In this parable, a man who had a hundred sheep had one of them stray into the rugged terrain of Palestine, where it could be caught in one of the many crevices, gullies, ravines, or caves.

A competent shepherd knew his flock (see John 10:1–18), and therefore knew instinctively when something was wrong or a sheep was missing. Shepherds were expert trackers, and their love for defenseless and totally dependent sheep would not allow them to quit until they had found and rescued a missing animal. When he found a lost sheep he would pour olive oil into any wounds and bind up any broken legs. Then he would carefully place the sheep on his shoulders and take it back to the fold.

This parable illustrates that Jesus' love, represented by the shepherd's, is personal and individual. He is equally concerned for any of His sheep who might stray—whether it's the respected church elder who stumbles, or the poor believer from the ghetto who wanders from Him.

ASK YOURSELF

How have you experienced the seeking, insatiable love of the Shepherd in your own life? How has it affected your reactions and responses toward others who are in need, in trouble, or in spiritual danger?

BELIEVERS' RELATION TO CHRIST: SHEEP AND SHEPHERD, PART 2

If it turns out that he finds [the sheep], truly I say to you, he
rejoices over it more than over the ninety-nine which have not gone astray.
—MATT. 18:13

This parable illustrates that Christ's care for His people is patient. He bears with their sinful, self-willed foolishness and will not abandon a single believer, even though some will seem to be the least promising, least faithful of all His children.

Our Lord here also illustrates the Father's seeking care. He does not wait for a wayward sheep to return on his own but goes to whatever lengths necessary to spiritually retrieve that one. Christ is far more desirous for a saint's restoration than is even the most caring and earnest human pastor.

As "the great Shepherd of the sheep through the blood of the eternal covenant" (Heb. 13:20), the Lord Jesus has an infinite concern about a single believer who goes astray. And when He regathers and restores the errant one, how great is the heavenly rejoicing "over it . . . than over the ninety-nine which have not gone astray?" (cf. Luke 15:3–7).

That special joy derives not from favoritism, but from a special concern the caring Shepherd has for the greater needs of the straying sheep. By analogy, a mother will devote much more attention and care to a seriously ill child than to any other of her children. And when that child recovers, the loving mother does not rejoice for the children who have been well but for that one who was sick and suffering.

Because our Lord has compassion on all His neediest ones, and their welfare brings Him great joy, we dare not despise such people.

ASK YOURSELF

Who are the two or three people on your prayer list who need to hear this message the strongest today? How could you go about expressing the seeking, caring love of Christ most clearly to them?

BELIEVERS' RELATION TO THE FATHER

It is not the will of your Father who is in heaven
that one of these little ones perish. —MATT. 18:14

The "Father who is in heaven" joins His Son and the angels in rejoicing over any believer who is restored, thus providing us another reason we should not despise one another.

The word rendered "perish" usually means destruction or death, but sometimes, as here, it refers to nonpermanent ruin or loss (cf. Rom. 14:15; 1 Cor. 8:11). Jesus uses the word in reference to a believer's spiritual progress. His Father doesn't want even one of "His little ones" to suffer spiritual hurt or damage (by falling into sin), even temporarily. Sin by Christians ruins their usefulness to God and the church. It also undercuts their happiness and the joy of a right relationship to Him and other believers.

Peter instructs us to cast all our cares on God, because He cares for us (1 Peter 5:7). The Father individually cares for each sinner who repents and comes to Him through faith in Christ. He makes sure that He brings back into the fellowship of His family and kingdom any of them who wander from Him.

William Arnot once observed, "If it did not please [God] to get me back, my pleasure would be small." It should comfort any and all Christians who might get ensnared by sin to realize that, when they repent and return to righteousness, their heavenly Father will have abundant joy. Thus for one believer to despise another is to defy God's will and be His antagonist. The Father, the Son, and all the holy angels seek the well-being of God's own—and so should we.

ASK YOURSELF

Having a healthy fear of God is naturally important to relating rightly to Him, honoring Him out of the extreme otherness of His character and the authority of His rule. But how motivating is it to know that Your Father has such an intense love and desire for you and your welfare?

THE CHRISTIAN WHO RECEIVES DISCIPLINE, PART 1

If your brother sins . . . —MATT. 18:15*a*

Who is a candidate for church discipline? Any believer who sins, with Jesus' implication here being that that person has continued to live for some time with a certain sin unconfessed. And our Lord's reference to "your brother" is absolutely inclusive—there are no exceptions. *Every* Christian—young or old, man or woman, educated or uneducated, rich or poor, leader or follower—must be confronted when he sins.

"Sins" is from *hamartanō*, literally meaning "to miss the mark." In the New Testament it's the basic term telling us we miss the mark of divine standards. All sin is an offense against God's holiness, damaging believers' sanctification and marring fellowship among believers, as well as between them and God. So all persistent sin, by any believer, demands church discipline.

If one is maligned, abused, deceived, or the like by another brother or sister, he should rebuke the offender but also forgive him if he repents. The one offended must remain meek and humble and approach the offender with the goal of restoring him to holiness. Thus vindictiveness has no place in the disciplining process; rather it all must be conducted in the spirit of love and forgiveness. The one confronting should have deep concern at the spiritual damage the sinning brother or sister has suffered, and possess a real desire for the person to be restored to his prior position of obedience and blessing.

ASK YOURSELF

How often have you seen church discipline practiced and enforced? What are the main reasons for neglecting to implement this important part of body life? How would the cause of Christ be advanced if churches would take this responsibility as seriously as they should?

THE CHRISTIAN WHO RECEIVES DISCIPLINE, PART 2

If your brother sins . . . —MATT. 18:15*a*

When a brother's or sister's offense is known, we must begin as soon as possible to rebuke them. This will turn the offender from his sin early on and minimize the potential for the offended one to have resentment or bitterness. Such emotions are also sinful and tend to simmer as long as a break in relationship stays unmended. If discipline does not begin right away, it becomes more difficult for the offender to turn from sin and for the one offended to extend forgiveness to the offender. But Paul exhorts all believers to "be kind to one another, tender-hearted, forgiving each other, just as God in Christ also has forgiven you" (Eph. 4:32).

A decisive discipline process is essential because, more broadly, any sin committed by any believer affects all other believers, at least indirectly. The apostle correctly pointed out "that a little leaven leavens the whole lump of dough" (1 Cor. 5:6). Quite awhile ago, a man in my church told an attorney friend what church he attended and the attorney reacted in shock, "I'd never go there! That's where the most crooked attorney in Los Angeles attends." The other attorney's sin indirectly affected our entire church and tainted the whole cause of Christ. So every sin not dealt with by an offending believer must be addressed by the church.

ASK YOURSELF

How have you seen this proven in your own life—the fact that sins and temptations handled with swift, immediate correction are exponentially easier to fend off and defuse? If you know of some sins right now that are still in the early stages, how do you intend to deal with them?

THE CONCEPT OF REPROOF

Go and show him his fault in private. —MATT. 18:15*b*

"Show him his fault" (sometimes translated "reprove him") at its root means "bring to light" or "expose." And here it makes it impossible for the offender to escape recognizing his sin.

This initial confrontation of the sinning brother must be "in private," or one on one. If the sinning person repents, no further action is needed and no one else needs to know of the matter. The more the sin becomes known, the more resentful the offender can become and the more difficult the restorative process may be. When the offender is corrected privately, in love and humility, a change of heart is much more likely.

If the sinning person does turn to righteousness, a wonderful bond of friendship can occur between the two brethren. When Paul confronted Peter for heeding the legalistic, Judaizing sentiments (Gal. 2:11), Peter confessed his sin, repented, and became very close to Paul (cf. 2 Peter 3:15).

Christians must be deeply concerned about bringing fellow Christians back from sin, when necessary. Smug indifference and self-righteous contempt have no place in the believer's life. Nor should he hide behind cowardice or false humility at the expense of not confronting a brother or sister. Instead, his overriding concern must be the spiritual welfare of the sinning Christian, the purity and integrity of the church, and the honor and glory of God—and that might mean reproving another from time to time.

ASK YOURSELF

Have you ever taken the courageous initiative to confront a brother or sister, concerned about the danger that a sinful habit, a deliberate offense, or a potential blind spot was threatening to unleash on them and others? What did you learn from this experience?

THE RETREAT FROM REPROOF

Go and show him his fault in private. —MATT. 18:15*b*

There have been excesses during the history of the church in overemphasizing the preaching of hell and damnation. But that is not the problem in the contemporary church. Even in the late nineteenth century, many churches drifted away from preaching on the holiness of God and His demand that saints be holy too. Now the majority of evangelical churches and organizations almost exclusively emphasize preaching the love of God, with little or no mention of His wrath and judgment.

Embracing that sort of emphasis in which God is all love and no wrath, all grace and no justice, all tolerant forgiveness and no condemnation, is man-centered and idolatrous. This approach also emasculates the gospel and hinders rather than promotes genuine discipleship, which always includes reproving of sin as necessary. Underlying this emphasis has also been a stress on self-esteem, self-acceptance, and the meeting of personal felt needs—and that can include teaching on health, wealth, and worldly success for all believers.

But Jesus repeatedly proclaimed that He came to earth only to accomplish His Father's will (e.g., John 5:19; 6:38; 7:16). And we can reduce that will to a single declaration, quoted by the apostle Peter, "You shall be holy, for I am holy" (1 Peter 1:16; cf. Lev. 20:7). Above all, the Father and the Son, with the Spirit's full support, want Christians to be holy. Believers promote this command when, with humility and according to Scripture, they reprove other church members who persist in sin.

ASK YOURSELF

Some may fear that an emphasis on discipline in the church will create a harsh, heavy-handed environment that drives people away, deeper into their sins. What are the important heart motives that need to be in place to ensure that grace and mercy are always part of the process?

A Willingness to Reprove, Part 1

Go and show him his fault in private. —Matt. 18:15*b*

The first necessary requirement in reproving a sinning believer is that of a general willingness to undertake the task. God does not mock us by demanding us to do something that He does not enable us to accomplish. Thus as believers we have no excuse for being unwilling to go to a brother or sister with discipline, because He will give us the necessary wisdom and boldness when we are sincerely willing.

God has commanded every believer to confront church members who are sinning. In today's church it's a ministry that's much needed but often neglected. When mature believers reprove their brethren with gentleness and humility, God can use them as effective tools to purify His church and restore His fallen children.

Unwillingness to reprove someone else in the church shows we do not love him enough to warn him of his spiritual jeopardy. Refusal to deal with such brethren can be worse than slandering them (cf. Lev. 19:16–17). Unlike slander, which mainly hurts another's reputation temporarily, not helping one turn from sin contributes to his spiritual downfall. The Christian who's unwilling to reprove a brother or sister is not only unloving and uncaring, but deceived about his duty. The truly loving believer, like his loving Father, desires the proper discipline of those he loves (see Heb. 12:5–11). So-called love that tolerates sin is not love at all but mere human sentimentality.

ASK YOURSELF

Can you think of a time when the Spirit gave you a particular burden for someone whose sin was beginning to wreak a destructive path through their lives—but you gave in to fear, afraid of coming off as judgmental? Have you ever wished you'd been obedient to your first inclination?

OCTOBER 9

A WILLINGNESS TO REPROVE, PART 2

Go and show him his fault in private. —MATT. 18:15*b*

A second requirement that accompanies willingness to reprove is righteous zeal. When Christ observed the Jewish leaders and the money-changers defiling God's house with their commercialism, "He made a scourge of cords, and drove them all out of the temple, with the sheep and the oxen; and He poured out the coins of the money changers and overturned their tables; and to those who were selling the doves He said, 'Take these things away; stop making My Father's house a place of business'" (John 2:15–16). Jesus' holy zeal to purify the Father's house (cf. Ps. 69:9) would not allow Him to allow God's name to be dishonored.

A third requirement attending the willingness to perform biblical church discipline is personal purity. Without that, a Christian will have no desire to protect the purity of the church's members. His concern about the sins of other brethren might be strong, but it will merely be censorious if not joined with a true concern to avoid sin himself. To this attitude Jesus said,

> Why do you look at the speck that is in your brother's eye, but do not notice the log that is in your own eye? Or how can you say to your brother, "Let me take the speck out of your eye," and behold, the log is in your own eye? You hypocrite, first take the log out of your own eye, and then you will see clearly to take the speck out of your brother's eye. (Matt. 7:3–5)

We can become ministers of holiness as we zealously pursue personal and corporate purity in the church.

ASK YOURSELF

How is the "nobody's perfect" mentality used as an excuse for never speaking up—even in caring, brotherly love—to address the sin in another's life? How do you feel this pressure the strongest? What parts of this reluctance are the direct result of the enemy's deceptions?

THE PURPOSE OF DISCIPLINE

If he listens to you, you have won your brother. —MATT. 18:15c

The purpose of church discipline is not to expel people from the church or encourage the self-righteousness of those administering it. Rather, discipline is to restore the sinning brother or sister (cf. Prov. 11:30). Paul instructs us, "Brethren, even if anyone is caught in any trespass, you who are spiritual, restore such a one in a spirit of gentleness; each one looking to yourself, so that you too will not be tempted" (Gal. 6:1). In certain cases, we may be confronting someone who is not actually saved (see James 5:19–20). Therefore, discipline can lead to someone realizing his lost condition and desiring true conversion.

Here Jesus uses "won," originally a commercial term, to refer to regaining something of value, namely, a sinning brother. As we have seen in recent looks at the parable of the lost sheep and the Lord's statement that He does not want "one of these little ones to perish" (Matt. 18:14), He is not satisfied if even one of His children strays or suffers harm.

When a church member gets entrenched in sin, the entire fellowship and each other member suffers loss—no one believer is reproducible. Each is unique and uniquely gifted. If we go to great lengths to recover lost wealth and possessions, how much more effort should we expend to regain a spiritual treasure—a fellow believer in church—who is more valuable than any earthly riches?

ASK YOURSELF

What could help you rediscover the great value in each person who calls your church home or claims the name of Christ? How have you let yourself lose appreciation for the worth and contributions of others? What kinds of blessing does this attitude cause you to forfeit?

CHURCH DISCIPLINE, SECOND STEP

But if he does not listen to you, take one or two more with you, so that by the mouth of two or three witnesses every fact may be confirmed. —MATT. 18:16

If the sinning church member does not respond to reproof from a single believer, the second step of discipline is to "take one or two more" believers and confront the errant member again. Moses originally established the fundamental procedure (Deut. 19:15) for verifying and corroborating the facts in a dispute or concerning an allegation of wrongdoing. This therefore was not a novel concept for Jesus' hearers. To guard against someone's being falsely charged with a crime or sin is an important safeguard against a wrongful accusation of an innocent person.

If the testimony of several witnesses becomes necessary, it will not only confirm that a sin was committed, but that the sinning believer was properly rebuked and whether or not he has repented. When we take one or two witnesses with us, we hope that this added behind-the-scenes confrontation will preclude the next step of presentation before the whole church. This second-stage rebuke should induce a change of heart in the offender that the initial reproof did not.

These built-in, biblical protections against abuse or unjust indictment are to protect church leaders as well as other congregants. Paul warned Timothy, "Do not receive an accusation against an elder except on the basis of two or three witnesses. Those who continue in sin, rebuke in the presence of all, so that the rest also will be fearful of sinning" (1 Tim. 5:19–20). Believers, high-ranking or low-ranking, deserve a God-honoring fairness and balance in the process of discipline.

ASK YOURSELF

Those who dismiss the notion of church discipline would perhaps be surprised that Jesus' instructions are actually as patient and multi-layered as they are. What does it tell you about our Lord to know He calls us to continue seeking the welfare of a straying brother or sister?

Church Discipline, Third Step

If he refuses to listen to them, tell it to the church. —Matt. 18:17a

If the second stage of church discipline fails to produce repentance from the sinning member, then the two or three witnesses must bring the matter before the entire church. The first two steps are to be private or semiprivate, but this step is to be public, with all church members eligible to be present. The straying member should be brought before the entire congregation to receive further reproof and encouragement to repent. All members who know the person must accept the task to call the man or woman back to holiness.

The custom in our church in Southern California has been, upon taking this third step, to encourage members of the congregation who know the person to pursue him and aggressively but lovingly plead with him to repent and avoid having to face the final step of discipline.

Jesus indicates here that the place for discipline is *within* the church. The familiar word for church, *ekklesia*, occurs here with its basic meaning of congregation or assembly. From the context it's clear that our Lord has in mind any local group of redeemed people who assemble in His name.

Such an understanding of "church" removes any justification for believers to take church discipline or any grievances between saints to a secular court. Paul asked the Corinthians, "Does any one of you, when he has a case against his neighbor, dare to go to law before the unrighteous and not before the saints?" (1 Cor. 6:1; cf. vv. 2–3). Only believers, no matter in a large church or small, can biblically administer proper discipline at this or any stage.

ASK YOURSELF

Jesus calls us to go to great lengths to avoid embarrassing those who are failing to live up to their calling or are rebelling against all they know to be right. How is even this third phase of discipline driven by a desire to protect the offender from experiencing any more shame?

CHURCH DISCIPLINE, FOURTH STEP

If he refuses to listen even to the church, let him be to you as a Gentile and a tax collector. —MATT. 18:17*b*

The fourth step in church discipline is ostracism. If a sinning believer won't listen to the church, the congregation must banish the person from the fellowship and treat him "as a Gentile and a tax collector." Both groups were considered despised outcasts by the Jews of that day. "Gentile" mainly referred to non-Jews who practiced their traditional paganism and were not part of the worship and social life of the Jews. But the Jewish "tax collector" was more hated than a Gentile because he was an outcast by choice, being a traitor to his people.

Christ here is not teaching prejudice toward non-Jews. He came to save all kinds of people—some of His most noted followers (Matthew and Zaccheus) were former tax collectors. And notable Gentiles (the centurion whose servant was healed) also believed. The point with church discipline is that any believer who persists in sin must be expelled and treated as an unbelieving outsider.

Stubbornly unrepentant church members, who resist all attempts at discipline, must be completely excluded from the blessedness of the assembly's company and encouragement. Such people willingly reject gospel standards, and like Hymenaeus and Alexander they shipwreck their faith. Paul "handed [them] over to Satan, so that they will be taught not to blaspheme" (1 Tim. 1:20; cf. 1 Cor. 5:4–6). We can do no other than urge those people to repent and be restored to fellowship, or to let them go in their impenitent sin over to the world and the devil.

ASK YOURSELF

This is indeed a hard teaching. It goes against our modern sensitivities. But what have we forgotten about what sin really means and what it costs? How much of our sensitivity have we lost concerning the evil of sin and the grave affront it is to God's holy nature?

FINAL DISCIPLINE NOT OPTIONAL

If he refuses to listen even to the church, let him be
to you as a Gentile and a tax collector. —MATT. 18:17b

The church has no option but to enact final discipline when the situation calls for it. Jesus commands it ("let him be" is imperative) and Paul ordered the Thessalonians to "keep away from every brother who leads an unruly life and not according to the tradition which you received from us" (2 Thess. 3:6). Then he admonishes them, "If anyone does not obey our instruction in this letter, take special note of that person and do not associate with him, so that he will be put to shame" (v. 14).

When we have done our scriptural best to restore the offender, but he has not responded, that person must be left to his sin and shame. If he genuinely believes, the Lord will not cast him away, though He might have to allow him to sink deeper into sin before returning.

The discipline process should continue until the person repents or dies. The purpose of putting the brother out is to protect the fellowship's purity and testify to the watching world. And for the offender himself, the purpose of exclusion is not simply to punish but awaken; therefore we must act with love and humility. Paul declares, "Yet do not regard him as an enemy, but admonish him as a brother" (v. 15).

Not to have fellowship with an unrepentant brother or sister does not exclude all contact. Opportunities to admonish or call back ought to be taken and even sought. But the sole purpose of these should be further admonishment.

ASK YOURSELF

What are some specific examples of what it would cost a person to be outside the fellowship of a church? By thinking through this unpleasant list, consider the flip side—what a blessing these allegiances are to those who enjoy and add to the privilege of church membership.

THE AUTHORITY FOR DISCIPLINE, PART 1

Truly I say to you, whatever you bind on earth shall have been bound in heaven;
and whatever you loose on earth shall have been loosed in heaven. . . . For where
two or three have gathered together in My name, I am there in their midst.
—MATT. 18:18, 20

Church discipline should always be done with the utmost of care. Undertaken in the wrong manner or with the wrong attitude, it can do much damage by fostering legalism or self-righteousness. On the other hand, discipline left undone can cause much damage to members by letting sin's effect spread like leaven throughout the congregation.

Some charismatics have seriously misinterpreted this passage and used it (along with ones such as Matt. 7:7 and 21:22) to claim every imaginable blessing and privilege. But in the larger context of Matthew 18, familiar rabbinical expressions, and the text's grammar, Jesus is not teaching that we can bend God's power to serve human will. Neither is the Lord saying we can force heaven to do anything. On the contrary, He promises that when believers conform their wills to His, He will endorse and empower their act of obedience.

This passage continues Jesus' instruction on church discipline and provides a basis for such actions. If it is not speaking about asking God for special blessings or privileges, the verses certainly do not teach that church members in and of themselves have power to absolve the sins of fellow members. Christ simply sets forth that the church has divine authority to discipline members who won't repent of ongoing sin.

ASK YOURSELF

Certainly nothing good comes from being outside the will of God or seeking Him to endorse our every whim and inclination. What area of your life would you confess is not being lived in accordance with His Word, causing you to forsake both the power and beauty of holiness?

THE AUTHORITY FOR DISCIPLINE, PART 2

Truly I say to you, whatever you bind on earth shall have been bound in heaven;
and whatever you loose on earth shall have been loosed in heaven. . . . For where
two or three have gathered together in My name, I am there in their midst.
—MATT. 18:18, 20

The rabbinical phrases "bound in heaven" and "loosed in heaven" indicate that something is forbidden or permitted by God's revealed and inspired Scriptures. Jesus' listeners would have understood that people
—and believers in particular—could not bend heaven's (God's) will to
their own, but that the Father had a specific principle with which the
church must conform.

The expressions "shall have been bound" and "shall have been loosed"
are future perfect passives in the original, with the idea that God is not
compelled to adhere to the church's verdict on discipline, but that when it
follows Jesus' directives it conforms its decisions to what God has already
done and receives His approval and authority (see also John 20:23).

When a person genuinely trusts Jesus Christ as Lord and Savior, we
in the church can confidently pronounce his sins forgiven because he has
met the divine criterion for forgiveness, namely saving trust in Christ.
However, if one refuses to acknowledge Him as Lord and Savior, we can
declare with equal confidence that his sins are *not* forgiven because he has
rejected the basic criterion for forgiveness.

Church discipline is serious business—something not to be approached with carnal eagerness. Saints must ask, "Who are we to do such
work and by what authority do we, as fellow sinners, do it?" Only when
we discipline according to Jesus' standards can we have perfect confidence that we're acting according to His power and authority.

ASK YOURSELF

The ability to see and declare things with spiritual confidence implies a
living understanding of the Word of God. What are one or two matters
of biblical principle you've learned in recent days as God by His Spirit
has illlumined the pages of Scripture to direct your thinking?

THE AUTHORITY FOR DISCIPLINE, PART 3

Truly I say to you, whatever you bind on earth shall have been bound in heaven;
and whatever you loose on earth shall have been loosed in heaven. . . . For where
two or three have gathered together in My name, I am there in their midst.
—MATT. 18:18, 20

When Christians sincerely seek through discipline to purify the church, they receive the needed energy, authority, and approval from above to carry it out.

Christ also assures us that He acts with us in all efforts to rightly purify the church—"where two or three have gathered together in My name, I am there in their midst." The context here demands that there be two or three witnesses to the discipline process. To invoke God's name for a task is not merely to utter His name but to ask and work according to His will and character. If we have gathered in His name to culminate discipline, we have faithfully performed our work—on the Lord's behalf—of verifying the penitence or impenitence of the offending person.

Dietrich Bonhoeffer offers these insights:

> Since the confession of sin is made in the presence of a Christian brother, the last stronghold of self-justification is abandoned. The sinner surrenders; he gives up all his evil. He gives his heart to God, and he finds the forgiveness of all his sin in the fellowship of Jesus Christ and his brother. The expressed, acknowledged sin has lost all its power. . . . It can no longer tear the fellowship asunder. Now the fellowship bears the sin of the brother. He is no longer alone with his evil for he has cast off his sin from him. Now he stands in the fellowship of sinners who live by the grace of God and the cross of Jesus Christ.

ASK YOURSELF

What are some of the great benefits of joining with other believers in matters of prayer, counsel, friendship, or any number of interactions? How are you making the most of God's desire to keep us connected and caring for each other, working together for His kingdom's sake?

Peter's Inquiry about Forgiveness

Then Peter came and said to Him, "Lord, how often shall my brother sin against me and I forgive him? Up to seven times?" —Matt. 18:21

In view of Jesus' teaching about church discipline, Peter here wonders how many times believers are obligated to forgive brethren who persist in transgression. How many times should they be allowed to repent and rejoin the fellowship?

To his credit, Peter personalized his Lord's instruction, and his primary concern about his own responsibility prompted the asking of this pertinent question.

Peter had a real penchant for asking questions. He always wanted to be sure he understood the implications of Christ's words and deeds, and thus he elicited much wonderful teaching from our Savior. God approves of genuine questions because He blesses those who truly seek to know Him and His truth. Jeremiah recorded this divine insight: "You will seek Me and find Me when you search for Me with all your heart" (Jer. 29:13).

Likely with magnanimous thoughts of himself, Peter suggests a limit of seven as the number of times a person ought to be forgiven and restored. Seven is more than twice the number allowed by rabbinical tradition (three; see Amos 1:3, 6, 9, 11, 13), which was made into a universal rule for limiting both God's times of forgiveness and His people's. The Jews had illogically reasoned that it is presumptuous for people to forgive one another more than three times, if that was God's limit.

Peter no doubt believed Jesus would be impressed with his generous suggestion of seven, which reflected his growing comprehension of his Lord's instruction and personal example regarding compassion and mercy.

ASK YOURSELF

When confronted with a challenging lesson from Scripture, are you more likely to apply its consequences and responsibilities to others than to yourself? In what ways do you need to look first to your own compliance before concerning yourself with what someone else is or isn't doing?

THE EXTENT OF FORGIVENESS

Jesus said to him, "I do not say to you, up to seven times,
*but up to seventy times seven." —*MATT. 18:22

Peter's question indicated his thoughts were much like the Jewish leaders or any other fallen person was inclined to think. His ideas on forgiveness were in the measurable, limited terms of the law rather than the
immeasurable, unlimited terms of grace.

But Jesus' answer here is not merely extending the legal limits of forgiveness—certainly not the bare number 490. His illustration simply indicates a number that, practically speaking, is beyond counting. Keeping
strict accounts is not considered, and neither is it by a believer with a sincere heart of forgiveness. That person forgives the thousandth offense as
readily as the first, because that's how God forgives him.

Jesus' statement may have been an allusion to Lamech's boast that
"if Cain is avenged sevenfold, then Lamech seventy-sevenfold" (Gen.
4:24). Sinful people always want to return evil for evil without limit. But
our Lord said to return good for evil without limit.

On another occasion, Jesus said even if a brother "sins against you
seven times a day, and returns to you seven times, saying, 'I repent,' forgive him" (Luke 17:4). This refers not to some daily forgiveness limit,
but to regular sinning committed many times daily, day after day, and the
corresponding forgiveness. The mature believer will never let his own
forgiveness be surpassed by a brother's sin. When callous sin against him
increases, so does his gracious forgiveness—which reflects the divine nature (cf. Rom. 5:20; Eph. 4:32).

ASK YOURSELF

Perhaps you struggle with a sin that, as much as you hate to admit it, has
been known to trip you up on a daily, sometimes hourly basis. Without
giving yourself permission to continue in disobedience, what does it
mean to you that your Lord and Savior's forgiveness is unlimited?

THE EXAMPLE OF FORGIVENESS, PART 1

The kingdom of heaven may be compared to a king who wished to settle accounts with his slaves. When he had begun to settle them, one who owed him ten thousand talents was brought to him.
—MATT. 18:23–24

The immeasurable, unpayable debt in this parable symbolizes the huge debt of sin that every person owes God. When the Holy Spirit convicts someone of his sin (John 16:8), that man or woman realizes their sin is beyond comprehension and humanly impossible to pay for. Like Paul, every convicted sinner sees the utter sinfulness of sin (Rom. 7:13). It is such a realization that caused Job to "repent in dust and ashes" (Job 42:6). Similarly, it is what caused Ezra, on behalf of himself and his countrymen, to pray, "O my God, I am ashamed and embarrassed to lift up my face to You, my God, for our iniquities have risen above our heads and our guilt has grown even to the heavens" (Ezra 9:6).

Unbelievers take life from God, but rather than living as wise stewards who invest the gifts of life for His glory, they squander everything on themselves. They're like the prodigal son (Luke 15:11–24) or the slave who buried his talent (Matt. 25:18, 24–30). Both of these wasted their "gospel privilege" from the Lord.

As much harm as sin does to humanity, every sin ever committed is primarily against God (Ps. 51:4) and an offense before His heavenly throne.

The slave here is any unbeliever who knows about God (Rom. 1:18 ff.), has life from Him (Acts 17:25), but wastes the opportunity to repay God His due and instead squanders it in sin—thus manifesting his dire need for forgiveness.

ASK YOURSELF

It is not wholly inaccurate (though an extreme underestimation) to consider your sins like a bill in the mail, calling for full and immediate payment of your mortgage. Consider again today the desperation of your sin load, contrasted against God's all-sufficient forgiveness.

THE EXAMPLE OF FORGIVENESS, PART 2

But since he did not have the means to repay, his lord commanded him to be sold, along with his wife and children and all that he had, and repayment to be made. So the slave fell to the ground and prostrated himself before him, saying, "Have patience with me and I will repay you everything." —MATT. 18:25–26

The king in this parable has been gracious simply by not demanding an accounting earlier. In an infinitely greater way, God extends common grace to the most hardened sinner by allowing him to go on living—perhaps the greatest gesture of divine mercy. But there is coming a day in the life of every person when he must account for his life. This is not final judgment but a time of conviction when all persons must face their sins and their need for repentance. It is a time when they hear the gospel or a Bible passage, or a personal testimony.

Like the slave here, they realize they must give an account, that their guilt is inexcusable, and that the king (God) is good and right. The slave's falling down and prostrating himself was more than the normal homage rendered to a monarch. It was an act of total submission in which he threw himself completely at the king's mercy.

Likewise, every sinner should be as overwhelmed by his sin as the slave was by his debt. Sinners convicted by the Spirit will realize their only hope is to humbly confess sin and throw themselves on God's mercy in Christ (see Luke 18:13). The slave realized he could never repay his debt, which prompted his plea, "have patience with me," and his unrealistic promise, "I will repay you everything." His understanding was flawed but his attitude right. As it were, he sensed the need of forgiveness and the chance to make good on his debt.

ASK YOURSELF

What are some of the times in your life when radical measures were the only way to sum up the situation, the only way to have any hope of getting the help you needed? Why does God demand that we often take radical steps? Are there any you need to take right now?

THE EXAMPLE OF FORGIVENESS, PART 3

The lord of that slave felt compassion and released him and forgave him the debt.
—MATT. 18:27

Jesus here presents an extraordinary portrait of the Father's compassionate love for the genuinely repentant sinner. The slave asks only for patience so he can repay his debt, but instead the king lets him go and forgives him the entire amount. That's what God does with the sin debt of those who confess their need, repent, and receive redemption. (The parable does not depict every aspect of salvation. Since Jesus wanted to illustrate forgiveness between believers, the story simply depicts a man with an unpayable debt who seeks and receives abundant mercy.)

Not until the prodigal son reached the bottom of his wretched lifestyle did he face up to his wicked foolishness (Luke 15:11–24). He had forsaken his family and lived a debauched life in a pagan land. When his money ran out, the only work the young man could find was slopping hogs, a most demeaning task for a Jew. The son then came to his senses and said, "How many of my father's hired men have more than enough bread, but I am dying here with hunger!" (v. 17). He then vowed to confess his sin to his father and return home. But even before the son reached home his father embraced him with forgiveness, had a celebration for him, and declared, "This son of mine was dead and has come to life again; he was lost and has been found" (v. 24).

In a far greater way, Christ was humiliated in His incarnation and lovingly "endured the cross, despising the shame" (Heb. 12:2) to redeem us.

ASK YOURSELF

Is there someone in your life who has come to you seeking forgiveness, but instead of lavishing it on them as your Father has done, you either gave it grudgingly or perhaps inwardly refused to do so? What is keeping you from granting forgiveness to this person . . . and why?

THE EXAMPLE OF FORGIVENESS, PART 4

That slave went out and found one of his fellow slaves who owed him a hundred denarii; and he seized him and began to choke him, saying, "Pay back what you owe." So his fellow slave fell to the ground and began to plead with him, saying, "Have patience with me and I will repay you." But he was unwilling and went and threw him in prison until he should pay back what was owed.
—MATT. 18:28–30

Sins against others are not insignificant but they are minute compared to the offenses against God for which He has freely forgiven us.

That sinful flesh still influences saints is seen in the first slave's hardheartedness against his fellow slave. The first man was much closer to his fellow slave than to the king, and the amount the king forgave him was hugely greater than the small amount he refused to forgive. Those realities should have made the first slave not only especially grateful but especially merciful. Obviously he is not merciful, but instead presumptuous and callous toward his fellow servant.

This unforgiving behavior is morally unthinkable, bizarre, and irrational. For believers to refuse to forgive one another is completely unacceptable. Yet Scripture, history, and personal experience show us this is the way believers sometimes treat each other. This parable is an unflattering illustration of the sin that still resides in every Christian disciple and causes much damage and conflict within the church. Although they have been completely and eternally forgiven, based on God's grace and trust in Christ's atoning work, believers often behave as if they have been forgiven because of their own merit. They might even look down on brothers and sisters with disdain and a sense of superiority, which does not in any way exemplify forgiveness.

ASK YOURSELF

Have you in any way accepted God's forgiveness as being even partially earned by your own good behavior? Turn your heart to the truth of the matter, that all you have been given is all of grace.

THE EXAMPLE OF FORGIVENESS, PART 5

When his fellow slaves saw what had happened, they were deeply grieved and came and reported to their lord all that had happened. Then summoning him, his lord said to him, "You wicked slave, I forgave you all that debt because you pleaded with me. Should you not also have had mercy on your fellow slave, in the same way that I had mercy on you?" —MATT. 18:31–33

Believers should be "deeply grieved" when another Christian is unforgiving. That rigidity of heart not only tends to drive the sinning believer deeper into sin, it can also create dissension and division within the church, taint its testimony, and deeply grieve our Lord Himself.

The other slaves' going to the king with the dreadful account of an unforgiving attitude offers us interesting insight into what the parable says about the Christian's duty to carry out discipline against a sinning brother, *and* the need, as necessary, to ask God to punish and remove the ungracious fellow believer.

The king is rightly incensed when hearing the news of the first slave's attitude, and properly calls him "wicked" because the slave allowed remaining sin to control his thoughts and deeds. Unforgiveness is much more sinful in a believer because that brother or sister is infinitely more capable of forgiving than is the person who has never experienced divine grace. How can someone receive God's mercy for the unpayable debt of sin and then not forgive another's small offense against him?

The king here does not expect the first slave to give his fellow slave an opportunity to repay the debt, but he did expect him to extend mercy and graciously forgive the man's entire debt—even as the king had done with the first slave's massive debt. The principle of Ephesians 4:32 applies: "Be kind to one another, tender-hearted, forgiving each other, just as God in Christ also has forgiven you."

ASK YOURSELF

Perhaps with some holy imagination, you could think of an opportunity to extend lavish mercy and blessing on another person who deserves none of it. How might such an encounter take place?

THE EXAMPLE OF FORGIVENESS, PART 6

His lord, moved with anger, handed him over to the torturers until he should repay all that was owed him. My heavenly Father will also do the same to you, if each of you does not forgive his brother from your heart. —MATT. 18:34–35

The Lord does not discipline His children out of hatred but out of love: "For those whom the Lord loves He disciplines, and He scourges every son whom He receives" (Heb. 12:6). God does this only to bring them back to Himself and His righteousness—"He disciplines us for our good, so that we may share His holiness" (v. 10). Thus every believer experiences God's chastening occasionally because every one deserves it from time to time. And it's only natural that His "discipline for the moment seems not to be joyful, but sorrowful; yet to those who have been trained by it, afterwards it yields the peaceful fruit of righteousness" (v. 11).

When we forget God's rich forgiveness to us and refuse to forgive fellow believers, Christ places us under such "torturers" (the word referred to inquisitors)—stress, hardship, pressure, or other tribulations—until we confess our sin and receive forgiveness. James warns us, "Judgment will be merciless to one who has shown no mercy" (James 2:13).

Christ is *not* teaching here of our receiving a forgiveness that brings salvation, as if God saves only those who are forgiving. That would be a form of works righteousness. But He *is* referring to saints' forgiving one another after experiencing God's free grace. Believers will—and surely ought to—display the redeemed and transformed life by having a forgiving attitude toward others (see Matt. 6:14–15). However, there will always be times when Christians will fall into the sin of unforgiveness, and this entire teaching is for those times.

ASK YOURSELF

What are some of the "torturers" that can show up in the life of an unforgiving person, causing him loss and unnecessary pain? How have you experienced some of these unpleasantries in your own life? How did God use them to draw you back into conformity with His Word?

FORGIVENESS OF ONE ANOTHER, PART 1

. . . if each of you does not forgive his brother from your heart. —MATT. 18:35*b*

Christians' forgiveness of each other is not as powerful as God's, which permanently absolves believers from sin and continually cleanses their hearts from daily iniquity. However, their forgiveness of each other must reflect these two kinds of forgiveness. They must possess an internal, all-encompassing attitude that is ready to forgive in advance, before the sin is known or the other person requests forgiveness. That spirit is unchanging and reflects love from God that "covers a multitude of sins" (1 Peter 4:8). If the offending believer repents, the other believer then offers relational forgiveness and God restores the broken relationship.

Disciples of Christ should be identified as forgiving people, because they've been forgiven as no other group. If they refuse to forgive other believers, they deny their redeemed nature and sever themselves from God's relational forgiveness that cleanses them from ongoing sins. They thereby forfeit inner peace, power, and sanctification that only a strong relationship with Jesus Christ can produce.

An anonymous saint once wrote many years ago, "Forgiveness is the image of God, the forgiving Father, and an advancement of Christ's kingdom in the world." The Beatitudes tell us, "Blessed are the merciful, for they shall receive mercy" (Matt. 5:7). If we desire mercy and blessing from Christ for our repeated sins against Him, we must have a heartfelt willingness to forgive fellow saints even for repeated sins against us. Then we can genuinely and confidently ask God to "forgive us our debts, as we also have forgiven our debtors" (6:12).

ASK YOURSELF

What does forgiveness "from your heart" entail? Can genuine forgiveness ever occur in any other way? What is set in motion (or allowed to continue) when a form of forgiveness is given that is less than authentic, less than wholehearted, less than the measure of God's grace?

FORGIVENESS OF ONE ANOTHER, PART 2

. . . if each of you does not forgive his brother from your heart. —MATT. 18:35b

True heart forgiveness is a trusting forgiveness, one that views the offending brother exactly as if he hadn't sinned. Even though sin against God, the church, and individual brethren can produce long-lasting hurt, the restoration process can be characterized by generosity and trust. If the sin was theft, we can again entrust the offender with something precious. If the sin was shirked responsibility, we can give him or her other important tasks to do. If slander was involved, we can again entrust them with our reputation—we will again fully love and trust one another.

The genuinely forgiving person will not dwell on an offense, but there can be reminders beyond his control that he can't forget. And real forgiveness will not merely excuse an offense—sin is always sin and we should never seek to dismiss it. However, true forgiveness will terminate bitterness, anger, and resentment that only exacerbate the sin rather than remove it.

Again, the sort of forgiveness we have discussed is impossible in our own strength. It is a supernatural trait and is possible only through the power of the indwelling Holy Spirit. Only as a believer walks by the Spirit is he able to "not carry out the desire of the flesh," which can include holding a grudge rather than forgiving (see Gal. 5:16–21). "But the fruit of the Spirit is love, joy, peace, patience, kindness, goodness, faithfulness, gentleness, self-control; against such things there is no law" (vv. 22–23). If we have such spiritual fruit, we will also have a constant attitude of mutual forgiveness (cf. vv. 24–26).

ASK YOURSELF

Should we treat continual sins any differently from one-time errors of the past? What kind of character is called on when forgiveness is not a single occurrence based on a former act but rather a heart attitude that must be repeatedly employed to deal with ongoing offenses?

JESUS DISCIPLING IN GALILEE

After these things Jesus was walking in Galilee, for He was unwilling to walk in Judea because the Jews were seeking to kill Him. —JOHN 7:1

The apostle John recorded nothing specific about Jesus' activities during the interval denoted by "after these things" (six months from Passover in April, 6:4, to the Feast of Tabernacles in October, 7:2) other than He "was walking in Galilee"—no doubt traveling and ministering (see Mark 8:22–26; Matt. 15:32–38; 17:14–18).

Jesus spent most of the interval, however, extensively discipling the apostles. That He spent only two days with the large crowd of John 6 but six months with His men demonstrates that our Lord's main ministry focus was not on mass meetings but discipleship. He poured His time and energy into the eleven servants (Judas Iscariot fell away; Matthias and Paul were later chosen) who would pick up His ministry legacy when He ascended back to heaven. The true church today is the result of those men who faithfully discipled others, who continued the process down to our day.

Discipleship must be our top priority as well. Jesus didn't commission the church to merely draw in large crowds, but to make disciples as it progressed (Matt. 28:19–20). Paul underscored this in his injunction to pastor Timothy: "The things which you have heard from me in the presence of many witnesses, entrust these to faithful men who will be able to teach others also" (2 Tim. 2:2). God wants us to judge the success of our churches by the depth of their discipleship, not the numerical size of their congregations.

ASK YOURSELF

What have been some of the benefits you've derived from up-close, one-on-one learning that would never have been yours any other way? What is cluttering your life too full to offer discipleship to another person, including your children? How could you change that?

OCTOBER 29

EARTHLY RELATIVES CHALLENGE JESUS

"For no one does anything in secret when he himself seeks to be known publicly. If You do these things, show Yourself to the world." For not even His brothers were believing in Him. —JOHN 7:4–5

Because the Feast of Booths was nearing, and was a mandatory one for Jewish men to attend, Jesus' half brothers (sons of both Mary and Joseph; see Matt. 13:55) assumed He would be going to Judea to celebrate it. They challenged Him to perform public miracles before the many who would be in Jerusalem for the feast. They likely reasoned that Christ's followers from Galilee and Judea would see works showing He was indeed Messiah. And maybe some who had recently abandoned Him would return. The brothers, however, were not eager for Him to show His glory, for they did not even yet believe in Him (v. 5).

Actually, these family detractors may have wanted to see more signs so they could decide for themselves if the works were authentic and credible. Like the crowd (6:14–15), they expected a political Messiah—a messiahship that would center in Jerusalem. If the Jewish leaders approved of Jesus' miracles and identity as Messiah, so would the half brothers.

The brothers' words about private versus public ministry, implying Jesus shouldn't remain secluded in Galilee, show they didn't fully understand His mission. Further, their challenge for Him to reveal Himself to the world simply manifests more skepticism. And the apostle John's footnote, "For not even His brothers were believing," confirms their faithless words. Earlier, they had thought Jesus had lost His mind (Mark 3:21, 31–34). Up to this point, nothing had changed their minds—only the Lord's resurrection would draw them to faith in Him (Acts 1:14).

ASK YOURSELF

Have you ever felt that some large gathering would be the best way for a friend or family member to be changed by a spiritual experience? While this can certainly occur, be praying for something more permanent—a deep-down, very personal encounter with the living God.

JESUS ANSWERS THE CHALLENGE

Jesus said to them, "My time is not yet here, but your time is always opportune. The world cannot hate you, but it hates Me because I testify of it, that its deeds are evil. Go up to the feast yourselves; I do not go up to this feast because My time has not yet fully come." Having said these things to them, He stayed in Galilee.
—JOHN 7:6–9

Our Lord never unveiled Himself before the appropriate time, the precise moment the Father chose (cf. John 2:4). So Jesus would not publicly enter Jerusalem and proclaim Himself to be Messiah until Passover (Luke 19:37–40), at which time that manifestation would lead to His death.

By contrast, Christ's unbelieving brothers knew nothing of God's plans and purposes, and were indifferent to His providence. They could go to the feast at any time because they would face no fatal hostility from the Jewish leaders. However, Jesus reminded His brothers that the world hated Him because of His testimony against it. The devil controls the world (1 John 5:19), hence it is intrinsically evil and sinful.

Besides reasons of divine timing, Jesus chose not to go to Jerusalem for other reasons as well. The probable large, public caravan of people (cf. Luke 2:44) might have invited another forcible attempt to make Him king, or it could have triggered a premature triumphal entry into Jerusalem. Either way, events could have caused His death before the proper time.

When our Lord did lay down His life six months hence, it would be exactly when God predetermined it (John 7:30; 8:20). Jesus would in no way allow his brothers' skepticism to dictate His actions. His sovereign Father orchestrated everything in His time and determined all the Son did.

ASK YOURSELF

Have you ever had to go against others' expectations in order to remain obedient to God's direction for your life? Or do you generally let these kinds of pressures do the dictating, even when it causes you to be less than faithful to God's calling?

THE PROPER TIME

There was much grumbling among the crowds concerning Him; some were say-
ing, "He is a good man"; others were saying, "No, on the contrary, He leads the
people astray." Yet no one was speaking openly of Him for fear of the Jews.
—JOHN 7:12–13

Activities in Jerusalem confirmed the wisdom of Jesus' caution in going there. There was much discussion among the people, revolving around two views of the Lord: "some were saying, 'He is a good man,'" whereas others claimed, "He leads the people astray." But both perceptions were incorrect. A mere good man would not claim to be God (cf. 8:24, 28, 58), and a deceiver would not perform the genuine miracles that Jesus did (10:25, 37–38; 14:10–11).

Tragically, the view that Christ led the people astray was the one most Jews eventually accepted. Although the leaders plainly rejected Him, the Sanhedrin had not officially passed judgment regarding Him. Therefore the masses guarded their words, speaking neither for nor against Him, until an official response came forth.

This passage shows us that Jesus always followed God's timetable perfectly. And He always did the Father's will precisely in line with God's infallible wishes. If we are genuine followers of Christ, we will be able to do the same—because we possess both His Word and Spirit. The Word informs us (Ps. 40:8), and the Holy Spirit enables us to obey with gladness (143:10; cf. 119:111). Unbelievers don't have these capabilities, but nonetheless, any day is right for them to turn to the Lord for salvation (2 Cor. 6:2).

ASK YOURSELF

Failing to act wisely in certain situations may have caused you a world of trouble in the past. Perhaps, in fact, you've lost confidence in your ability to make smart choices. Always remember that the beginning of wisdom is to fear the Lord. What might this lead you to do?

THE SOURCE OF JESUS' KNOWLEDGE

But when it was now in the midst of the feast Jesus went up into the temple,
and began to teach. The Jews then were astonished, saying, "How has this
man become learned, having never been educated?" So Jesus answered them
*and said, "My teaching is not Mine, but His who sent Me." —*JOHN 7:14–16

J esus' sudden appearance during the feast caught the Jewish authorities off guard, thwarting any plans they might have made to seize Him (cf. v. 11). As they listened to Jesus' unequalled teaching, the Jews were astonished: "How has this man become learned, having never been educated?" Their point was that Jesus had received no formal training in the prescribed rabbinic schools. In today's terms, He had not been to seminary or been ordained by any formal ecclesiastical body. Since they could not refute Jesus' teaching, they questioned His credentials—challenging His authority to teach because He lacked an authorized education and the legitimate right to teach.

The Lord's reply was direct and devastating. He "answered them and said, 'My teaching is not Mine, but His who sent Me.'" It is true that His knowledge was not derived from any human institution. But that did not mean it was merely His personal opinion, as the authorities implied. That Jesus' teaching was directly and immediately from God was thus an indictment of the Jewish leaders. By disagreeing with Him, they revealed that their teaching was not from God (8:47).

ASK YOURSELF

How much of what you think you know is based on your own opinions and experiences, rather than on the sure Word of God, the eternal truths of the ages? When was the last time you had your own conclusions shaken by an encounter with God's ultimate truth?

JESUS' SURETY

If anyone is willing to do His will, he will know of the teaching,
whether it is of God or whether I speak from Myself. —JOHN 7:17

Jesus promised the person who honestly seeks the truth revealed by God, the one who is willing to do God's will, that he will know the truth about Christ's teaching, whether it is of God or not. The Lord's challenge to the crowd was simple: if they would humble themselves before God's Word to know and obey it, they would come to a sure realization that His teaching was true. Such confidence comes through the Holy Spirit, who confirms the truth about Christ to the willing heart (1 John 2:20, 27), both internally through His testimony (1 Cor. 2:10–15), and externally, through manifestations that demonstrate the truth of the gospel (John 3:2; 5:36).

Accepting or rejecting the claims of Jesus Christ is never a purely intellectual decision; there are inescapable moral and spiritual implications. Those who willingly seek and obey the truth will find it and will be set free from their slavery to ignorance and sin (John 8:32). But those who reject the truth prove themselves to be children of their "father the devil, [who] want to do the desires of [their] father. He was a murderer from the beginning, and does not stand in the truth because there is no truth in him" (v. 44). Unless they repent, they will share his fate.

ASK YOURSELF

Perhaps there's someone in your life—a spouse, a child, a friend, a coworker—who knows Christ but is just not grasping or living by a particularly clear truth from His Word. Rather than continuing to confront, have you considered praying that the Spirit would do His own convicting?

Jesus' Selflessness

He who speaks from himself seeks his own glory; but He who is seeking the glory
of the One who sent Him, He is true, and there is no unrighteousness in Him.
—John 7:18

There are at least two characteristics of every false teacher and would-be messiah. First, he "speaks from himself"; that is, on his own authority, not God's. And second, he "seeks his own glory," not God's.

Jesus, however, never sought His own glory (cf. John 5:41; 8:50), since He "did not come to be served, but to serve, and to give His life a ransom for many" (Matt. 20:28), for He is "gentle and humble in heart" (Matt. 11:29; cf. 2 Cor. 10:1). False teachers are materialistic, but "the Son of Man [had] nowhere to lay His head" (Luke 9:58). False teachers are self-seeking and demanding, but Jesus stooped to wash the disciples' feet (John 13:4–5)—thus performing a menial task normally reserved for the lowliest slaves.

That Jesus came "seeking the glory of the One who sent Him," instead of glorifying Himself, verified His claim to be the true Messiah, and showed that there was "no unrighteousness in Him." It is not surprising that the Jewish leaders rejected the One who sought God's glory, since they were those who received "glory from one another and . . . [did] not seek the glory that is from the one and only God" (John 5:44).

ASK YOURSELF

Hopefully you know a pastor or church leader who lives out this truth in his own life—being devoted to God's Word and His people at whatever cost to personal reputation, safety, or comfort. Would you encourage his heart by calling or writing to thank him for his example?

JESUS' INDICTMENT OF THE JEWS

"Did not Moses give you the Law, and yet none of you carries out the Law?
Why do you seek to kill Me?" The crowd answered, "You have a demon!
Who seeks to kill You?" —JOHN 7:19–20

Aware of the Jewish authorities' venomous hatred and desire to kill Him (cf. 5:18; 7:1), Jesus pronounced judgment directly on the people with the rhetorical question, "Did not Moses give you the Law"—to which they would, of course, have answered emphatically, "Yes" (cf. Rom. 2:17–20)—"yet none of you carries out the Law?" That was the most accurate statement the Lord could make as to the truth of human sinfulness. No one can keep the Law; that is the reality in every human life.

Our Lord's sentence on them came in His question, "Why do you seek to kill Me?" They prided themselves on being disciples of Moses (John 9:28), yet their treatment of Jesus was an outrage before the God who gave the Law and sent His Son to deliver them from its curse. Specifically, they were seeking to murder the Lord, proving themselves to be blasphemous and unworthy descendants not only of Moses, but also of Abraham (8:40).

The crowd resented His allegation, and accused Him of being possessed by an evil spirit. The sentence of guilt for violating the Law is confirmed by their hatred of the Son of God, who fulfilled the Law blamelessly (Matt. 3:17; Heb. 7:26).

ASK YOURSELF

Has spiritual pride blinded you to any weaknesses in your character? Have you given yourself permission to be disobedient in certain areas because you are so obedient in others? Pray that God would continue His sanctifying work in you, leaving no stone unturned.

JESUS ON SIGNS AND THE SABBATH

Jesus answered them, "I did one deed, and you all marvel. For this reason Moses has given you circumcision (not because it is from Moses, but from the fathers), and on the Sabbath you circumcise a man. If a man receives circumcision on the Sabbath so that the Law of Moses will not be broken, are you angry with Me because I made an entire man well on the Sabbath? Do not judge according to appearance, but judge with righteous judgment." —JOHN 7:21–24

Here Jesus defends His right to heal a sick man by pointing out the Jewish leaders' misinterpretation of the Sabbath regulations. Every male Jewish child was circumcised when he was eight days old (Gen. 17:12; Lev. 12:3). Yet if the eighth day happened to fall on the Sabbath, the Jews would circumcise the baby anyway—despite the injunction in the Law against working on the Sabbath (Ex. 20:10).

Jesus' argument is irrefutable. If the Jews themselves broke the Sabbath law to circumcise children, how could they object to His making an entire man well on the Sabbath?

The Lord's concluding exhortation, "Do not judge according to appearance, but judge with righteous judgment," was both an indictment of their lack of moral and theological discernment and a plea for it. Jesus was urging His hearers to abandon their misconceptions regarding Him and judge His claims with righteous judgment. Those who do so will find Him to be exactly who He claimed to be, just as He promised they would (John 7:17).

ASK YOURSELF

Can you think of an inconsistency in your beliefs or practices? Do you condemn a particular action, yet only up to a point? What are the costs of such hypocrisy in terms of both your testimony as well as freedom of relationship with God? How seriously are you ready to take this?

PROFOUND CONFUSION REGARDING JESUS

*"We know where this man is from; but whenever the Christ may come, no knows
where He is from." Then Jesus cried out in the temple, teaching and saying,
"You both know Me and know where I am from; and I have not come of Myself,
but He who sent Me is true, whom you do not know." —JOHN 7:27–28*

Based on misinterpretations of Isaiah 53:8 and Malachi 3:1, the leaders
believed that the Messiah would be unknown until He suddenly appeared
to redeem Israel. Since they knew Jesus' background (cf. Matt. 13:55–
56), they assumed this meant He could not be the Messiah.

A comparison of the Lord's words, "You both know Me and know
where I am from," with His declaration in 8:19, "You know neither Me
nor My Father," reveals that His comment here was intended as irony.
Jesus was asserting that they did not know Him, saying in effect, "So you
think you know Me and where I am from, do you?"

To counter the leaders' accusation that He was a self-appointed false
prophet, Jesus declared, "I have not come of Myself, but He who sent Me
is true." He had not come on His own, but rather had been sent by the
true God. But to the unbelieving crowd, and more shockingly to the religious leaders, Jesus said, "You do not know [the God you profess]." Despite all their privileges, they were woefully ignorant of the very God
they so proudly claimed to know.

ASK YOURSELF

Along with the joys and comforts of familiarity with God, do you also
know what it's like to be surprised by God? How has He caught you off
guard in recent days and years, amazing you with elements of His
character or His dealings with you that were not what you expected?

PEOPLE DIVIDED REGARDING JESUS

They were seeking to seize Him; and no man laid his hand on Him, because His hour had not yet come. But many of the crowd believed in Him; and they were saying, "When the Christ comes, He will not perform more signs than those which this man has, will He?" The Pharisees heard the crowd muttering these things about Him, and the chief priests and the Pharisees sent officers to seize Him.
—JOHN 7:30–32

Infuriated by what they considered blasphemy, Jesus' enemies "were seeking to seize Him." John says the real reason "no man laid his hand on Him" was "because His hour had not yet come." Jesus always operated according to God's sovereign timetable. Nothing, including impulsive mob violence, could precipitate His death before the appointed hour.

However, "many of the crowd believed in Him." Their rhetorical question, "When the Christ comes, He will not perform more signs than those which this man has, will He?" explains what convinced them of Jesus' authenticity. They could not imagine that the Christ would do more than what Jesus had done (cf. 2:23; 3:2; 6:2).

When "the Pharisees heard the crowd muttering these things" about Jesus, they became alarmed. After consulting with each other, "the chief priests and the Pharisees sent officers to seize Him."

This section illustrates the nation's division over Jesus: some hailed Him as the Messiah, while others sought desperately to silence Him. And the leaders, who should have been the first to recognize His authenticity, led the effort to have Him eliminated.

ASK YOURSELF

Still today, the living Christ continues to generate a response and reaction even from those who claim not to care. Why is Jesus such a lightning rod of opinion? What are His opponents truly saying about Him, even when they are so vocal in their ridicule of Him?

Derisive Contempt of Jesus

Jesus said, "For a little while longer I am with you, then I go to Him who sent Me. You will seek Me, and will not find Me; and where I am, you cannot come." The Jews then said to one another, "Where does this man intend to go that we will not find Him? He is not intending to go to the Dispersion among the Greeks, and teach the Greeks, is He? What is this statement that He said, 'You will seek Me, and will not find Me; and where I am, you cannot come'?" —JOHN 7:33–36

Instead of heeding the Lord's warning, the unbelieving Jews merely ridiculed Him. "Where does this man intend to go that we will not find Him?" they scoffed. "He is not intending to go to the Dispersion among the Greeks, and teach the Greeks, is He?" They found the idea that He would minister to Gentiles to be preposterous. Mockingly, they offered Jesus' statement, "You will seek Me, and will not find Me; and where I am, you cannot come," as support for their derision.

Tragically, these scoffers missed Jesus' point completely. Like Isaiah, who wrote, "Seek the Lord while He may be found; call upon Him while He is near" (Isa. 55:6), Jesus was warning His opponents not to delay conversion until it is too late. Paul wrote, "Behold, now is 'the acceptable time,' behold, now is 'the day of salvation'" (2 Cor. 6:2). If you are unsure of your salvation, don't delay.

ASK YOURSELF

What makes you most certain of your salvation? Despite the devil's propensity for casting doubt, to what do you stake your hopes each day, certain beyond all doubt that this same Jesus has come to rescue you, to deliver you, to conform you to His very character?

JESUS OFFERS SALVATION AT THE FEAST

Now on the last day, the great day of the feast, Jesus stood and cried out, saying,
*"If anyone is thirsty, let him come to Me and drink." —*JOHN 7:37

Drawing on imagery from Isaiah's prophecy (12:3; 55:1), Jesus' reference to salvation as living water would have been familiar to His hearers. In the relatively dry land of Israel, thirst was an appropriate picture of one's need for salvation. By using water to illustrate the truth about Himself, Jesus capitalized on a prominent water ritual that took place on each of the seven days of the feast. It commemorated God's miraculous provision of water during Israel's wilderness wandering (Ex. 17:6).

It was against this backdrop that Jesus made His stunning invitation, "If anyone is thirsty, let him come to Me and drink." Our Lord was inviting thirsty souls to come to Him for spiritual, eternal, life-giving water, instead of the physical, temporal water of the ceremony.

Three key words summarize Jesus' gospel invitation. First, the thirsty ones are those who recognize their spiritual "thirst" (cf. Isa. 55:1; Matt. 5:6). Next, if they are to find relief, such individuals must "come" to Jesus, the only source of living water. But not all who acknowledge their need and approach Him have their thirst quenched. Many are unwilling to take the final step and "drink"; that is, appropriate Him by faith.

Make sure you have thirsted for salvation, have come to Jesus as the source of salvation, and have drunk, or appropriated Him by faith.

ASK YOURSELF

Try your hand at identifying the various thirsts of your life—those things that cause you to feel dry and fatigued without them. How has Jesus satisfied these longings in your heart? Why are His ways of quenching your thirst so far superior to any alternative remedies?

THE HOLY SPIRIT AND SALVATION

"He who believes in Me, as the Scripture said, 'From his innermost being will flow rivers of living water.'" But this He spoke of the Spirit, whom those who believed in Him were to receive; for the Spirit was not yet given, because Jesus was not yet glorified. —JOHN 7:38–39

God did not intend for believers to be ponds in which the living water of salvation stagnates. Believers are to be channels through which the rivers of living water flow to others. By evangelizing the lost and edifying the saints (1 Cor. 12:4–11; 1 Peter 4:10–11), believers allow the spiritual life within them to impact others.

Jesus "spoke of the Spirit," through whom eternal life is imparted to those who believe (John 3:5–8). The Spirit also empowers them to bring the living water of salvation to other thirsty souls (cf. Acts 4:31).

When the Lord spoke, the promise that "those who believed in Him were to receive" the Holy Spirit was still future, "for the Spirit was not yet given, because Jesus was not yet glorified."

Our Lord is not saying the Holy Spirit was not present or active at that time, or in past redemptive history. He was saying there was to come for believers a giving of the Spirit by which unique power would be provided for ministry and evangelism. Since the close of the transitional period in the book of Acts, however, all Christians receive the Holy Spirit at the moment of salvation.

ASK YOURSELF

Perhaps "rivers of living water" would not best describe what you're experiencing right now as you do your best to live for Him. What do you think might be keeping you from partaking of this refreshing flow? Where might the leak be occurring that's crimping your "living water" supply?

RESPONSES TO SALVATION'S OFFER: THE CONVINCED

Some of the people therefore, when they heard these words, were saying,
"This certainly is the Prophet." Others were saying, "This is the Christ."
—JOHN 7:40–41a

When some of the people heard Jesus' gracious words of invitation, they became convinced He was "the Prophet" of whom Moses wrote (Deut. 18:15–18; the correct interpretation). Others viewed him as a forerunner of the Messiah. At the very least, these people viewed Jesus as a great prophet (cf. Matt. 21:11, 46; Mark 6:15; Luke 7:16; 24:19; John 4:19; 6:14; 9:17), possibly even the Messiah. While their knowledge may not have been complete, they were at least convinced that He was sent from God.

Others had a clearer understanding of Jesus' identity and were saying of Him, "This is the Christ." They earlier had been intimidated into silence by fear of the Jewish authorities (7:13; cf. 9:22; 12:42; 19:38; 20:19). But now, having become convinced of Jesus' identity, they boldly proclaimed it. These people were part of the believing remnant of Israel (2 Kings 19:30–31; Isa. 10:20–22); members of the "little flock" (Luke 12:32); those who entered through the narrow gate that leads to eternal life (Matt. 7:13–14); thirsty souls who accepted Christ's invitation, came to Him, and drank of the living water that He provides. In short, the convinced are those who have been saved.

ASK YOURSELF

You just never know who might be convinced of Christ's reality if you were to present Him as the answer to all human questions. Perhaps the biggest question of all is whether or not you're utterly convinced yourself that He is the only way, the only truth, the only life.

Responses to Salvation's Offer: The Contrary

Still others were saying, "Surely the Christ is not going to come from Galilee, is He? Has not the Scripture said that the Christ comes from the descendants of David, and from Bethlehem, the village where David was?" So a division occurred in the crowd because of Him. Some of them wanted to seize Him, but no one laid hands on Him. —John 7:41b–44

Not all were convinced of Jesus' authenticity: "Surely the Christ is not going to come from Galilee, is He?" they scornfully asked. The idea that the Messiah could come from the boondocks of Galilee seemed ludicrous to the sophisticated Judeans (cf. v. 52; 1:46). Besides, they insisted, "Has not the Scripture said that the Christ comes from the descendants of David, and from Bethlehem, the village where David was?"

If the scoffers had examined the facts, they would have discovered that Jesus met both of those qualifications. He was a descendant of David (Matt. 1:1; Luke 1:32), and had been born in Bethlehem (Luke 2:4–7). They hastily assumed that since Jesus had grown up in Nazareth (Matt. 2:21–23; Luke 4:16), He must have been born there. They had no interest in investigating His messianic credentials.

As a result of the differing opinions regarding Jesus, "a division occurred in the crowd." This incident illustrates the truth that Jesus divides people. You are either for Him or against Him; there is no middle ground (Matt. 12:30).

ASK YOURSELF

If you could summarize what most people today think of Jesus, what would be the top entries on your list? How do these miss the mark of what the Bible actually tells us about Him, not to mention what you have come to learn of Him by actually being indwelt by His Spirit?

RESPONSES TO SALVATION'S OFFER: THE CONFUSED

*The officers then came to the chief priests and Pharisees, and they said to them,
"Why did you not bring Him?" The officers answered, "Never has a man spoken
the way this man speaks." The Pharisees then answered them, "You have not
also been led astray, have you? No one of the rulers or Pharisees has believed in
Him, has he? But this crowd which does not know the Law is accursed."*
—JOHN 7:45–49

The officers of the temple police had been sent several days earlier by
the chief priests and Pharisees to arrest Jesus (v. 32). When they returned
empty-handed, their superiors demanded, "Why did you not bring
Him?" They expressed confusion and amazement, answering, "Never
has a man spoken the way this man speaks." These men were religiously
trained Levites, yet Jesus' words left them stunned. While they did not
accept Him as the Messiah, neither did they openly reject Him. They did
not know what to do with Him. Caught between the power and grace of
His message and the hatred of their leaders, they were paralyzed into in-
decision and inactivity.

Infuriated at the officers' failure to arrest Jesus, the Pharisees chided
the officers not for their lack of professionalism (as police officers), but
for their alleged lack of religious discernment (as Levites). They accused
them of naively being duped by a religious charlatan.

In contrast, the Pharisees viewed themselves as the spiritual elite, men
who were above the possibility of being wrong about religious matters.

ASK YOURSELF

What does it tell you about Jesus' courage and confidence—not to
mention His boundless patience—to know that He remains true to
Himself no matter what others may say or do about Him? How deeply
do you desire to have the same kind of unflappable assurance?

RESPONSES TO SALVATION'S OFFER:
THE CONTEMPLATIVE

Nicodemus (he who came to Him before, being one of them) said to them, "Our Law does not judge a man unless it first hears from him and knows what he is doing, does it?" They answered him, "You are not also from Galilee, are you? Search, and see that no prophet arises out of Galilee." —JOHN 7:50–52

The Pharisees' claim that the religious establishment had unanimously rejected Jesus was not true (cf. 12:42). The prominent rabbi Nicodemus, perhaps the preeminent teacher in all of Israel, was the most notable exception. He was probably not a disciple of Jesus at this point, but he was open to the Lord's claims. While not openly defending Jesus, Nicodemus did raise a procedural point in His favor, "Our Law does not judge a man unless it first hears from him and knows what he is doing, does it?"

But the Sanhedrin turned on Nicodemus savagely. "You are not also from Galilee, are you?" they taunted him. To identify Nicodemus with the despised, unsophisticated Galileans was the most demeaning insult they could make.

Then they mockingly invited him to "search, and see that no prophet arises out of Galilee," conveniently overlooking the fact that Jonah was from Galilee. They implied that he was ignorant of the most basic theological truths.

Despite their derision, Nicodemus continued to pursue the truth (cf. 7:17), and eventually found it in Christ (cf. 19:39). Jesus commits Himself not to the scoffing unbeliever, but to the contemplative, honest seeker.

ASK YOURSELF

Have you ever found yourself as a lone voice of conviction in a crowd of allied dissenters? They called it peer pressure when we were younger, but we know now that it doesn't stop once we escape adolescence. Where are you even now being challenged to stand up against opposite opinions?

JESUS EXHIBITS HUMILITY

Early in the morning He came again into the temple, and all the people were coming to Him; and He sat down and began to teach them. —JOHN 8:2

Jesus, the Creator of all things, had no place of His own to stay. This fact strikingly illustrates the humiliation and condescension of the Incarnation. At birth His mother "wrapped Him in cloths, and laid Him in a manger, because there was no room for them in the inn" (Luke 2:7). During His ministry He said to a would-be follower, "The foxes have holes and the birds of the air have nests, but the Son of Man has nowhere to lay His head" (Matt. 8:20). Jesus Christ, God in human flesh, was not given the reception even the most minor human dignitary would have received (cf. 1:11).

The text notes that, simply and without fanfare, early the next "morning He came again into the temple" to teach. No angelic herald announced Jesus' arrival, nor did He perform any sensational miracles to draw a crowd. But such was the power of His teaching that "all the people were coming to Him." In His humility, the Lord used no gimmicks to market or promote Himself, but offered His teaching freely to all who would listen. In typical rabbinical style, He sat down somewhere in the temple complex and began to teach the people.

Throughout Jesus' ministry He exhibited this kind of humility and sets the example for us to follow.

ASK YOURSELF

What are some of the surroundings and comforts we now refer to as requirements—comforts that Jesus was able to minister quite effectively without? Could it be that these actually inhibit us from serving Him as we ought? Is there something God is calling you to do without?

HARMONIZING DIVINE JUSTICE AND MERCY

The scribes and the Pharisees brought a woman caught in adultery, and having set her in the center of the court, they said to Him, "Teacher, this woman has been caught in adultery, in the very act. Now in the Law Moses commanded us to stone such women; what then do You say?" They were saying this, testing Him, so that they might have grounds for accusing Him. —JOHN 8:3–6a

Bringing with them a woman caught in adultery, some scribes and Pharisees barged into the crowd of people listening to Jesus. Addressing Him with mock politeness as "Teacher," they demanded a ruling from Him on what to do with her.

The Pharisees' motive was obvious: They were using the woman in an attempt to trap Jesus. They were "testing Him, so that they might have grounds for accusing Him."

This challenge raised an important issue: how are divine justice and mercy harmonized? God is holy and His "Law is holy" (Rom. 7:12). The Law knows nothing of forgiveness (Rom. 3:20). How then can God forgive sinners without violating His holy law?

The answer is, through the Lord Jesus Christ. His sacrificial death fully satisfied the demands of God's justice. In Jesus Christ divine justice and mercy harmonize. Because His sacrificial death paid the penalty for the sins of all who believe in Him, God can "be just and the justifier of the one who has faith in Jesus" (Rom. 3:26). God poured out His wrath against sin on Jesus so He can pour out His grace and mercy on believers.

ASK YOURSELF

Perhaps you feel guilty and condemned today by your failure to live up to God's standard. Through your faith in the Lord Jesus Christ, you have both the assurance of forgiveness as well as His empowerment to live in submitted obedience to Him. Will you stand absolved and encouraged?

JESUS EXHIBITS WISDOM

Jesus stooped down and with His finger wrote on the ground. But when they persisted in asking Him, He straightened up, and said to them, "He who is without sin among you, let him be the first to throw a stone at her." Again He stooped down and wrote on the ground. —JOHN 8:6b–8

Seemingly oblivious to what was going on, "Jesus stooped down and with His finger wrote on the ground." Thinking they finally had Jesus trapped, the scribes and Pharisees persisted in asking Him. Always the master of the moment, Jesus remained silent, allowing them to reveal their hatred and hypocrisy as they insistently pressed their attack.

At last, "He straightened up, and said to them, 'He who is without sin among you, let him be the first to throw a stone at her.'" Then He calmly stooped down once more and wrote on the ground, and said nothing.

The Lord's reply was simple, yet profound. It upheld the Law, since He did not deny the woman's guilt, and broadened the Law's power by exposing the sins of the accusers. It also avoided the charge of instigating an execution in violation of Roman authority. And it mercifully spared the woman from being stoned for her sin.

Jesus' masterful answer neither minimized the woman's guilt, nor denied the Law's sanctity. But it cut the ground out from under the scribes and Pharisees by revealing that they were unfit to be her judges and executioners.

ASK YOURSELF

As for us, we are wise to stand in awe of our Lord, who does all things well, who accomplishes all His holy will, who never wavers for one moment, even when all around us is in turmoil. Are you feeling the pressure of the day's battles? Jesus is here, and He knows just what He's doing in you.

JESUS EXTENDS FORGIVENESS

*When they heard it, they began to go out one by one, beginning with the older ones, and He was left alone, and the woman, where she was, in the center of the court. Straightening up, Jesus said to her, "Woman, where are they? Did no one condemn you?" She said, "No one, Lord." And Jesus said, "I do not condemn you, either. Go. From now on sin no more." —*JOHN 8:9–11

After the departure of the scribes and Pharisees, Jesus was left alone with the woman, who remained standing where she was, "in the center of the court."

For the first time someone addressed the woman. "Straightening up" from His posture of stooping to write, "Jesus said to her, 'Woman, where are they? Did no one condemn you?'" The term "woman" was a polite, respectful form of address, one with which Jesus addressed His mother (2:4; 19:26), the Samaritan woman at the well (4:21), and Mary Magdalene (20:13, 15). With her accusers gone, there was no one left to condemn her. Exercising His divine prerogative to forgive sin (Matt. 9:6; cf. John 3:17; 12:47), Jesus said, "I do not condemn you, either. Go. From now on sin no more."

Forgiveness does not imply license to sin. Jesus did not condemn her, but He did command her to abandon her sinful lifestyle.

This wonderful story paints a marvelous picture of the Lord Jesus Christ, whose gracious humility, infinite wisdom, convicting speech, and tender forgiveness are its central themes.

ASK YOURSELF

We spent a good deal of time in past weeks looking at Jesus' call for the church to discipline believers who are rebelling against God. How does this account differ in scope? What should our reaction be toward those outside the faith who are living in opposition to His Word?

JESUS, THE LIGHT OF THE WORLD, PART 1

Jesus again spoke to them, saying, "I am the Light of the world; he who follows Me will not walk in the darkness, but will have the Light of life." —JOHN 8:12

By claiming to be the Light of the world Jesus was clearly claiming to be God (cf. Ps. 27:1; Isa. 60:19; 1 John 1:5), and to be Israel's Messiah, sent by God as the "light to the nations" (Isa. 42:6).

The analogy of light was particularly relevant to the Feast of Tabernacles. The daily water-pouring ceremony had its nightly counterpart in a lamp-lighting ceremony. In the very Court of the Women where Jesus was speaking, four huge candelabra were lit, pushing light up into the night sky like a searchlight. These served as a reminder of the pillar of fire by which God had guided Israel in the wilderness (Ex. 13:21–22). The people danced exuberantly around the candelabra through the night, holding blazing torches and singing songs of praise. It was against this backdrop that Jesus made the stunning announcement that He is the true Light of the world.

Jesus Christ alone brings the light of salvation to a sin-cursed world. To the darkness of falsehood He is the light of truth; to the darkness of ignorance He is the light of wisdom; to the darkness of sin He is the light of holiness; to the darkness of sorrow He is the light of joy; to the darkness of death He is the light of life.

ASK YOURSELF

All of us come to forks in the road where the way ahead is confusing and uncertain. But most of our decisions are not between shades of gray but between darkness and light. Are there some choices you know you need to make—paths He has clearly illumined for you to follow?

JESUS, THE LIGHT OF THE WORLD, PART 2

*Jesus again spoke to them, saying, "I am the Light of the world; he who follows Me will not walk in the darkness, but will have the Light of life." —*JOHN 8:12

Unlike the temporary and stationary candelabra of the feast, Jesus is a light that never goes out and a light to be followed. Just as Israel followed the pillar of fire in the wilderness (Ex. 40:36–38), so Jesus called men to follow Him (John 1:43; Matt. 9:9). The one who follows Him, Jesus promised, "will not walk in the darkness" of sin, the world, and Satan, "but will have the Light" that produces spiritual life (cf. John 1:4). Having been illumined by Jesus, believers reflect His light in the dark world (Eph. 5:8).

The Greek word for "follows" is sometimes used to speak of the crowds who followed Jesus. But it can also refer, more specifically, to following Him as a disciple. In that context, it connotes complete submission to Jesus as Lord. God does not accept a halfhearted commitment to following Christ—of receiving Him as Savior, but not following Him as Lord. The person who comes to Jesus comes to Him on His terms, or he does not come at all.

The Lord was not interested in making salvation artificially easier for people, but genuine. He wanted their absolute allegiance, obedience, and submission. Following Christ is not burdensome, as walking in the light illustrates. It is far easier than stumbling around in the dark (cf. Jer. 13:16).

ASK YOURSELF

The Word, we know, is said to be like a lamp to our feet and a light along the path. How can you read and interact with the Scriptures in such a way that God can do this illuminating work more effectively in your life? Where are some places you need His light to shine most clearly?

A FAITHLESS ACCUSATION

The Pharisees said to Him, "You are testifying about Yourself;
*Your testimony is not true." —*JOHN 8:13

Not unexpectedly, the Pharisees reacted negatively to Jesus' claim. According to the Old Testament Law, every fact in a legal matter had to be established by the testimony of more than one witness (Num. 35:30; Deut. 17:6; 19:15). In typical fashion, the Pharisees refused to consider the possibility that Jesus' claim might be true. Instead, they arbitrarily dismissed it on a legal technicality.

In reality, of course, there were others who could testify to the truthfulness of Jesus' claims (e.g., John the Baptist [John 1:7–8, 19–27, 34, 36; 3:26; 5:33], the apostles [John 1:49; 6:69], the Samaritan woman [John 4:39], Martha [John 11:27], those who witnessed His raising of Lazarus [John 12:17], Jesus' works [John 5:36; 10:25], the Scriptures [John 5:39], and, above all, the Father [John 7:17–18]). He was not, as the Pharisees alleged, the only witness who could verify His claims.

The Pharisees' skeptical response illustrates just how obtuse unbelief is; it is never convinced no matter how compelling the evidence. Jesus performed miracles unparalleled in human history (John 15:24). Yet "though He had performed so many signs before them, . . . they were not believing in Him" (John 12:37). Nonetheless, to those who honestly seek the truth Jesus promised, "If anyone is willing to do [the Father's] will, he will know of the teaching, whether it is of God or whether I speak from Myself" (John 7:17).

ASK YOURSELF

Is there an area where you're failing to exercise your faith in God's wisdom and reliability? Do you doubt that He is working in your life, using even unpleasant circumstances to advance His will for you and for His kingdom? How do you plan to do battle against this faithless tendency?

JESUS' TESTIMONY OF HIMSELF, PART 1

Jesus answered and said to them, "Even if I testify about Myself, My testimony is true, for I know where I came from and where I am going; but you do not know where I come from or where I am going. You judge according to the flesh; I am not judging anyone. —JOHN 8:14–15

Knowing it was pointless to argue, Jesus rebuked the Pharisees for their hard-hearted ignorance. In so doing, He offered three reasons that validated the truthfulness of His witness concerning Himself, one of which we'll consider in today's entry, two more in tomorrow's.

First, Jesus supported His claim by referring to His divine origin and destiny, while the Pharisees were ignorant of both. Therefore He was qualified to testify about Himself, but they were not. "For I know where I came from and where I am going," He told them, "but you do not know where I come from or where I am going." The Lord's self-knowledge and divine omniscience (cf. 2:25; 16:30; 21:17) thoroughly confirmed His testimony. His opponents, however, did not know either where He came from or where He was going.

Jesus further exposed their ignorance when He declared to them, "You judge according to the flesh," according to earthly standards, as sinful men in a fallen world. They understood nothing of His heavenly origin, and even what they thought they knew about Him was incorrect.

But as believers who have spiritual understanding, we see Christ for who He really is, and even see all other people as spiritual and eternal souls.

ASK YOURSELF

Pray with thanksgiving today that the Lord has revealed to you who He really is. Realize afresh that you could never have figured this out on your own. If you were ever to know Him, it could be only by His gracious disclosure. Never let yourself grow tired of recalling His mercy.

JESUS' TESTIMONY OF HIMSELF, PART 2

"Even if I do judge, My judgment is true; for I am not alone in it, but I and the Father who sent Me. Even in your law it has been written that the testimony of two men is true. I am He who testifies about Myself, and the Father who sent Me testifies about Me." So they were saying to Him, "Where is Your Father?" Jesus answered, "You know neither Me nor My Father; if you knew Me, you would know My Father also." —JOHN 8:16–19

The second support for the credibility of Jesus' testimony is based on His divine nature shared with the Father. "But even if I do judge," the Lord said, "My judgment is true; for I am not alone in it, but I and the Father who sent Me." By insisting He was one with the Father in judgment, Jesus was claiming essential equality with Him.

As a final vindication for His self-witness, Jesus rebutted the Pharisees' false allegation that He was His only witness (v. 13). The Lord provided two witnesses instead, declaring, "I am He who testifies about Myself, and the Father who sent Me testifies about Me." In perfect agreement, the Father and the Son bear witness to the truth of Jesus' claims.

Predictably, even that did not satisfy the Pharisees. Their response proves that they did not know the Father. Although they prided themselves on knowing Him, the Pharisees—blinded by their own hardheartedness—were actually ignorant of spiritual reality (Matt. 15:14; 23:16, 24).

ASK YOURSELF

Some people have a much different perception of God the Father than they do of God the Son. And yet Jesus said, "If you knew Me, you would know My Father also." How does this affect the way you think of your heavenly Father? How does Jesus reflect the Father's nature?

THE DANGER OF SELF-RIGHTEOUSNESS, PART 1

He said again to them, "I go away, and you will seek Me, and will die
in your sin; where I am going, you cannot come." So the Jews were
saying, "Surely He will not kill Himself, will He, since He says,
'Where I am going, you cannot come'?" —JOHN 8:21–22

Jesus warns the self-righteous religious leaders that their unwillingness
to believe in Him means they would die in their sins. Faced with that
startling pronouncement, the Jews turned His sobering warning into a
venomous joke. "Surely He will not kill Himself, will He?" they asked
sarcastically. Ironically, those who were plotting to take His life asked if
He intended to commit suicide. They understood that when He said,
"Where I am going, you cannot come," Jesus was speaking of His death.
Since they assumed that they were going to heaven, the Jews mockingly
suggested that Jesus must be speaking of killing Himself, in which case
He would go to hell.

Smugly confident in their self-righteousness, they were not just deaf
to Jesus' words, but they mockingly, blasphemously twisted their meaning. It is true that Jesus would give up His life voluntarily (cf. John
10:17–18), but He would not die by His own hand; rather, He would die
at the hands of those very men who now mocked Him (Acts 2:23). And
the place to which He was referring—where He would go but they could
not follow—was not hell, but heaven.

ASK YOURSELF

Is there even a tinge of self-righteousness in your own assessment of
yourself? How often do you find yourself comparing your actions,
attitudes, and motives against those of others? Train yourself to be very
sensitive to these airs, knowing how noxious they can become.

THE DANGER OF SELF-RIGHTEOUSNESS, PART 2

*The Jews were saying, "Surely He will not kill Himself, will He,
since He says, 'Where I am going, you cannot come'?"* —JOHN 8:22

Self-righteousness is a deadly deception, utterly contrary to genuine salvation. The Judaism of Jesus' day was an intricate legalistic system of salvation by human achievement. The apostle Paul wrote, "Not knowing about God's righteousness and seeking to establish their own, they did not subject themselves to the righteousness of God" (Rom. 10:3). Tragically, the scribes and Pharisees failed to understand what Paul, who had been raised a zealous Pharisee (Acts 23:6; Gal. 1:13–14), later came to understand, that "by the works of the Law no flesh will be justified in [God's] sight" (Rom. 3:20), because to break the Law in one place, one time, is to be guilty of all (James 2:10).

External compliance to the Law will save no one; salvation comes only from Christ's righteousness imputed to those who believe (2 Cor. 5:21). Genuine righteousness far surpasses the outward, legalistic righteousness of the scribes and Pharisees. Though the latter impresses men, it does not result in salvation (Matt. 6:1; cf. Rom 3:20).

The scribes and Pharisees were the epitome of self-righteous human achievers. Those who follow their example and trust in good works, morality, and religious activities to save them; who refuse to admit their inability to contribute anything to saving themselves and cry out, "God, be merciful to me, the sinner!" (Luke 18:13), will likewise die in their sins.

ASK YOURSELF

Humility is something you can't really notice in yourself, yet it yields benefits and healthy side-effects that the self-righteous are never able to enjoy. What are a few of the key indicators that tell you the false front of spiritual arrogance is yielding to a heart of genuine spirituality?

THE DANGER OF WORLDLINESS

He was saying to them, "You are from below, I am from above;
*you are of this world, I am not of this world." —*JOHN 8:23

Jesus elaborated on His warning in verse 21 that those who didn't believe in Him would die in their sin and not go where He was going (heaven). The Lord pointed out that their origin, like their destiny, was altogether different from His.

Kosmos (world) refers in this context to the invisible spiritual system of evil that opposes the kingdom of God and is controlled by Satan (John 12:31; 1 John 5:19). The world does not recognize Jesus' true identity (John 1:10), or that of believers (1 John 3:1). It is also ignorant of the Holy Spirit (14:17). Those engulfed in it hate Jesus (and His followers) for rebuking their sinful lifestyle (John 15:18).

Materialism, humanism, immorality, pride, and selfishness (1 John 2:16) are the world's hallmarks, which are utterly opposed to divine truth, righteousness, virtue, and holiness. Its opinions are wrong; its aims are selfish; its pleasures are sinful; its influences are demoralizing; its politics are corrupt; its honors are empty; its smiles are phony; and its love is false and fickle.

Though they were once "without God in the world" (Eph. 2:12), believers are no longer part of the world system. But those who remain "worldly-minded" are "devoid of the Spirit" (Jude 19) and will die in their sins and be consigned to hell.

ASK YOURSELF

Are you aware of worldly attitudes and enticements that are keeping you from a life of pure, uninterrupted fellowship with God? Is it any wonder that these allures are so difficult to relinquish? Yet what do we always lose by being satisfied with temporary gratification?

THE DANGER OF UNBELIEF

Therefore I said to you that you will die in your sins; for unless you believe that I am He, you will die in your sins. —JOHN 8:24

Repeating His warning from verse 21, Jesus declared that those who reject Him will die in their sins because they refuse to "believe that I am He."

The Lord Himself says that those who reject Him cannot be saved, but will die in their sins. To be a Christian one must believe the full biblical revelation about Jesus: that He is the eternal second person of the Trinity, that He entered space and time as God incarnate, that He was born of a virgin, that He lived a sinless life, that His death on the cross is the only sufficient, substitutionary sacrifice for the sins of all who would ever believe in Him, that He rose from the dead and ascended to the Father in heaven, that He now intercedes for His own redeemed people, and that He will one day return in glory.

Persistent unwillingness to believe the truth about Jesus Christ, by its very nature, precludes the possibility of forgiveness, since salvation comes only through faith in Him (3:16, 36; 6:40; Rom. 10:9–10; 1 John 5:10–13). Those who continue in unbelief, refusing to embrace in faith all that Jesus is and has done, will die in their sin and be lost forever (cf. 3:18, 36; Heb. 2:3). Apart from the knowledge of the gospel of Jesus Christ, no one can be saved.

ASK YOURSELF

It is tempting to devote oneself to spiritual growth and understanding while leaving behind the basics on which all Christian maturity exists, as well as forgoing the call of God to be ambassadors of His gospel message. How are you keeping this spirit alive in your own daily life?

THE DANGER OF WILLFUL IGNORANCE

They were saying to Him, "Who are You?" Jesus said to them, "What have I been saying to you from the beginning? I have many things to speak and to judge concerning you, but He who sent Me is true; and the things which I heard from Him, these I speak to the world." They did not realize that He had been speaking to them about the Father. —JOHN 8:25–27

The Jews' incredulous question, "Who are You?" was amazing in light of all the miraculous signs Jesus had performed (5:36) and the repeated claims He had already made. There may have been an undercurrent of mockery in the question: "Who are You to tell us we are going to die in our sins?" But the query does reflect their stubborn, willful ignorance. The overwhelming evidence made it patently obvious who Jesus was, so He merely replied that He was who He had been claiming to be "from the beginning" of His ministry.

Jesus did have "many things to speak and to judge concerning" them. They had been given more than enough revelation to be responsible; their ignorance was inexcusable. His judgment of them would be in perfect harmony with the Father's will, for it was the Father who sent Him, and Jesus "spoke only the things which" He "heard from Him."

Incredibly, they still "did not realize that He had been speaking to them about the Father." Such was the deceptive power of their willful unbelief.

ASK YOURSELF

They just didn't get it. Have you ever been accused of this, whether over some kind of dispute at home, or in a work setting, or through a disagreement at church? Whenever this charge is accurately leveled, what are some of the most productive ways for us to respond?

THE PATHWAY TO FREEDOM:
BELIEF IN JESUS CHRIST

Jesus was saying to those Jews who had believed Him . . . —JOHN 8:31*a*

Belief is the initial point of contact with Christ. But the Bible warns that
not all faith is saving faith. Jesus would later describe these same "Jews
who had believed" as those who were still slaves of sin (v. 34). They did
not really love Jesus (v. 42), but were actually children of the devil
(vv. 38, 41, 44) who refused to believe in Him (vv. 45, 46), blasphemed
Him (vv. 48, 52), and sought to kill Him (vv. 37, 40, 59).

Genuine faith will manifest itself in a person's changed lifestyle
(v. 18), as well as an enduring love for and devotion to Christ.

Saving faith consists of three elements, commonly referred to by the
Latin terms *notitia, assensus,* and *fiducia. Notitia* (knowledge) is the intellectual component of faith. It involves an understanding of the basic biblical facts regarding salvation. *Assensus* (assent) goes one step beyond
notitia and confidently affirms those facts to be true. *Fiducia* (trust) acts
on them by personally appropriating Jesus Christ as the only hope for
salvation.

The classic biblical definition of faith in Hebrews 11 embraces all
three of these elements: *notitia* ("by faith we understand"; v. 3); *assensus*
("faith is the assurance of things hoped for"; v. 1), and *fiducia* ("[faith is]
the conviction of things not seen"; v. 1). In saving faith the entire person—the intellect (knowledge), the emotions (assent), and the will
(trust)—embraces Jesus Christ as Savior and Lord.

ASK YOURSELF

It's possible that not everyone who shares a pew with you on Sunday
morning has truly repented of their sins, truly trusted Christ for salvation,
truly surrendered their life to His lordship. What would be some ways to
stay sensitive to the genuine spiritual health of others in your church?

THE PATHWAY TO FREEDOM:
CONTINUE IN THE WORD

If you continue in My word, then you are truly disciples of Mine.
—JOHN 8:31*b*

Those who are "truly" (actually, in reality) disciples of Jesus Christ will "continue" (remain, abide) in both faith and obedience to His Word. The present tense of the verb *eimi* (are) suggests that Jesus was not telling them the requirements for becoming a disciple. Instead, He declared that the nature of true discipleship consists of continued obedience to His Word.

Scripture repeatedly affirms that only those who obey Christ are truly His disciples: "For whoever does the will of My Father who is in heaven, he is My brother and sister and mother" (Matt. 12:50). "You are My friends if you do what I command you" (John 15:14). "For this is the love of God, that we keep His commandments" (1 John 5:3).

Such passages make it clear that there can be no dichotomy between truly accepting Christ as Savior and also obeying Him as Lord. It is not possible to be saved without confessing Christ as Lord and giving willing obedience to His lordship.

True disciples are Word oriented. They recognize that it is "the word of His grace, which is able to build [them] up" (Acts 20:32). They understand the importance of being "doers of the word, and not merely hearers who delude themselves" (James 1:22). True believers are "like newborn babies, [they] long for the pure milk of the word, so that by it [they] may grow in respect to salvation" (1 Peter 2:2).

ASK YOURSELF

What has characterized some of your best experiences in Bible reading and study? When are you most aware that you've let yourself become drawn away from its value and importance? How would you describe the level of dependency you feel for being constantly reoriented by the Word?

THE PATHWAY TO FREEDOM: KNOWING THE TRUTH

You will know the truth. —JOHN 8:32a

The New Testament tells us, "Grace and truth were realized through Jesus Christ" (John 1:17), that He is "the way, and the truth, and the life" (14:6), that the "truth is in Jesus" (Eph. 4:21). Such knowing of truth is radical in today's world that despairs of finding absolute truth. Just prior to Jesus' crucifixion, Pontius Pilate disparagingly asked Him, "What is truth?" (John 18:38). Likewise, contemporary skeptics have nothing but their own ignorance and pessimism, which results from a pointless search for meaning apart from God.

As the Holy Spirit—the "Spirit of truth" (16:13; 1 John 5:6)—teaches them, believers can also know the truth regarding Jesus. In his first letter, John refers to this vital operation:

> As for you, the anointing which you received from Him abides in you, and you have no need for anyone to teach you; but as His anointing teaches you about all things, and is true and is not a lie, and just as it has taught you, you abide in Him. (2:27)

Scripture is the ultimate revelation, imparting to us God's truth. It reveals the truth incarnate in the person of Jesus, and its words, inspired by the Holy Spirit, teach us the truth. Thus Christ asked the Father, "Sanctify them in the truth; Your word is truth" (John 17:17; cf. Ps. 119:142). The Bible is completely sufficient for all who believe because it is "inspired by God and profitable for teaching, for reproof, for correction, for training in righteousness; so that the man of God may be adequate, equipped for every good work" (2 Tim. 3:16–17).

ASK YOURSELF

When was the last time the truth of a certain passage sounded as current as the morning newspaper, speaking specifically to a pressing matter in your life, just at that moment? What feels different about a timely nugget of Scripture compared to any quote from any other book?

REALIZING THE PATHWAY TO FREEDOM

. . . and the truth will make you free. —JOHN 8:32*b*

Once believers begin to know the truth in the Lord Jesus Christ, they will realize the pathway to genuine spiritual freedom. Such liberating truth includes freedom from Satan's bondage of falsehood (1 John 5:18), condemnation (Rom. 8:1), judgment (John 3:18), spiritual ignorance (8:12), spiritual death (8:51), and most important, sin (Rom. 6:18, 22).

This is why Christ first came to this world—to lay out this pathway and liberate all lost sinners who truly believe (Luke 19:10). At His hometown synagogue in Nazareth, Jesus applied crucial words from the prophet Isaiah to His ministry: "The Spirit of the Lord is upon Me, because He anointed Me to preach the gospel to the poor. He has sent Me to proclaim release to the captives, and recovery of sight to the blind, to set free those who are oppressed" (Luke 4:18; cf. Isa. 61:1). If we are truly set free in Jesus Christ, we must obey the apostle Paul's admonition to the Galatians: "It was for freedom that Christ set us free; therefore keep standing firm and do not be subject again to a yoke of slavery" (Gal. 5:1).

ASK YOURSELF

Notice the verb tenses in the Galatians passage above. Freedom is an established fact, accomplished by the work of Christ on the believer's behalf. But the admonition about how to apply this freedom is an ongoing decision to "keep standing." How do you go about doing that?

THE PRETENSE OF FREEDOM

They answered Him, "We are Abraham's descendants and have never
yet been enslaved to anyone; how is it that You say, 'You will become free'?"
Jesus answered them, "Truly, truly, I say to you, everyone
who commits sin is the slave of sin." —JOHN 8:33–34

The freedom Jesus talks about here has nothing to do with racial or religious identity, as the Jews thought. Paul reminds us, "For he is not a Jew who is one outwardly, nor is circumcision that which is outward in the flesh. But he is a Jew who is one inwardly; and circumcision is that which is of the heart, by the Spirit, not by the letter; and his praise is not from men, but from God" (Rom. 2:28–29; cf. Rev. 2:9).

Christ's answer to the Jews' claim of freedom was blunt: "Truly, truly, I say to you, everyone who commits sin is the slave of sin." The word "commits" is a present tense participle that sees sin as a life principle of innate fallenness and basic wickedness—much more than just various individual actions. Despite their pretentious, pious claim to freedom, the Jews were actually slaves to sin, because "by what a man is overcome, by this he is enslaved" (2 Peter 2:19). Sin, like a despotic master, completely enslaves unbelievers "to various lusts and pleasures" (Titus 3:3) "in the bondage of iniquity" (Acts 8:23). As people in that predicament, the Jews desperately needed Jesus to free them from their spiritual bondage.

Saving faith in Jesus Christ is the only way people can receive release from sin's damning control (Rom. 6:1–7). Once they die to sin (v. 2; cf. Gal. 2:19–20), it will no longer be their master (Rom. 6:14, 18). After that, people can freely be servants of righteousness (1 Peter 2:16).

ASK YOURSELF

If you are smothering under the guilt of sin that continues to draw you back to its deceptions, realize that as a new creature in Christ Jesus, condemnation is no longer a word that applies to you. What would keep you from returning wholeheartedly to the Lord today?

THE PROMISE OF FREEDOM

The slave does not remain in the house forever; the son does remain forever.
So if the Son makes you free, you will be free indeed. —JOHN 8:35–36

Even though as descendants of Abraham and part of God's chosen nation the Jews seemed to have much privilege, they were slaves at risk of forfeiting all spiritual privileges. Jesus elsewhere warned them, "I say to you that many will come from east and west, and recline at the table with Abraham, Isaac and Jacob in the kingdom of heaven; but the sons of the kingdom will be cast out into the outer darkness; in that place there will be weeping and gnashing of teeth" (Matt. 8:11–12).

Christ's second statement here repeats the promise He had just made in verse 36 that "if the Son makes you free, you will be free indeed." He is the Son who rules over the Father's house (Heb. 3:6), and as such, God authorizes Him to free believers from their slavery to sin and make them children of God. Jesus thus sets them "free from the law of sin and of death" (Rom. 8:2). And He furthermore brings them into God's adopted family (Gal. 4:5; Eph. 1:5), taking them from slavery to sonship (cf. Rom. 8:17).

Charles Wesley's classic hymn summarizes God's promise beautifully:

> Long my imprisoned spirit lay
> Fast bound in sin and nature's night;
> Thine eye diffused a quick'ning ray,
> I woke, the dungeon flamed with light;
> My chains fell off, my heart was free;
> I rose, went forth and followed Thee.

ASK YOURSELF

"Free indeed." If this is not what you're experiencing on a daily basis as you fellowship with God and interact with life, you are being resistant to a reality that Christ died to provide you. Think back to a time when you felt "free indeed." What was different then? Why not now?

ABRAHAM'S PHYSICAL CHILDREN

. . . therefore you also do the things which you heard from your father.
—JOHN 8:38*b*

The Jews' descent from Abraham and their physical circumcision mean nothing without "circumcision . . . which is of the heart" (cf. Deut. 10:16; Col. 2:11)—the cleansing of sin that the Holy Spirit accomplishes in salvation. Paul asserts, "They are not all Israel who are descended from Israel" (Rom. 9:6; see v. 27; Isa. 10:22). And he teaches further, "Even so Abraham believed God, and it was reckoned to him as righteousness. Therefore, be sure that it is those who are of faith who are sons of Abraham. . . . So then those who are of faith are blessed with Abraham, the believer" (Gal. 3:6–7, 9).

Abraham looked ahead in faith to the coming of Messiah, yet the Jews hearing Jesus sought to kill Him—the very Messiah for whom Abraham had hoped. And unlike their ancestor, who believed God's word (Gen. 15:6), these Jews rejected Jesus' divine instruction (Matt. 13:19; cf. 1 Cor. 2:14). The Lord's words penetrated their hardened hearts no deeper than the seed that fell beside the road (Matt. 13:4, 19). By contrast, "the word of God . . . performs its work in [those] who believe" (1 Thess. 2:13).

Jesus spoke to the Jews of the divine truth that He only as Son could reveal directly from His Father (cf. John 15:15; 17:8). But they rebuffed His teaching and preferred to obey other words—from their father Satan. Their conduct proved Satan was their spiritual father, even as Jesus' conduct proved His Father was God. Because the Jews didn't know the Son, they didn't know His Father either, despite their physical descent from Abraham.

ASK YOURSELF

What are some of the greatest plusses we derive from being born into families in which many generations have trusted Christ for salvation? Are there any challenges this also presents? How do you counteract the self-righteous tendencies that can flow from this dynamic?

ABRAHAM'S SPIRITUAL CHILDREN

They answered and said to Him, "Abraham is our father." Jesus said to them, "If you are Abraham's children, do the deeds of Abraham. But as it is, you are seeking to kill Me, a man who has told you the truth, which I heard from God; this Abraham did not do. You are doing the deeds of your father." —JOHN 8:39–41a

Abraham was a man of tremendous faith. Genesis 15:6 tells us that he "believed in the Lord; and He reckoned it to him as righteousness." The New Testament reinforces the truth of Abraham's genuine saving faith, as Paul devotes much to the subject (Rom. 4; Gal. 3:6–14). The author of Hebrews similarly extols the patriarch's testimony (Heb. 11:8–12, 17–19).

Jesus' Jewish opponents, however, with their self-righteous good deeds that tried to gain God's favor, did not follow Abraham's example, because it is "those who are of faith [who] are blessed with Abraham, the believer" (Gal. 3:9). Salvation comes only through faith in Christ, "the way, and the truth, and the life; no one comes to the Father but through [Him]" (John 14:6; cf. Acts 4:12; 1 Tim. 2:5).

If they had really been Abraham's spiritual children, the Jewish elite would have done the sort of works he did. God Himself testified that "Abraham obeyed Me and kept My charge, My commandments, My statutes and My laws" (Gen. 26:5). But Jesus' enemies sought to kill Him, even though He told them the truth He had heard from the Father. Such homicidal intentions did not at all reflect Abraham's obedience. Their hostility and disdain toward the Son of God demonstrated beyond a doubt that many of the Jews could not be Abraham's spiritual children— the things they did and said "Abraham did not do."

ASK YOURSELF

We cannot judge another's salvation with absolute certainty, but what are some of the works that should follow genuine conversion to Christ? Which of these are you not exhibiting yourself in any noticeable manner? How is God working to stir these traits within you?

FALSE CLAIM TO BE GOD'S CHILDREN

They said to Him, "We were not born of fornication; we have one Father: God."
Jesus said to them, "If God were your Father, you would love Me, for I proceeded
forth and have come from God, for I have not even come on My own initiative, but
He sent Me. Why do you not understand what I am saying? It is because you cannot
hear My word. . . . Which one of you convicts Me of sin? If I speak truth, why do
you not believe Me? He who is of God hears the words of God; for this reason you do
not hear them, because you are not of God." —JOHN 8:41b–43, 46–47

W hat our Lord had earlier only implied He now stated directly: physically, the Jews were children of Abraham, but morally and spiritually they were children of the devil (cf. Matt. 13:38; 1 John 3:12).

As Jesus concluded this session, He posed two questions to His foes. The first, "Which one of you convicts Me of sin?" boldly affirms our Lord's utter holiness. Second Corinthians 5:21 says He "knew no sin"; Hebrews 4:15 says that He "has been tempted in all things as we are, yet without sin" (see also 7:26; 1 Peter 2:22). Only Someone perfectly holy and in close communion with the Father could issue such a challenge (cf. John 18:23). Though the Jewish leaders believed He was guilty of sin, they couldn't prove any charge.

His second question pressed the point: "If I speak the truth, why do you not believe Me?" If sinless, Jesus could not be worthy of indictment. The Lord then summarized: "He who is of God hears the words of God; for this reason you do not hear them, because you are not of God." Christ destroyed the false security of the Jews who claimed spiritual heritage from Abraham. Unless they repented, they faced hell's doom. Such is the fate of any who trust in redemption apart from Christ's saving work.

ASK YOURSELF

Knowing our propensity and struggle with sin, let the thought settle around you that our Lord never sinned. Therefore, what could keep you from being totally confident in His power to aid you in righteousness, knowing the power it must have taken to lead a sinless life?

DISHONORING JESUS

The Jews answered and said to Him, "Do we not say rightly that You
are a Samaritan and have a demon?" Jesus answered, "I do not have
a demon; but I honor My Father, and you dishonor Me." —JOHN 8:48–49

Here the Jews took their blasphemous accusations to the limit by claiming Jesus had a demon (cf. Matt. 10:25; Mark 3:22; John 10:20). To say a
person had a demon was the same as calling him insane, since the demon-
possessed often behaved irrationally. With obvious spiritual blindness,
the Jews concluded that a demon had driven Jesus mad.

However, our Lord did not respond in kind to these malicious
claims—"while being reviled, He did not revile in return" (1 Peter 2:23).
Instead He simply told them, "I do not have a demon." Rather than serving Satan, Jesus was busy honoring His Father (cf. John 6:38; 14:31;
15:10). He could not have a demon because demon-possessed people did
not honor God.

Unlike His critics, who acclaimed themselves (cf. Luke 16:15), Jesus
did not seek His own glory. If that had been His goal, He could have continued to dwell in the glories of heaven, as He had from eternity past (John
17:5, 24). But the Son of Man willingly came to earth "to seek and to save
that which was lost" (Luke 19:10; cf. Heb. 9:28) and to "save His people
from their sins" (Matt. 1:21). For our sakes the Lord disregarded any future
dishonor to Himself, and as Creator and sustainer of the universe,

> Left His Father's throne above,
> So free, so infinite His grace;
> Emptied Himself of all but love,
> And bled for Adam's helpless race.

ASK YOURSELF

When was the last time someone leveled an unjust accusation against
you? Do you know of someone right now who believes something
untrue and unflattering about you? How have you responded to this in
the past? How do you intend to respond to it in the future?

HONORING JESUS

There is One who seeks and judges. Truly, truly, I say to you, if anyone keeps My word he will never see death. —JOHN 8:50*b*–51

Although Christ didn't seek to glorify Himself, His Father always seeks to honor Him. Unlike sinful humanity, God always judges rightly and has decided the Lord Jesus is worthy of honor. At both Christ's baptism and transfiguration (Matt. 3:17; 17:5), God said of His Son, "This is My beloved Son, in whom I am well-pleased." Because Jesus was humbly obedient to being our Substitute on the cross,

> God highly exalted Him, and bestowed on Him the name which is above every name, so that at the name of Jesus every knee will bow, of those who are in heaven and on earth and under the earth, and that every tongue will confess that Jesus Christ is Lord, to the glory of God the Father. (Phil. 2:9–11; cf. Pss. 2:6–12; 110:1; Isa. 52:13)

To all men and women who honor Christ by heeding His call to salvation, He promises that they "will never see death." The one who obeys His Word (Matt. 5:19; John 15:10, 20) is a genuine child of God (1:12), in His kingdom (3:3–5), and His real disciple (8:31) who will never experience spiritual death (Rev. 2:11; 20:6). Jesus declares to everyone this great gospel truth: "Truly, truly, I say to you, he who hears My word, and believes Him who sent Me, has eternal life, and does not come into judgment, but has passed out of death into life" (John 5:24; cf. 3:16; 6:50; 11:25–26).

ASK YOURSELF

Of all the glorious benefits afforded you by means of Christ's salvation, which one or two are particularly precious to you at this point in your life? What has brought these to the forefront during this period of time? How has Jesus confirmed their reality and value in your heart?

ANSWERING THE DOUBTERS

"Your father Abraham rejoiced to see My day, and he saw it and was glad." So the Jews said to Him, "You are not yet fifty years old, and have You seen Abraham?" Jesus said to them, "Truly, truly, I say to you, before Abraham was born, I am."
—JOHN 8:56–58

Jesus' statement to the Jews, "Your father Abraham rejoiced to see My day, and he saw it and was glad," is in marked contrast to their unbelieving rejection of Him. The writer of Hebrews suggests that Abraham and others looked ahead to Christ's incarnation and ministry: "All these died in faith, without receiving the promises, but having seen them and having welcomed them from a distance" (11:13). Abraham saw in his son Isaac the beginning of the divine covenant with him (Gen. 12:3; 15:1–21; 17:1–8), which would eventuate in Messiah's coming. The Lord again contrasted His enemies' attitudes and actions with those of Abraham to prove that they could not be the patriarch's spiritual children. Abraham had rejoiced in His coming; these Jews wanted to murder Him.

The Jews persisted in their unbelief when they cynically wondered, "You are not yet fifty years old, and have You seen Abraham?" They also distorted Jesus' words—He had not said He'd *seen* Abraham, but that the patriarch had *prophetically* seen *Him*.

Our Lord's decisive response that He existed before Abraham was born was a claim to complete deity. Jesus once again applied to Himself the sacred name ("I am") of God. Therefore, as a member of the eternal Godhead (John 1:1–2), He was alive well before Abraham's time. The Jews' dishonoring, doubting claims were effectively smashed, as Homer Kent notes: "By using the timeless 'I am' rather than 'I was,' Jesus conveyed not only the idea of existence prior to Abraham, but timelessness—the very nature of God himself (Exod. 3:14)."

ASK YOURSELF

The crispness and conciseness of Jesus' rebuttals are impressive to read. How happy are you with your ability to defend your faith with poise and excellence? What could make you more effective at it?

THE CONCERN OF MARY AND MARTHA

So the sisters sent word to Him, saying, "Lord, behold, he whom You love is sick." But when Jesus heard this, He said, "This sickness is not to end in death, but for the glory of God, so that the Son of God may be glorified by it." Now Jesus loved Martha and her sister and Lazarus. —JOHN 11:3–5

Mary and Martha believed Jesus would heal their brother because He loved him so deeply. And they were sure He had the power to do so.

The sisters' words to Jesus are beautifully simple. They gave no details of Lazarus's condition and didn't manipulate the Lord to do anything specific. They simply appealed to their Lord's love for Lazarus and in humble faith made known his need (cf. 1 Peter 5:7).

Christ's reply that the brother's illness would not result in death did not mean he wouldn't die, but that death wouldn't be the final outcome. Sometimes sickness and death are God's will for believers, and Lazarus's situation would bring glory to both the Father and the Son (cf. John 9:3; 12:23, 28).

Given Jesus' close relationship with Mary, Martha, and Lazarus, it is puzzling He did not go to Bethany immediately. Instead, He "stayed two days longer in the place where He was (11:6)." This was a delay not to allow the brother to die—he had likely already passed away. The delay does however highlight several divine purposes: it forced the sisters to wait and strengthen their faith through trust in Jesus; it showed that Lazarus was really dead and that Jesus' raising him would be a miracle; and it again demonstrated that our Lord ministers according to His timetable, not ours.

ASK YOURSELF

Are you boldly, bravely trying to exercise your faith during a difficult situation, yet finding that your trust and patience is seeming to go unheeded? God alone knows how long this season must last. Keep waiting, keep believing. He is doing His work where you cannot see it.

DECEMBER 12

JESUS' CLAIMS TO MARTHA, PART 1

Jesus said to her, "Your brother will rise again." Martha said to Him,
"I know that he will rise again in the resurrection on the last day." Jesus said
to her, "I am the resurrection and the life; he who believes in Me will live even
if he dies, and everyone who lives and believes in Me will never die. Do you
believe this?" She said to Him, "Yes, Lord; I have believed that You are the
Christ, the Son of God, even He who comes into the world." —JOHN 11:23–27

The Lord's assurance to Martha that Lazarus would arise again meant
he would be resurrected immediately, but Martha misunderstood. Like
the other mourners had done, Jesus was comforting her with a reminder
that her brother would be raised at the end of the age, Martha assumed.
That was a truth she was already aware of because the Old Testament
taught the resurrection of the body (Job 19:25–27; Dan. 12:2). Martha
also knew it was Jesus' teaching (John 5:21, 25–29; 6:39–40). It's ironic
that she believed Jesus could accomplish a distant resurrection, but she
did not consider He could raise Lazarus now.

Christ therefore challenged Martha to move beyond an abstract faith
in a final resurrection to a complete faith in Him—"I am the resurrection
and the life." She was looking to the end of this age, but time is not an
obstacle to Him who has the power of resurrection and life (cf. 5:21, 26).
Our Lord will indeed raise the dead in the future resurrection, but He
was also poised to raise her brother that very day. Jesus was calling
Martha, as He does all sinners, to a personal, saving trust in Him as the
One who alone has power over death.

ASK YOURSELF

Does your belief in God reside more in the abstract and philosophical
and perhaps not enough in the concrete and practical? Would you dare
to believe today that the trust you've placed in Him for eternity could
also be the trust you place in Him on a matter of pressing concern?

JESUS' CLAIMS TO MARTHA, PART 2

Jesus said to her, "Your brother will rise again." Martha said to Him,
"I know that he will rise again in the resurrection on the last day." Jesus said
to her, "I am the resurrection and the life; he who believes in Me will live even if
he dies, and everyone who lives and believes in Me will never die. Do you believe
this?" She said to Him, "Yes, Lord; I have believed that You are the Christ,
the Son of God, even He who comes into the world." —JOHN 11:23–27

Our Lord's statement, "He who believes in Me will live even if he dies, and everyone who lives and believes in Me will never die," teaches two related truths. The follower of Christ will live even after he dies physically because Christ will raise him on the last day. And because every believer has eternal life (John 3:36; 6:47), he will never die spiritually because physical death can never eradicate eternal life. Thus everyone who by faith embraces Jesus Christ can exult, "O death, where is your victory? O death, where is your sting?" (1 Cor. 15:55).

Martha's affirmation of faith stands beside other great gospel confessions of faith (John 1:49; Matt. 14:33). It looks forward to the wonderful purpose statement at the end of John's gospel: "These have been written so that you may believe that Jesus is the Christ, the Son of God; and that believing you may have life in His name" (20:31). Here Martha emphatically declares three essential truths about our Lord: He is the Christ, or Messiah (see 1:41); He is the Son of God (see Matt. 14:33; John 1:34, 49); and He is the deliverer sent by the Father (see Isa. 9:6; Luke 7:19–20).

Because of His endless love for Martha, Christ pointed her to Him, the sole source of spiritual life and well-being.

ASK YOURSELF

How often does the fear of death cast a shadow over your ordinary day? Dealing with the reality of death is not a cause for either recklessness or despondent fatalism. But what could biblical freedom from the fear of death alleviate from your life? How could it change you?

JESUS' COMPASSION FOR LAZARUS'S FAMILY

When Jesus therefore saw her weeping, and the Jews who came with her also weeping, He was deeply moved in spirit and was troubled, and said, "Where have you laid him?" They said to Him, "Lord, come and see." Jesus wept. So the Jews were saying, "See how He loved him!" —JOHN 11:33–36

Mary seems to have been the more emotional of the two sisters, as she fell down at Jesus' feet and repeated Martha's lament that if He had been there earlier, Lazarus would not have died. This was not a reproach to the Lord but simply an expression of grief.

At seeing Lazarus's family and others mourning, Jesus "was deeply moved in spirit and was troubled." "Deeply moved" includes the connotation of indignation, and the Lord felt this over the fatal results of sin and the reaction of the mourners, who were behaving more like the pagans who have no hope (1 Thess. 4:13). "Troubled" further underscores the intensity of Jesus' response to the situation. It typically denotes strong emotions, such as Zacharias's fear when seeing the angel (Luke 1:12), the apostles' terror when seeing Jesus walk on water (Matt. 14:26), and Jesus' reaction to His impending death (John 12:27).

Like the others, "Jesus wept." This verb has the connotation of the person silently bursting into tears. Such a tearful response stemmed from Christ's love for Lazarus and his sisters and His grief over the relentless, heinous effects of sin on a fallen world. This shortest of Scripture verses emphasizes Jesus' true humanity—He was indeed "a man of sorrows and acquainted with grief" (Isa. 53:3). The stage was now set for the compassionate Lord to convincingly demonstrate His power over death by raising Lazarus from the grave.

ASK YOURSELF

Too often our exterior emotions are forced and disingenuous, derived more from societal expectations than deep conviction. Where have you noticed this happening in your own life? What could change your outward expressions from false fronts to true feelings?

JESUS' PROMISE TO MARTHA

Jesus said to her, "Did I not say to you that if you believe,
you will see the glory of God?" —JOHN 11:40

Martha's general anxiety and despair concerning the death of her brother Lazarus prompted Jesus to give her a statement partially of hope as well as gentle rebuke. Scripture does not record a precise duplicate statement our Lord might have given to Martha earlier in this episode. Thus it may refer to a much earlier comment that is not in the Gospels, or to a composite of previous remarks He made to the apostles and the sisters before this moment.

No matter, Christ challenged Martha not to worry about Lazarus's body but to focus instead on Jesus Himself. His promise here did not, of course, make the impending miracle dependent on Martha's faith. What the Lord would soon do would be a sovereign and divine work, intended to glorify Himself and the Father by displaying the mighty power of resurrection. Although everyone present would see His miracle, only the ones having genuine faith in Jesus would grasp its full significance. Commentator Leon Morris writes,

> For [Jesus] the "glory of God" was the one important thing. This means that the real meaning of what He would do would be accessible only to faith. All who were there, believers or not, would see the miracle. But Jesus is promising Martha a sight of the glory. The crowd would see the miracle, but only believers would perceive its real significance, the glory.

ASK YOURSELF

Are you faced with a situation in which you need to be content with the ways and purposes of God, even if it means not getting what you want? Or perhaps a harder question—Can you be the most pleased that God is receiving glory when He gives you what you do want?

THE POWER TO RAISE LAZARUS, PART 1

He cried out with a loud voice, "Lazarus, come forth." The man who had died
came forth, bound hand and foot with wrappings, and his face was wrapped
around with a cloth. Jesus said to them, "Unbind him, and let him go."
—JOHN 11:43b–44

The words describing Christ's calling Lazarus back from the grave emphasize the loudness of His command. The shout may have symbolized the power necessary to raise the dead; or maybe it distanced our Lord from the mutterings of unbelieving sorcerers and magicians (cf. Isa. 8:19).

Students of Scripture have often noted that Jesus' power is so great that had He not addressed Lazarus specifically, *all* those buried would have come forth. Earlier He taught, "Do not marvel at this; for an hour is coming, in which all who are in the tombs will hear His voice, and will come forth; those who did the good deeds to a resurrection of life, those who committed the evil deeds to a resurrection of judgment" (John 5:28–29). This resurrection is a preview of the tremendous divine power we'll witness on the last day.

Unlike the circus atmosphere that so often surrounds contemporary "faith healers" (who can't really raise the dead anyway), Lazarus's raising was not marked by showmanship, theatrics, or man-centered hype. Christ's divine power simply spoke for itself. At His short but forceful command, the king of terrors (death; cf. Job 18:14) gave back his lawful captive. Jesus nullified the victory of the tomb (1 Cor. 15:55) and concurrently unlocked the door of death and Hades—He alone possesses the authoritative keys for such an action (Rev. 1:18).

ASK YOURSELF

Have you lost some of your confidence in the power of God to meet your needs according to His riches in glory (Phil. 4:19)? Would you lay aside all your doubts and remember that your God can do anything, without even trying hard?

THE POWER TO RAISE LAZARUS, PART 2

He cried out with a loud voice, "Lazarus, come forth." The man who had died
came forth, bound hand and foot with wrappings, and his face was wrapped
around with a cloth. Jesus said to them, "Unbind him, and let him go."
—JOHN 11:43b–44

Immediately following the miracle of Lazarus's resurrection, the Lord
gave the practical order to unbind his grave clothes and let him go unfettered. Leon Morris notes that "Jesus was never so carried away by the
wonder of His miracles that He forgot the needs of the person."

There is more than the practical, mundane aspect to note in the significance of Jesus' involving the eyewitnesses in the unwrapping of
Lazarus. Gerald Borchert's commentary points out, "The very mourners
who doubted [Jesus] were agents in the completion of the miracle. In
their participation the mourners in fact became part of the sign and therefore were undeniable witnesses to the power of Jesus."

Although this was the culminating miracle of Jesus' earthly ministry,
this sign pales in significance to what yet would occur before His mission
was completed. Not long after this, Christ would Himself rise from the dead
(Luke 24:1–11). Lazarus would one day die again, having merely a corruptible human body. But the Lord rose as the conqueror of death and "the first
fruits of those who are asleep" (1 Cor. 15:20). Paul writes of the glorious
benefits of that for all believers: "This perishable will have put on the imper-
ishable, and this mortal will have put on immortality, then will come about
the saying that is written, 'Death is swallowed up in victory'" (15:54).

ASK YOURSELF

These things, Paul later said, were written for our encouragement. So
how can you apply the hope and confidence of certain resurrection to
the ordinary business of this day? What change of perspective does this
afford to the issues causing you the most concern?

MANY BELIEVE IN JESUS

Many of the Jews who came to Mary, and saw what
He had done, believed in Him. —JOHN 11:45

The apostle's statement that many who saw Lazarus raised "believed in [Jesus]" sounds simple, but it is crucial and profound. That's because genuine saving faith always rests solely on Jesus Christ (see John 6:29, 35, 40; 11:25–26; 14:6; 1 John 5:10, 13). This is true because "there is salvation in no one else; for there is no other name under heaven that has been given among men by which we must be saved" (Acts 4:12).

Scripture also makes plain, however, that not everyone who seems to believe in Jesus will actually demonstrate genuine saving faith (John 2:23–25; 8:30–31; James 2:16). Nevertheless, the people here, for several reasons, appear to have had true faith. The Lord's main reason for bringing Lazarus back from the grave was to glorify Himself and the Father, and Christ is glorified when people truly believe unto salvation (2 Cor. 4:15). Second, the Jewish leaders apparently considered these people as true believers (John 11:48), because these individuals were deemed a threat to the religious establishment. Third, John contrasts the ones said to believe with unbelievers who reported the miracle to the Pharisees (v. 46), and he always made a clear distinction between the two groups. Lastly, although faith that derived from Jesus' miracles was not always authentic, this one was so powerful and persuasive that it likely produced only genuine believers of those who professed faith in Him that day. This miracle left no room for shallow or superficial responses of faith.

ASK YOURSELF

As you pray for God's miraculous intervention in your own life, in the life of a close family member, in the life of a dear friend, do you also use this prayer to ask that God would stir saving faith and belief in those who are on the periphery of the circumstance? God can do it all.

Principles of Kingdom Equality, Part 1

*When those hired about the eleventh hour came, each one received a denarius.
When those hired first came, they thought that they would receive more; but each
of them also received a denarius. When they received it, they grumbled at the
landowner, saying, "These last men have worked only one hour, and you have
made them equal to us who have borne the burden and the scorching heat of the
day." But he answered and said to one of them, "Friend, I am doing you no
wrong; did you not agree with me for a denarius? Take what is yours and go, but I
wish to give to this last man the same as to you. Is it not lawful for me to do what
I wish with what is my own? Or is your eye envious because I am generous?" So
the last shall be first, and the first last.* —Matt. 20:9–16

This parable of the laborers in the vineyard contains many principles il-
lustrating that God's gift of eternal life is equal for all believers. Overarching is that He is sovereign in salvation. The landowner (God) sought
laborers to work in his vineyard. Because God is sovereign in the entire
redemptive process, people have no demands on His grace and mercy.
Everyone who believes is first sought by the Father and given to the Son
(John 6:39). Whether that occurs early or late in the person's life, all
glory belongs to God.

Second, only God sets up the terms of salvation. The vineyard
workers labored a different number of hours and no doubt with varying
degrees of productivity, but they received the same pay. Only God's unchanging grace determines the worth of his gift, not human merit.

Third, God continues to call all kinds of sinners to His kingdom. This
will continue until the very last hour of the present age. While it is day, before the night of judgment, the Holy Spirit will keep drawing all who believe into God's eternal kingdom, because our Lord does not wish "for any
to perish but for all to come to repentance" (2 Peter 3:9).

ASK YOURSELF

Do you often find yourself comparing gifts with other believers,
either seeing yours as being better or perhaps as being inferior?

PRINCIPLES OF KINGDOM EQUALITY, PART 2

But he answered and said to one of them, "Friend, I am doing you no wrong; did
you not agree with me for a denarius? Take what is yours and go, but I wish to
give to this last man the same as to you. Is it not lawful for me to do what I wish
with what is my own? Or is your eye envious because I am generous?" So the last
shall be first, and the first last. —MATT. 20:13–16

J esus' parable of the laborers reveals four more principles of kingdom
equality. A fourth is that God saves all who are willing. All the vineyard
laborers realized their neediness, gave up dependence on their own resources, and looked only to the landowner (God).

Next, God is compassionate on all who acknowledge their utter
poverty and hopelessness. When anyone comes to the Lord understanding he has no other prospect for eternal life but in Him, God always graciously and lovingly receives that person for His own.

A sixth principle is that all who came into the vineyard (God's kingdom) worked. Even if they entered at the final hour, the landowner valued their work the same as those who had been there all day. Throughout
the history of redemption, God has used many late-in-life and deathbed
conversions to lead others to Himself and bring Him much glory.

Seventh, God has the supreme authority and ability to keep His promises. Just as the landowner had ample funds to pay each worker his promised amount, Christ's atonement was sufficient to pay for the sins of all
who believe. The only reason a man or woman misses salvation is because
they refuse to believe. God's gracious promises are always more than sufficient—where sin increases, grace increases all the more (Rom. 5:20).

ASK YOURSELF

How have you noticed God's sensitivity and ability to meet each person
at his or her point of need, working differently in their lives than He
does in others, although for the same eternal purpose?

PRINCIPLES OF KINGDOM EQUALITY, PART 3

But he answered and said to one of them, "Friend, I am doing you no wrong; did
you not agree with me for a denarius? Take what is yours and go, but I wish to
give to this last man the same as to you. Is it not lawful for me to do what I wish
with what is my own? Or is your eye envious because I am generous?" So the last
shall be first, and the first last. —MATT. 20:13–16

Today we come to the final three principles of kingdom equality, as derived from this parable. Number eight is that God always gives more than is deserved. The landowner was no more obligated to hire the first workers than the last, and not at all required to pay ones more than the others. All received more than they were worth. In an infinitely greater fashion, no Christian is qualified to receive the Lord's least favor, much less salvation.

Ninth, humility and a genuine sense of unworthiness are the only attitudes anyone should bring before God. The daylong laborers lost much of their humility at the end of the day because of jealousy at not earning more wage than the last-hour workers. But all the laborers had come to the vineyard with the same submissiveness and willingness to receive the landowner's payment.

Finally, from beginning to end, the parable pictures God's sovereign, boundless grace. The laborers' work had absolutely no bearing on what they were paid. Likewise, people's supposed good works have no relationship to what they may receive through faith in Jesus Christ. Just as sin is the great equalizer that causes every person to "fall short of the glory of God" (Rom. 3:23), His grace is the ultimate equalizer, forgiving sin and making every believer equally acceptable as His adopted children in Christ.

ASK YOURSELF

Which of the laborers bears the closest resemblance to you? How has your personal situation, whether as a daylong laborer or an afternoon recruit, proven to be God's perfect plan for you?

The Plan of Jesus' Suffering

The Son of Man will be delivered to the chief priests and scribes,
and they will condemn Him to death, and will hand Him over to the Gentiles.
—Matt. 20:18b–19a

The apostles knew they were now headed for Jerusalem to celebrate Passover with Jesus, but they did not understand that He would be the ultimate Passover Lamb (cf. Rev. 13:8), as Scripture predicted. Even after His resurrection, He had to rebuke two disciples for their skimpy knowledge of this: "O foolish men and slow of heart to believe in all that the prophets have spoken! Was it not necessary for the Christ to suffer these things and to enter into His glory?" (Luke 24:25–26). Several decades later, Peter wrote:

> As to this salvation, the prophets who prophesied of the grace that would come to you made careful searches and inquiries, seeking to know what person or time the Spirit of Christ within them was indicating as He predicted the sufferings of Christ and the glories to follow. (1 Peter 1:10–11; cf. Luke 24:46; 1 Cor. 15:3–4)

Jesus' suffering was always in God's plan (Acts 2:23). When the Lord was an infant, His parents brought Him to the temple to present Him to God, at which time Simeon told Mary, "Behold, this Child is appointed for the fall and rise of many in Israel, and for a sign to be opposed—and a sword will pierce even your own soul—to the end that thoughts from many hearts may be revealed" (Luke 2:34–35). When John the Baptist announced His earthly ministry, he declared, "Behold, the Lamb of God who takes away the sin of the world!" (John 1:29; cf. Rev. 5:6, 12).

ASK YOURSELF

The fact that suffering is a necessary component to life in our fallen world may be a notion we deplore, but it is reality all the same. How do you approach pain and trials differently and more maturely now than you did in earlier days? What has God taught you in the midst of it?

THE PROPORTION OF JESUS' SUFFERINGS

*. . . to mock and scourge and crucify Him, and on the third day
He will be raised up.* —MATT. 20:19*b*

It was customary for the Romans to mock and scourge prisoners who
were not Roman citizens, as they did to Jesus even before His conviction
to death. First the soldiers flogged Him with a leather whip that had
sharp pieces of bone and metal attached. Then they put a scarlet robe on
Him and jammed a crown of thorns on His head and mockingly hailed
Him as King of the Jews (see Matt. 27:26–30). Only after these humilia-
tions did they crucify Him.

We must not minimize Jesus' sufferings. He felt every laceration of
the whip and every sting of the reed. His bruised and torn muscles
strained to carry the cross to Golgotha. He felt each nail in His hands and
feet—His entire weight rested on them when the cross was upright. And
He suffered great thirst and the sense of suffocation. Yet His greatest sufferings were emotional and spiritual:

> He was despised and forsaken of men, a man of sorrows and ac-
> quainted with grief; and like one from whom men hide their face He
> was despised, and we did not esteem Him. Surely our griefs He
> Himself bore, and our sorrows He carried; yet we ourselves es-
> teemed Him stricken, smitten of God, and afflicted. But He was
> pierced through for our transgressions, He was crushed for our iniq-
> uities; the chastening for our well-being fell upon Him, and by His
> scourging we are healed. (Isa. 53:3–5)

ASK YOURSELF

We speak often of "stress" in our life experience, as something that seems
to increase with each passing year. Is it helpful to you, at the end of
another trying day, to lay your various stresses alongside those endured by
your Savior, and to realize that He well understands your pain?

THE POWER OF JESUS' SUFFERINGS, PART 1

. . . to mock and scourge and crucify Him, and on the third day
He will be raised up. —MATT. 20:19b

Jesus' final sufferings were indeed powerful, encompassing more than just the physical. He suffered the pain of disloyalty as Judas Iscariot betrayed Him to the chief priests. He could agree with the psalmist, "Even my close friend in whom I trusted, who ate my bread, has lifted up his heel against me" (Ps. 41:9). One whom He had called, taught, and loved cooperated with Jesus' enemies. There's nothing much more grievous than suffering the violation of trust and intimacy at the hands of a friend.

Our Lord also suffered the pain of rejection. God's chosen people rejected Him as Messiah and treated Him instead as a criminal who should be executed (John 1:11). His disciples deserted Him for a time, afraid to be seen as His friends, much less His servants. Even His heavenly Father forsook Him while Jesus was on the cross, so as not to have to behold the sin borne by the Son.

Further, Christ suffered the pain of humiliation. Not only the Gentiles who carried out His execution mocked Him, but so did the leaders of His own people. The Romans thoroughly humiliated Him by furnishing Him with a mock crown, scepter, and robe of royalty—and then rendering derisive obeisance to Him. Of course their ultimate scorn was to nail the Lord to a wooden cross, between two thieves, in full public display.

ASK YOURSELF

As our thoughts turn to Christmas today and tomorrow, do not let the candy-coated Christianity of the stores and TV specials dim the reality of what Jesus' coming actually cost. He came for you to die for you. Worship Him as the Lamb of God, even as the babe in Bethlehem.

THE POWER OF JESUS' SUFFERINGS, PART 2

*. . . to mock and scourge and crucify Him, and on the third day
He will be raised up.* —MATT. 20:19*b*

As we continue to look at the power of Jesus' sufferings so firmly arrayed against Him, we see two additional areas. He suffered the pain of unjust guilt. The guilt that He willingly took upon Himself, as He suffered and died, was not His own. The Father placed all the guilt of every sinner who ever believed in Jesus on His shoulders. Perhaps the prospect of bearing such overwhelming guilt and shame is what caused our Savior to sweat great drops of blood as He prayed in the garden the night before His death.

Christ also suffered the great pain of death itself. Physiologically, He most likely died from the suffocation caused by crucifixion. But a more painful and profound source of suffering that proved fatal was the massive weight of cumulative grief He bore due to the heavy penalty of sin—the penalty He accepted in place of His chosen ones. To save sinners whom He loved with an infinite love, Jesus had to become for them the sin He hated with an infinite, righteous hatred. The Father "made Him who knew no sin to be sin on our behalf, so that we might become the righteousness of God in Him" (2 Cor. 5:21).

Contrary to what His foes hoped, Jesus' sufferings and death did not signal the end for Him. God would never allow His "Holy One to undergo decay" (Ps. 16:10). Therefore Jesus arose "on the third day" so that those of us who believe in Him will never have to die spiritually.

ASK YOURSELF

With Christmas in our minds and hearts today, celebrate not only the miracle of Jesus' birth but also the miracle of His coming again to redeem for all eternity those who have placed faith in Him, who have heard His gracious call and responded with humble repentance.

HOW NOT TO BE GREAT:
THE POLITICAL POWER PLAY

She said to Him, "Command that in Your kingdom these two sons of mine may sit one on Your right and one on Your left." —MATT. 20:20b

People have long sought to get ahead by manipulating friends and relatives to gain political office, a business promotion, a lucrative contract, or admission to a prestigious college. As the old adage asserts, "It's who you know that really counts."

James and John, with help from their mother, may here have been seeking to capitalize on family ties to Jesus. It's clear that this mother was Salome, a sister of Jesus' mother, Mary, and thus Jesus' aunt (making James and John His cousins; see Matt. 27:56; Mark 15:40; John 19:25).

Salome used an ancient act of obeisance—bowing down—to flatter Jesus and appeal to His sense of monarchy and power. Near Eastern rulers were noted for drawing on resources to grant favors and requests (Mark 6:23), and the apostles' mother hoped she could so manipulate the Lord.

That this was such an open-ended request of Jesus suggests it was not legitimate but rather self-seeking. If He granted the request, their mother could bask in the apostles' prestigious positions. James and John were in effect demanding Jesus to give them the two most honorable positions in His kingdom.

At this moment James and John were behaving too much like the Jewish leaders who loved "the place of honor at banquets and the chief seats in the synagogues" (Matt. 23:6). They craved prestige and elevation over the other disciples, which is not the way to kingdom greatness.

ASK YOURSELF

How have you seen a sense of entitlement and importance hinder a person's effectiveness in ministry? How have you felt the tug of it on yourself, considering yourself to be above certain tasks or too good for certain people? Run as far and fast as you can from such arrogance.

How Not to Be Great: Self-serving Ambition

He said to them, "My cup you shall drink; but to sit on My right and on My left, this is not Mine to give, but it is for those for whom it has been prepared by My Father." And hearing this, the ten became indignant with the two brothers.
—Matt. 20:23–24

The full measure of Jesus' cup was taking the weight of sin and God's wrath against it upon Himself. It was a prospect so horrible that He prayed, "My Father, if it is possible, let this cup pass from Me" (Matt. 26:39).

James and John's answer about the cup reflects a complete misunderstanding of Jesus' meaning, or a self-confident, foolish attitude. Thus they declared, "We are able." Their carnal confidence was later exposed as they and the other apostles fled when Jesus was arrested (26:56).

Our Lord lovingly assured the brothers, "My cup you shall drink." They would indeed share in the "fellowship of His sufferings" (Phil. 3:10; cf. Acts 12:2; Rev. 1:9); however, that was only by the power of the Holy Spirit, not their own.

Nevertheless, it was still presumptuous for James and John to request what they did, and not Christ's prerogative but the Father's to grant it. Only God's sovereign choice, not favoritism or selfish ambition, would bestow such prestigious honors in the kingdom.

Although their response seems righteous at first glance, the other apostles actually reacted more from envious resentment than holy concern about the brothers. All the disciples had on other occasions argued about who should be the greatest (e.g., Mark 9:33–34). Such arrogant and self-centered quibbling arose even at the Last Supper (Luke 22:24). But self-serving ambition is *not* the way for any believer to attain spiritual greatness.

ASK YOURSELF

What grand promises have you made to the Lord before, only to fail and forget them? This should not keep us from aspiring to obedience, but rather to realize that it is not worked up from the inside.

THE PRECEPT OF GENUINE GREATNESS, PART 1

It is not this way among you, but whoever wishes to become great
among you shall be your servant, and whoever wishes to be first
among you shall be your slave. —MATT. 20:26–27

The path to God's greatness is through pleasing Him and serving others in His name. In His view, the person who is truly great is the one willing to be a servant. "Servant" here is from *diakonos*, from which we get the term *deacon*. Originally, the Greek word denoted someone who did menial labor such as housecleaning or waiting on tables. It simply described the lowest level of blue-collar workers, those who had little formal training, and didn't need it.

Jesus elevated "servant" to a position of much importance, using it to describe His most faithful disciples. He chose this term because it best exemplifies the selfless, humble life He honors and modeled in His earthly ministry. Further, the true servant manifests a willingness to sacrifice for others in the name of Christ (cf. 1 Cor. 3:5; 4:1).

It is not wrong but very much acceptable to seek greatness and eternal glory in a scriptural fashion, because such glory is God-given. Paul instructed the Thessalonian believers, "It was for this He called you through our gospel, that you may gain the glory of our Lord Jesus Christ" (2 Thess. 2:14; cf. v. 6). The way to genuine greatness and eternal glory, both deriving from God, is the way of renouncing worldly and temporal glory that derives from fallen human beings—which is basically the way of the servant. Our goal must be to render spiritual service at the highest level of excellence and leave the outcome of that service to God.

ASK YOURSELF

What opportunities for service are available to you today, perhaps in very simple, practical ways around the house or in more creative, complicated ways that require a bit more forethought and initiative? What is so important today that it could keep you from pursuing greatness?

THE PRECEPT OF GENUINE GREATNESS, PART 2

It is not this way among you, but whoever wishes to become great among you shall be your servant, and whoever wishes to be first among you shall be your slave. —MATT. 20:26–27

Here Christ repeats and underscores God's way to genuine greatness: "Whoever wishes to be first among you shall be your slave." It was much lower and more demeaning to be a slave than even to be a servant in those days. Whereas a servant had a few possessions and could freely go when he wanted and work where he wanted, a slave belonged completely to his master and had to go wherever and do whatever the master commanded.

In some of his epistles, the apostle Paul calls himself the Lord's slave even before calling himself an apostle (Rom. 1:1; Phil. 1:1; Titus 1:1). Slaves were the property of their masters and thus could be bought and sold. As such, believers "have been bought with a price" (1 Cor. 6:20; cf. Rom. 14:8) and are Christ's property, having been bought with His own blood (1 Peter 1:18–19).

Humble, sacrificial service characterizes the precept of genuine greatness. If we desire to be first and great in Christ's kingdom, we must preeminently be willing to serve in the difficult, uncomfortable, lonely, and demanding place—where we might not be appreciated and even be persecuted. Realizing this life is transient and the next life eternal, we will be glad to spend and be spent for the sake of the Lord (see also Matt. 25:21).

When faithful saints have served to the best and full limit of their abilities, they'll then humbly tell Christ, "We are unworthy slaves; we have done only that which we ought to have done" (Luke 17:10).

ASK YOURSELF

How would it change the way you approach the day by echoing the sentiment of Paul, considering your highest station to be a servant of the most high God? What implications does this have on your work, your relationships, your various obligations and duties?

The Pattern of Genuine Greatness: Jesus Christ

The Son of Man did not come to be served, but to serve,
and to give His life a ransom for many. —MATT. 20:28

To discover the pattern of the truly great and godly servant of God, we need look no further than the Son of Man Himself. Many years after the apostle John wanted to sit at Jesus' side in the kingdom, he humbly stated, "The one who says he abides in Him ought himself to walk in the same manner as He walked" (1 John 2:6). John no longer sought to manipulate Jesus for personal advancement but only to follow His example of service.

Jesus attained greatness in the eyes of His Father when, in His earthly mission as the Son of Man, He came to serve (cf. John 13:4–5, 12–17), not merely to be served by others.

Although He existed in the form of God, [He] did not regard equality with God a thing to be grasped, but emptied Himself, taking the form of a bond-servant, and being made in the likeness of men. Being found in appearance as a man, He humbled Himself by becoming obedient to the point of death, even death on a cross. For this reason also, God highly exalted Him, and bestowed on Him the name which is above every name. (Phil. 2:6–9)

As Paul's instruction to the Philippians shows, Christ's ultimate act of servanthood was when He gave His life as an atonement for sinners: "Greater love has no one than this," Jesus said, "that one lay down his life for his friends" (John 15:13).

ASK YOURSELF

What benefits have you derived from Christ's willingness to cast off His own rights and privileges in order to serve your deepest needs? What benefits could you inspire in others' lives by modeling the heartbeat of Jesus, pouring yourself out so that others will be blessed?

JESUS' SELFLESS RANSOM

The Son of Man did not come to be served, but to serve,
and to give His life a ransom for many. —MATT. 20:28

At the end of this statement, our Lord gives the first New Testament teaching regarding His redemptive work as Messiah. He would vicariously suffer as a ransom for those sinners who trust in Him. Jesus didn't merely sacrifice Himself as an example for others. And He was not just a martyr for some righteous cause. Nor does He simply exemplify life-giving selflessness, although He is indeed the ultimate example of that. Christ was much more than one who lived and died for others—He died as a ransom for others.

Without faith in Christ, a person is a slave to sin, the flesh, the devil, and death, and it was to redeem people from these slaveries that Jesus came "to give His life a ransom for many." The apostle Paul explained this to Roman believers:

> Therefore there is now no condemnation for those who are in Christ Jesus. For the law of the Spirit of life in Christ Jesus has set you free from the law of sin and of death. For what the Law could not do, weak as it was through the flesh, God did: sending His own Son in the likeness of sinful flesh and as an offering for sin, He condemned sin in the flesh. (Rom. 8:1–3)

"Having been freed from sin, you became slaves of righteousness," Paul earlier wrote to the Romans (6:18). Jesus' once-and-for-all sacrifice has bought back from slavery to sin all who trust in Him.

ASK YOURSELF

At the close of one year and the crisp edge of another, resolve that you will let Jesus take the center seat in your heart and life—loving others through you, serving others through you, exuding His righteousness through your mortal body, all for the praise of His name.

Daily Readings from the Life of Christ, Volume 1

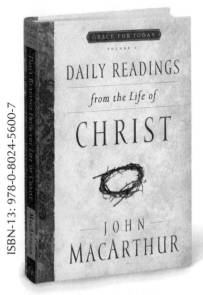

ISBN-13: 978-0-8024-5600-7

"If you are the Son of God, tell these stones to become bread." Jesus answered, "It is written: 'Man does not live on bread alone, but on every word that comes from the mouth of God.'"

Matthew 4:3–4

It's time to stop gorging ourselves on bread and start living like Jesus. In this daily devotional by highly acclaimed author John MacArthur, your hungry heart will be focused on God and His Word. With insights on the life of Jesus, thoughts to ponder, and wisdom gleaned from years of careful study, this devotional will feed your daily walk. *Daily Readings from the Life of Christ* delivers a fresh realization of the grace of God in Christ for today.

1-800-678-8812 • MOODYPUBLISHERS.COM

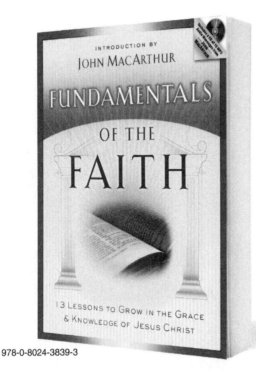

JOHN MACARTHUR

FUNDAMENTALS

OF THE

FAITH

13 LESSONS TO GROW IN THE GRACE
& KNOWLEDGE OF JESUS CHRIST

978-0-8024-3839-3

"On Sunday mornings at Grace Community Church, small groups of people gather together in Fundamentals of the Faith classes to use this manual of thirteen lessons, which blend basic biblical truths with personal obedience and service." With topics ranging from "God: His Character and Attributes" to "The Church: Fellowship and Worship," *Fundamentals of the Faith* is an ideal study to disciple new believers or realize afresh what it means to believe in Jesus.

Fundamentals of the Faith contains a CD with thirteen audio messages from John MacArthur to accompany each lesson.

Introduction by John MacArthur

www.MoodyPublishers.com
Sign up for Moody Publishers Book Club on our website.

978-0-8024-0728-3

Not only is Revelation the inspired Word of God, it is also the only New Testament book that includes a promised spiritual blessing for those who heed its message. If you read and obey the words of Revelation, God promises that you will be blessed.

Is Revelation even possible to understand? Sadly, no book in Scripture has been more misunderstood or misinterpreted than Revelation. Does this mean its message is hopelessly obscure? Certainly not. God is a God of clarity. And He gave us the book of Revelation "to show to His bond-servants, the things which must soon take place." He did this in a way His people could understand. Does the End of the Story matter? Some Christians seem to think it doesn't, or at least not very much. But God certainly considers it important.

by John MacArthur

Find it now at your favorite local or online bookstore.

www.MoodyPublishers.com
Sign up for Moody Publishers Book Club on our website.

978-0-8024-7845-0

It is absolutely essential that a church perceive itself as an institution for the glory of God, and to do that, claims John MacArthur, the local church must adhere unfalteringly to biblical leadership principles. Christ never intended church leadership to be earned by seniority, purchased with money, or inherited through family ties. He never compared church leaders to governing monarchs, but rather to humble shepherds; not to slick celebrities, but to laboring servants. Drawing from some of the best-received material on church leadership, this updated edition guides the church with crucial, effective lessons in leadership. This book is valuable not only for pastors and elders, but for anyone else who wants the church to be what God intended it to be.

by John MacArthur
Find it now at your favorite local or online bookstore.

www.MoodyPublishers.com
Sign up for Moody Publishers Book Club on our website.